Argumentation Schemes for Presumptive Reasoning

LEA TITLES IN ARGUMENTATION

Argumentation Schemes for Presumptive Reasoning

Douglas N. Walton
University of Winnipeg

 LAWRENCE ERLBAUM ASSOCIATES, PUBLISHERS

1996   Mahwah, New Jersey

Lawrence Erlbaum Associates
10 Industrial Avenue
Mahwah, NJ 07430

Cover design by Gail Silverman

Library of Congress Cataloging-in-Publication Data

Walton, Douglas N.
    Argumentation schemes for presumptive reasoning /
Douglas Walton.
        p. cm.
    Includes bibliographical references and index.
    ISBN 0-8058-2071-X (alk. paper). — ISBN 0-8058-2072-8
(alk. paper)
    1. Hypothesis. 2. Presupposition (Logic) 3. Reasoning. I.
Title.
BC183.S25   1996
168—dc20   95-20169
                                                              CIP

Books published by Lawrence Erlbaum Associates are printed on
acid-free paper, and their bindings are chosen for strength and
durability.

Printed in the United States of America
10 9 8 7 6 5 4 3 2 1

For Karen, with love.

TABLE OF CONTENTS

PREFACE

As a member of a research group on "Fallacies as Violations of Rules of Argumentative Discourse" at Netherlands Institute for Advanced Study in the Humanities and Social Sciences (NIAS) in 1989-1990, the author heard a lot of talk about argumentation schemes as the glue that holds argumentation in a critical discussion together, making it "reasonable." But, what are these argumentation schemes and where do you find them? Frans van Eemeren, in answer to these questions, said that they are found in the (1963) doctoral dissertation of Arthur Hastings. This, indeed, did turn out to be the best source of material on argumentation schemes, called "modes of reasoning" by Hastings. Although Hastings' account was incomplete, and insufficiently structured to be as useful as one would like (in the current state of the art), it proved to be the most helpful treatment of argumentation schemes, in the scant literature on this subject.

My own previous research in the field of argumentation has been in the area of informal fallacies. It seems to be a recurrent pattern with these fallacies that the basic tool required to work out an analysis of the fallacy is some kind of argumentation scheme, or structure of inference underlying the fallacy. It seems that to understand the fallacy, or incorrect (erroneous) argument, you first of all have to understand the correct type of argumentation that was abused or misused.

The basic problem with many of the traditional examples of the informal fallacies given in textbooks is that they are not clearly fallacious. Indeed, in many cases, arguments of the same kind as that identified with the fallacy are quite reasonable, provided we lower our standard of what is a reasonable argument by including presumptively reasonable arguments. These are inconclusive and defeasible arguments that nevertheless have a practical function of shifting a burden of proof in a dialogue. This notion of presumptive reasoning will be defined dialectically in chapter two. But for the present, we need to see that an argument can be weakly or presumptively reasonable, even if it is inconclusive, and yet not be a fallacious argument.

Many of the fallacies are misuses of presumptive inference, a kind of reasoning that is neither knowledge-based nor probability-based, but has the function of shifting a weight of presumption onto the other party in a dialogue. Presumptive inference has been analyzed in Walton (*Plaus. Arg.*, 1992), and this research is extended and applied to argumentation schemes in chapter two. Presumptive inference has been in the past systematically ignored by logicians, but it is the basis of kinds of argumentation that are very common in everyday arguments like the argument from sign, the argument from consequences, and the appeal to expert opinion in argument. The analysis of forms of these kinds of arguments is the subject of this book.

A good example is the use of appeal to authority in argumentation. Appeal to expert opinion in argument has, especially during some historical periods, been rejected as inherently fallacious. However, currently, with the advent of expert systems as a practically useful technology, the trend is to accept appeal to expert opinion as a legitimate kind of argumentation. But what kind of argument is it? The best answer is that it is a presumptive kind of argumentation which can correctly be used in a context of dialogue–expert consultation dialogue, a species of information-seeking dialogue–to shift a weight of presumption for or against a proposed course of action in practical reasoning. The presumption is shifted back and forth in dialogue, depending on whether critical questions to the argumentation scheme are properly raised or adequately replied to. When expert consultation dialogue is adjoined to critical discussion correctly in a form of dialectical shift or mixed dialogue, the appeal to expert opinion can be correctly used to support an argument advanced in the critical discussion.

This type of argument can be used to support the goals of a critical discussion by making the discussion informed and up-to-date, with scientific developments for example. Such a mechanism enables the carefully solicited opinion of an expert to be reasonably, if tentatively, accepted by non-experts "for the sake of argument" in a critical discussion without stifling the discussion or delaying it by holding an extensive scientific inquiry into a body of evidence that may be massive, sophisticated and specialized. Presumptions are something we could hardly do without in everyday arguments, for without them, a discussion would be stultified by endless calls for lengthy inquiries.

Presumptions are shifted back and forth in dialogue through the filter of an argumentation scheme, a formal pragmatic structure of arguments that is the counterpart to logical forms of inference in semantics. The concept of an argumentation scheme was originally developed by Hastings (1963), who postulated several types of schemes that are highly relevant to the study of fallacies.

In view of our interest in the *argumentum ad verecundiam* as a fallacy, Hastings' ninth argumentation scheme, for the argument from authority, provides a relevant example of how an argumentation scheme functions. Note that Hastings saw the argument from authority as (in principle) a reasonable kind of argumentation. Hastings saw it as a form of sign reasoning of the following kind: the fact that a speaker asserts a conclusion is taken (by a hearer) to be a sign that the conclusion is true.

As an example of the argument from authority, Hastings cited the following argument.

Case 0.1:   The first concerns the ability of these nations to obtain these nuclear weapons. We suggest that they certainly do have this ability, that many nations have come into the ability in recent years. The London Disarmament Conference, in its follow-up report in 1957, said–and I note this opening phrase–"On their own without outside help the following nations can achieve nuclear weapons"–a long list follows–"Belgium, Canada, Sweden, Switzerland, France, Japan, India, Italy, Argentina, West Germany, Egypt, Israel . . ." and many other nations. We note that many sources, such as the Senate's Disarmament Sub-committee, have all echoed this very important and very strategic possibility. (p. 126)

According to the analysis given by Hastings, the conclusion of this argument is that (probably) these thirteen nations can get nuclear weapons on their own. To prove this conclusion, the speaker presents an authority that says it is true, and backs that up by citing (without direct quotation) another authority who is said to agree.

Hastings goes on to add that we test this kind of argument by posing a number of questions which focus on the reliability of the cited authority, including the following tests: (1) What are the qualifications of the sources? (2) How are they regarded by other authorities in the field? (3) Do they have any biases or prejudices that would influence their conclusions? (4) Do the sources have knowledge of the immediate topic? (5) Are the sources known to be reliable? These critical questions are indeed shown to play an important role in the analysis of the reasoned use of expert opinion in chapters one, two, and three that follow. The reader might also note the allusion to bias in (3) which will come to play an important role in the study of the various kinds of *ad hominem* argumentation studied in chapter three. It is also significant to note the linkage of appeals to authority with *(ad hominem)* criticisms of bias by Hastings, for future reference (see chapter 3).

These ideas about argumentation schemes were developed further in Windes and Hastings (1965). Particularly interesting in this regard is their discussion of the *argument from consequences,* a type of argument that occurs in a context of argumentation where the conclusion is said to be a "should" or "ought to" directive (imperative), expressing a policy or kind of action (the subject of chapter six). According to Windes and Hastings, one simple argumentation scheme of this type occurs in the kind of argument where an advocate lists and proves the benefits (positive consequences) that will result from the proposed course of action. The critic then replies by asking whether some of these consequences (negative side-effects) might be harmful or even "downright dangerous" (p. 226). One type of negative argument from consequences that is perfectly legitimate in the right context of dialogue is the slippery slope argument. The slippery slope argument is a method of warning someone who is contemplating a course of action that taking the first step may (presumptively) lead to a chain of consequences culminating in a disaster, a bad outcome that the person being warned will not like. This is a presumptive type of argumentation, but it is not inherently fallacious (in all cases), according to our analysis of it in chapter three.

Presumption is a practical notion that is used to enable a dialogue or an action to go ahead on a provisional basis in time to be of some use in providing a tentative solution to a practical problem. Presumptions can be based on routine ways of doing things, on fashions or customs, on conventional wisdom, and on cooperation and politeness. Presumptive inferences, however, are subject to withdrawal or rebuttal in exceptional cases. They are defeasible and provisional in nature, as analyzed in chapter two.

Presumptive arguments can be used fallaciously if pressed ahead too hard in a dogmatic manner that does not allow for rebuttal, because presumptive arguments are defeasible. But in many cases, they are nonfallacious.

For example, taking the "say so" of a stranger on the street would normally be quite a weak evidential basis for accepting a proposition as a presumption to act upon, but in some cases this kind of argumentation can meet a burden of proof that is a reasonable basis for action. A case from Walton (*Inf. Log.*, 1989) illustrated the point.

Case 0.2:   If a lecture starts in two minutes, and I do not know which room of a large building it is scheduled for, I may go to room 128 just because a colleague says: "I heard someone say that the lecture is in room 128." Now hearsay of this sort is an extremely weak form of proof. But if I have no better evidence to go on, and finding more conclusive evidence by going to the conference desk would mean my being late for the lecture, then I may reasonably decide to act on my colleague's report, despite its very weak argumentative force. This decision may be reasonable, however, because I would probably be late anyway, no matter what else I did. Hence, in the absence of the facts, it is reasonable to act on a very weak presumption. The burden of proof tilts the balance in the direction of walking toward room 128. (p. 26)

In this case, the conclusion that it was prudentially reasonable to walk in the direction indicated was set up by the lack of any definite or hard knowledge available within the practical constraints of the situation. The decision to act was based on little more than a weak conjecture. Still that decision could have been a perfectly reasonable way of proceeding in the situation. By contrast, going on hearsay of this sort in another situation, where the requirements of burden of proof are different, could be a premature conclusion that is not prudentially reasonable.

In assertions, the burden of proof is on the proponent (assertor) to prove or provide evidence if challenged by a respondent in dialogue. With presumptions, this dialectical arrangement is reversed according to our analysis, given in chapter two. A proponent can put forward a presumption "for the sake of argument" for purely practical reasons, without offering evidence to back it up. It is then up to the respondent to rebut the presumption by bringing forward evidence against it. If the respondent does not, the presumption holds, provisionally, at least until some subsequent point in the dialogue where someone brings forward evidence to refute it. With presumption then, the burden of (dis)proof lies on the respondent, not on the proponent.

Presumptive generalizations, and argumentation schemes based on them apply to normal or nonexceptional cases, and are inherently subject to exceptions in particular cases, according to the analysis of them given in chapter five. Consider the presumptive generalization: "If it walks like a duck, quacks like a duck, and looks like a duck, it's a duck." This presumptive conditional is based on the cumulative increment use of the argument from sign. As the positive signs that it is a duck pile up, the conclusion accrues a greater weight of presumption in its favor. But quite possibly, in a particular case, we are confronted with something that looks a lot like a duck, but is not. Perhaps it's a clever illusion, devised by social psychologists for an experiment. Or perhaps it's really a type of bird that looks a lot like a duck but does not have webbed feet, or some other important duck characteristics. In such a case, the presumptive inference defaults, or fails due to an exception.

Presumptive reasoning, according to the analysis given in this book, is based on pragmatic implicatures drawn out by a hearer on the basis of what a speaker's remarks suggest, as opposed to logical inferences that necessarily follow from what a speaker asserts. Hence presumptive reasoning is more rough-and-ready, more simplistic, and also more subject to defeat (and also error) than the logically tight deductive inferences that have traditionally been studied in formal logic. Even so, it will be argued here, the structures of presumptive reasoning are well worth investigating, both for their own sake, and in order to understand how argumentation can influence people (both correctly and incorrectly) in everyday speech, on all kinds of controversial issues.

After this book had been written, I received a copy of a new book on argumentation schemes (Kienpointner, 1992), and would like to thank the author, Manfred Kienpointner, for sending this book, and other papers of his on the subject. Despite my very limited reading knowledge of German, I have tried to take this important new contribution into account.

The work in this project was supported by a Fellowship from the Netherlands Institute for Advanced Study in the Humanities and Social Sciences (NIAS) and a research grant from the Social Sciences and Humanities Research Council of Canada. Thanks are due to Erik Krabbe for discussions, and to the members of the NIAS Research Group on "Fallacies as Violations of Rules of Argumentative Discourse": Frans van Eemeren, Rob Grootendorst, Sally Jackson, Scott Jacobs, Agnes Haft van Rees, Agnes Verbiest, Charles Willard, and John Woods.

My thanks especially to Amy Merrett for word-processing the manuscript, including the figures.

Finally, I would like to thank the editor of the *American Philosophical Quarterly*, for permission to reprint a revised version of my article, "Non-fallacious Arguments from Ignorance" (1992, *29*, 381-387) as part of chapter four, the editor of *Pragmatics and Cognition*, for permission to reprint a revised version of my article "The Speech Act of Presumption" (1993, *1*, 125-148) as part of chapter two, and the editor of *Logique et Analyse*, for permission to reprint "Ignoring Qualifications (*Secundum Quid*) as a Subfallacy of Hasty Generalization" (1990, *129-130*, 113-154), that appears in this book, with only minor changes, as chapter five.

CHAPTER ONE

INTRODUCTION

Recent work in informal logic and argumentation has come to rely more and more on the idea that certain common forms of argumentation–like argument from precedent, argument from authority, argument from analogy, and so forth[1]–are, in some instances, "valid" or correct modes of reasoning. If so, they must have structures or "forms." But what are these forms of argument, or so-called argumentation schemes? That is the question addressed in this book.

Following the usual methods of logic, we would expect to find logical calculi, systems of propositional calculus, or the probability calculus, that would model these types of reasoning as valid or invalid. However, we will argue that this approach, at least by itself, is not the answer.[2] Instead, we hope to show, these argumentation schemes can best be revealed as normatively binding kinds of reasoning when seen as moves, or speech acts in the setting of dialogue. In this pragmatic framework, two participants are reasoning together in a goal-directed, interactive, conventionalized framework called a *dialogue*. An argument is evaluated as good (correct, reasonable) to the extent that it contributes to the goal of the dialogue. An argument is evaluated as bad (incorrect, fallacious) to the extent that it blocks the goals of the dialogue.

According to this type of analysis, each of the types of argumentation modelled will have a distinctive argumentation scheme (structure, form) that allows it to function as a way of making a point or shifting a burden of proof in a dialogue.

NEED FOR A SYSTEMATIC STUDY

The reliance on argumentation schemes as a central component in the normative structure of argument evaluation and analysis by theorists like van Eemeren and Grootendorst (1984; 1992) has acutely raised the need for a more systematic study of these schemes. In particular, what is vital is to see whether or how these schemes can function–like the forms of argument in deductive logic–to test or verify that instances of them in natural language argumentation are in some sense correct or reasonable. Although the term valid does not seem to be quite the right word to use with many of these argumentation schemes, still, when they are rightly or appropriately used, it appears that they are meeting some kind of standard of correctness of use. What is important to come to know is what this standard is, for the most common and widely recognized schemes especially, and how each of the schemes can be tested against this standard.

---

[1]See chapter 3 for an account of the types of argumentation studied.
[2]See van Eemeren and Grootendorst (1989).

Blair (1991) put his finger on the central problem when he cited van Eemeren and Kruiger (1987) as identifying several different types of arguments like argument from analogy, causal arguments of various kinds, arguments from rules and principles, argument from consequences, and argument from precedent. But, Blair pointedly asked, what does it mean to say of such an argument that its premises are sufficient for its conclusion? According to the pragma-dialectical theory of van Eemeren and Grootendorst, Blair noted, "sufficiency is a function of appropriately meeting the critics' challenges to premises and inferences" (p. 332). Blair also noted that this means that an argument can rightly be said to be sufficient for its conclusion in this sense when it meets its burden of proof[3] relying on "what may be presumed without or accepted without further question" (p. 333). This answer seems exactly right, and points us in a promising direction. For many of the most common and basic types of argumentation schemes that require a new kind of analysis are inherently presumptive and dialectical in just the way Blair describes.

But as Blair noted, van Eemeren and Kruiger (1987) only give a few examples of these argumentation schemes, and clearly work is needed to more sharply define these types of argumentation before we can see better how they can be used as an aid to determine when an argument (of one of these types) is sufficient for its conclusion.

When we look to the literature on argumentation schemes, there is very little to be found. Quite a few argumentation schemes can be found in Perelman and Olbrechts-Tyteca (1969), but they are woven in with the general themes of the book. The single, outstanding best source is the doctoral dissertation of Hastings (1963), which presents nine "modes of reasoning" along with other "patterns of reasoning." Each mode of reasoning represents what we call an argumentation scheme. Hastings presents an illustrative example of each from everyday argumentation, and supplies a set of critical questions to match each scheme. Thus, Hastings (1963) is a uniquely valuable source that in effect founded the systematic study of argumentation schemes as a subject for further development.

Aside from this unique resource, however, there is very little to go on. Kienpointner (1987) gave a useful historical and analytical overview of the subject. The ancient and medieval classifications of the different "topics" identify many of the same types of argumentation that we associate with argumentation schemes. However, their way of presenting these schemes, by mixing them with logical doctrines like essentialism, that are now outdated and unfamiliar to modern readers, detracts from the usefulness these accounts might have.

Other than the occasional paper on the subject, for example by van Eemeren and Kruiger (1987), and scattered remarks by van Eemeren and Grootendorst (1984; 1992), there is really nothing else to turn to in attempting to get a grasp of what argumentation schemes are, or how they can be applied.

Just recently however, a new book has appeared which gives a comprehensive typology of argumentation schemes, and identifies sixty of these schemes.

The typology of Kienpointner (1992) is made on the basis of the kind of warrant *(Schlussregel)* used in an argument to provide the transition or inference from the premise(s) to the conclusion. The typology (Kienpointner, 1992) has

---

[3] Walton (1988).

three main categories of argumentation schemes: (I) those where the warrant is one of use *(Schlussregelbenützende Argumentation schemata)*, (II) inductive argumentation schemes, and (III) a third category comprising argument from example, analogy argument, and argument from authority. The first category is quite large, and comprises four subcategories: 1. classifying schemes–including definition, genus-species and part-whole arguments. 2. identity *(Gleichheit)*–including arguments based on similarity and difference. 3. against the proposition *(Gegensatz)* schemes–these are arguments used negatively for refutation (what Perelman and Olbrechts-Tyteca, 1969, called schemes of dissociation). 4. causal schemes.

Kienpointner's typology turns out to be quite useful to help us gain a perspective on the variety of argumentation schemes studied in this book. We have also adopted the policy of identifying and classifying the argumentation schemes on the basis of the warrant or rule (we think of it as expressing a type of generalization) that links the premise(s) of an argument to the conclusion. However, the scope of our inquiry is more narrow than that of Kienpointner. We analyze only what we call presumptive argumentation schemes, (i.e., ones where the generalization is presumptive in nature, and meant to admit of exceptions). Therefore, we do not include, for example, inductive arguments, part-whole arguments, or genus-species arguments, presuming that (by and large, at any rate) these types of argumentation are not presumptive in nature.

A number of the argumentation schemes we study in the subsequent chapters do, however, fit nicely into Kienpointner's typology. A number of them (especially the *ad hominem* variants in chapter 3) fit into the *Gegensatz* category. Several others are clearly causal in nature. Arguments based on example, authority, and analogy also fit into Kienpointner's typology. However, we classify arguments from authority, or at least the subspecies we call the argument from expert opinion, as a species of argument from position to know (see chapter 3).

Thus there are some points of difference between Kienpointner's way of classifying argumentation schemes and our own. But the main difference is that we are concentrating on what we call presumptive reasoning, and that makes the scope of our inquiry, and also, to some extent the basis on which it is made, different from Kienpointner's. Certainly the problem remains of understanding how many of the most common of these argumentation schemes in everyday conversation are inherently different from the usual models of deductive and inductive reasoning–these are the presumptive argumentation schemes.

Perhaps part of the problem is that this kind of project never appealed to logicians very much because it seemed to have more to do with rhetoric and the discovery of persuasive arguments, for example, in making a speech. If so, it seemed questionable whether it was appropriate to try to see presumptive arguments as, in some sense, logically valid. More often, they have been portrayed as fallacious. This apparent ambiguity has dogged the subject from its beginnings.

ARISTOTLE'S TOPICS

The history of the systematic study of argumentation schemes begins with Aristotle's (1939) *Topics*. The purpose of this treatise was to apprehend what Aristotle called *dialectical reasoning,* in which two parties reason together on the basis of premises that are *endoxa,* usually translated as "generally accepted opinions" (*Topica* 100b18). Dialectical reasoning contrasts with *demonstration,* a kind of reasoning which "proceeds from premises which are true and primary," for example, the first principles of science (100a28).

Aristotle also recognized a third kind of reasoning he called *contentious* (or *eristic*), which is "based on opinions which appear to be generally accepted but are not really so" (*Topica* 100b26).

In the *Topics,* Aristotle was taking a point of view on argumentation that subsequently came to be pushed to one side and forgotten. He saw reasoning as being used in different ways in different types of dialogue. And he set out to study and evaluate the uses of different types of argumentation as used within the norms or conventions of these different types of dialogue.

Such an approach has long seemed unfamiliar and even alien, and especially so in the 20th century, where logic, and reasoning generally, is seen exclusively from a semantic and formalistic point of view. Modern symbolic logic, a development of Aristotle's syllogistic (deductive) logic, came to abstract reasoning from its uses in a context of dialogue entirely. According to the formalistic viewpoint that became very dominant in the positivistic era of the first half of the 20th century, an "argument" came to be seen as a set of propositions with "truth-values" attached to them. The idea of the use of an argument in different types of conventionalized dialogues, or structures of interactive reasoning, dropped out of the picture. The idea was reverted to in Wittgenstein's "language-games" in his later philosophy, but has not begun to be investigated in any systematic way until the recent advent of argumentation as a field.

For these reasons, it is difficult for a 20th-century reader, especially one familiar with formal logic in some form, to have much of a grasp of what Aristotle was up to when he wrote about dialectical argumentation. The ideas in the *Prior Analytics* are familiar, because Aristotle was presenting a theory of objective validity, concerned with universal and absolute propositions, for example, of the form "All F are G," where the individuals that have property F all have property G (without considering exceptions). However in the *Topics,* Aristotle was presenting a theory of dialectical argumentation, in which an argument is evaluated relative to another person (*Topics* 155b10).

However, although dialectical argumentation, by its nature, involves two people reasoning together, Aristotle was not attempting to consider any particular pair of individuals, or the varying reactions of all individuals. Instead, according to Evans (1977), he is "contrasting the art which pays attention to the views of each individual, however eccentric these views be, with that which organizes and selects certain views as typical and specially relevant to the subject under consideration" (p. 76). Thus Aristotle's position is not an extreme relativism, but a qualified relativism that judges the worth of an argument in relation to an *endoxon,* which could perhaps be called a plausible or typical point of view on an issue where opinions differ. An argument is judged good or not, in relation to a point of view.

As Evans (1977) pointed out, the translation of the word *endoxon* presents difficulties. Evans did not think that it represents probability of any sort, and can instead be taken, in a basic sense, as meaning "representative of someone's view"

(p. 78). Aristotle also makes a distinction between a qualified and an unqualified *endoxon* (*Topica* 159a39 - 159b1). Something *endoxon* "may be so either without qualification or in a way which is qualified by reference to some person (Evans, 1977, p. 80). Evans came to the view that the unqualified *endoxon* could be translated as "absolute plausibility, unqualified by reference to this person" (p. 83), whereas the qualified *endoxon* refers to something that is plausible to a particular person, or participant in dialectical argumentation. The plausible, in other words, can take an absolute or relative form.

Those schooled in traditional (formal) logic might have difficulty in seeing how this notion of plausibility represents or relates to some logical, as opposed to rhetorical method of evaluating reasoning. But evidently, Aristotle thought that it does. According to De Pater (1968, p. 188), the Aristotelian topic or *topos* has two functions. In its *selective function*, a topic is a device to find arguments within a possible set of types of arguments. Using this function, an orator can run over the list of topics, representing different kinds of argumentation, and pick out the best or most appropriate one to make his case on a given issue. This is more of a rhetorical or inventive function of a topic. Van Eemeren, Grootendorst and Kruiger (1987) called this function a "tactical aid" or "search formula," in setting up an argument (p. 65).

In its *guarantee function*, the topic is a kind of inference link that grants "the plausibility of the step from arguments to controversial claim" (Kienpointner, 1987, p. 280). The guarantee function uses the argumentation scheme as a bridging structure of inference or Toulmin warrant that connects a set of premises to a conclusion. Used as a guarantee function, an argumentation scheme works in much the same way a deductive form of inference like *modus ponens* does, in sanctioning a form of argumentation as valid or invalid, correct or incorrect, in accord with a given standard of correct reasoning.

Whereas the selective function is rhetorical, a device to aid in the invention of useful argumentation, the guarantee function is logical, in the sense that it gives a standard to evaluate reasoning as correct or incorrect, in a normative sense.

INFORMAL FALLACIES

Recent work of the author on informal fallacies has shown, time and time again, with the major, traditional fallacies, that each of them is a species of argumentation that is not inherently incorrect or fallacious in itself, in every instance of its use.[4] What has been shown, instead, is that each of these types of argumentation is tentative and inconclusive–open to critical questioning–while still being strong enough, in many cases, to have some degree of bindingness or logical correctness in transferring acceptance from the premises to the conclusion. However, the bindingness is not of an unconditional or absolute kind–like deductive validity. Instead, it is a kind of tentative or provisional acceptance that is involved, (i.e., "Now I have accepted these premises, I am bound to tentatively accept the conclusion, for the sake of argument or discussion, unless some definite evidence comes

---

[4] Walton (1987; *Prag. Theory,* 1995).

in that is sufficient to indicate rejecting it"). The "validity" such an argument has (if that is the right word) is presumptive and provisional in nature.[5] It is frail, and subject to default.

Even so, such presumptively based arguments can be very useful and important in cases where action must be taken, but firm evidence is not presently available. Examples would be in planning, where the future holds many uncertainties, or in practical deliberation, where prudent action often requires acting on provisional hunches and guesswork, always subject to revision, as better information comes in.

This new approach to fallacies raises two problems. One is the problem that if these types of argumentation are not always fallacious, how do you tell the difference between the fallacious and the nonfallacious cases? The beginning of the answer to this question is to see that each individual case has to be examined on its merits, by bringing forward and analyzing the textual evidence of the case.

The other problem is even more fundamental. If these types of argumentation can be correct, in some sense, and nonfallacious in some instances of their use, what form or structure do they have as correct arguments? By what standard can we measure or test their correctness (or incorrectness) in a given case? In a nutshell, this is the problem of argumentation schemes.

This problem has been expressed perspicuously by Marks (1988), who used the following example.

Case 1.1:   The prisoner confessed to the crime.
                Therefore, the prisoner is guilty.

The truth of the premise of this argument does not conclusively prove the truth of the conclusion, because there might be many reasons why a prisoner might confess to a crime of which he is not guilty. Marks called the argument "informally fallacious," (p. 307) and admittedly it is a kind of argument that would tend to be labeled as fallacious in the standard treatment of the logic textbooks (see Hamblin, 1970, chapter 1). Even so, the argument does seem to have a measure of worth, subject to what is, or comes to be known about the circumstances of its use.

Marks (1988) considered that we could understand the argument as having a suppressed premise, "If a person confesses to a crime, then that person is guilty of that crime." This move makes the argument deductively valid–it now has the form of *modus ponens*–but does not save the argument. For any criticism of the non-explicitized form (as expressed in the version in Case 1.1), would apply equally well to the suppressed premise.

Marks saw a problem here, for the argument in question (once explicitized) is unsound, containing a false premise, but what has become of the sense of "fallaciousness" that was invoked by the initial presentation of it in Case 1.1?

---

[5] See chapter 2.

The solution to Marks' problem advanced in this book will take the following form of argumentation. Because the prisoner was presumably in a position to know whether he committed the crime or not, then his confessing does give a "push," or a weight of evidence towards the hypothesis that he did commit the crime. However, such a conclusion could easily turn out to be mistaken. The prisoner may have been coerced into a confession, or have had some reason for making a confession (e.g., to protect someone else), even though, in fact, he did not commit the crime. Perhaps the confession was even an outcome of a session of plea-bargaining. Hence the argument in Case 1.1 is best described (as things stand) as a fragile or slender, provisional kind of basis for inferring the conclusion from the premise, but not such a bad argument that it deserves to be called fallacious.

This is not to say that the argument in Case 1.1 could never be fallacious, depending on how the case is filled out. If the prosecuting attorney ignored genuine evidence that the confession was coerced by the police, and kept pushing the argument in Case 1.1 forward dogmatically, it could become appropriate to speak of a fallacy having been committed.

But by itself, the argument in Case 1.1 is not fallacious, even with the suppressed premise added.

If we were to view this suppressed premise as a universal generalization of the form, "For all x, if x confessed to a crime, then x is guilty of that crime," then we would have to concede that, in fact, this premise is false. One counterinstance is all that is needed to refute an (unqualified) universal generalization of this form. Interpreted in this way, the argument in Case 1.1 could be alleged to be a fallacy.

But would this be an appropriate or justifiable way of interpreting the argument in Case 1.1? In general, it would not be. In fact, it could quite legitimately be described as an instance of the *straw man* fallacy of interpreting the point of view of an arguer. In this instance, the fallacy is that of exaggerating the claim or viewpoint expressed to make it appear much stronger, or more extreme, than the case would justify.

How then should we interpret the implicit premise that links the explicit premise to the conclusion in the argument in Case 1.1? It is argued in this book that this conditional ought to be cast in a form that expresses the idea that normally if x confesses to a crime, then it is reasonable to move forward in subsequent investigation, discussion, or actions, on the assumption that x committed the crime. However, such an assumption follows neither by logical necessity nor by probability or inductive reasoning (at least of any straightforward kind). Instead, the conditional licenses only a permissible conclusion to be drawn from the premise as antecedent, on the assumption that the case of x is typical, in the sense that no known circumstance of the case defeats the application of the conditional to that case.

According to this interpretation, the argument in Case 1.1, when supplemented with a nonexplicit conditional premise or warrant, linking the explicit premise to the conclusion, has a function in dialogue of shifting an obligation, or weight of questioning, from one participant to another. Once put forward by a proponent in a dialogue (for example, in a legal trial), the argument creates a presumption that shifts a weight or burden onto anyone who would doubt it to ask appropriate critical questions, or to give evidence to indicate that this case is some-how not typical in a relevant respect.

Thus this argument is not a strong argument, and it is far from being con-clusive. But on our interpretation, it should not be called a fallacious argument.

Obviously, however, such an argument could easily become fallacious, or be used fallaciously, where it has been pushed forward too strongly in a dialogue, in a way that ignores, or suppresses the proper kind of qualifications that always need to be attached to such presumptive generalizations. In fact, there is actually a traditional name for this generic type of fallacy. It is called *secundum quid,* or neglect of qualifications.

Arguments like the one in Case 1.1 lie on a razor's edge: They are somewhat weak and unreliable, and apt to fail occasionally, but they are not so bad or inher-ently erroneous that they should be called "fallacious" in all instances. On the other hand, they can turn out to be fallacious, in some cases. And, in particular, they run the risk of committing the *secundum quid* fallacy as quite a general sort of failure they are prone to. If this is right, a new approach to fallacies is called for—an approach that takes more care in assessing the particulars of a given case.

In arguments like the one in Case 1.1, the premise, if true in a given case, does give a reason for accepting the conclusion. But it is not a conclusive reason, and it is subject to default relative to what is known (or becomes known) of the further circumstances of the case. The problem then is to find the underlying struc-ture of inference in such a case that enables one to identify and test the correctness (or incorrectness) of the argument as an instance of an argumentation scheme.

HOW ARE SCHEMES NORMATIVELY BINDING?

Van Eemeren and Grootendorst (1992) introduced the concept of an argumentation scheme by looking at ways people typically argue when a speaker has a standpoint or conclusion in mind, and tries to convince a listener to come to accept that con-clusion.

> In his endeavor to transfer the acceptability of the premises to the conclusion and to achieve the interactional effect that the listener accept his standpoint, the speaker tries to put forward his argument in such a fashion that it convinces the listener. He communicates, as it were, that he knows the way that leads from what is already accepted to the standpoint. In arguing in one of these ways, he relies on a ready-made *argumentation scheme:* a more or less conventionalized way of representing the relation between what is stated in the argument and what is stated in the standpoint. (p. 96)

This way of defining the concept of an argumentation scheme appears to make it a matter of what people conventionally or typically accept as a pattern of argumen-tation linking premises to a conclusion. Thus, it does not appear, by this descrip-tion, that the argumentation scheme binds the speaker or listener (or anyone else) to accept the conclusion as following from the premises logically.

Indeed, in a footnote, van Eemeren and Grootendorst seem to confirm that, as they see it, an argumentation scheme does not imply that the given argument it applies to is logically valid, in some sense.

> On this point, logic has not much to offer. In spite of important differences in the way logicians define the object, scope, and method of their work, they seem unanimous in thinking that their concern with validity is about formal rather than substantive relations between premises and conclusions, syntactico-semantic rather than pragmatic aspects, reasoning in isolation rather than in context, implications rather than inferences and—most important to us at this juncture—transmission of truth rather than acceptance. (p. 96)

It seems at this point that argumentation schemes have more of a rhetorical or persuasive function than a logical function. They represent ways of communicating an argument in a dialogue, in relation to the conventions of what kinds of moves or speech acts are conventionally accepted in that type of dialogue.

Kienpointner (1987) judged that argumentation schemes require a different kind of approach from the way arguments are evaluated in a deductive, formal logic. With argumentation schemes, it does not seem possible "to construct an algorithm to test the validity of natural language argumentation by translating it into a formal language." Apart from considering the context of use in a particular case, there seems to be no way to judge between "sound" and "fallacious" instances of argumentation schemes. Consequently, Kienpointner drew the conclusion that evaluating instances of argumentation schemes is best done by taking into account the context of dialogue of the given case.

> . . . the soundness of argumentation can't be judged independently of semantic and pragmatic standards underlying the argumentation, i.e. the language game played by subgroups of a speech community (in the sense of the late Wittgenstein). Consequently, the use theory of meaning can be seen as an adequate theoretical frame to understand and describe the diversity of soundness-concepts and soundness-judgments in a community. (p. 279)

This means that an argumentation scheme could be used correctly in one type of dialogue (language game) and fallaciously, or incorrectly, in relation to another type of dialogue.

For example, a thinly veiled threat could be inappropriate, and even rightly judged fallacious, in the context of a critical discussion. If the same threat were to occur in a negotiation dialogue however, it could be an acceptable, and not wholly inappropriate move or tactic, in that context of dialogue.

It is well known that van Eemeren and Grootendorst have the goal of studying argumentation normatively, and not just descriptively, as they have often stated (van Eemeren and Grootendorst, 1984). And in fact, a few years later (1992), we found them saying that argumentation schemes are the key means of evaluating many arguments in everyday conversations, and that the argumentation scheme does "correspond to" certain "assessment criteria."

A person who puts forward an argumentation anticipates criticism, and by choosing a particular type of argumentation, using the one argumentation scheme rather than the other, he implies that he thinks he knows which route will lead to the justification of his standpoint. At any rate, whether he really thinks this or not, if he is to be taken seriously by the other party, he may be held to be committed to deal with the critical questions which pertain to a justification via the argumentation scheme that is inherent in his argumentation.

In relying on a certain argumentation scheme, the arguer invokes a particular testing method in a dialectical procedure, in which certain critical reactions are relevant, and others not. Each argumentation scheme calls, as it were, for its own set of critical reactions. In conjunction with each other, these reactions constitute a well-rounded test for checking the soundness of an argumentation of the type concerned. (p. 98)

This way of describing argumentation schemes suggests that they are normatively binding, in the following sense. If the hearer accepts the premises of the speaker's argument, and the argument is an instance of a genuine and appropriate argumentation scheme (for the type of dialogue they are engaged in), then the hearer must or should (in some binding way) accept the conclusion. This does not appear to be "validity" in the same sense in which the word is familiarly used in deductive (or perhaps even inductive) logic. But it does appear to express a normative or broadly logical sense of validity, bindingness, conditional acceptability, or whatever you want to call it.

The sense of "validity" expressed here expresses a commitment to deal with critical questions appropriate for an argument. It appears, moreover, to be a dialogue-relative (or dialectical) concept of validity or bindingness (obligation). It appears, judging from the previous quotation, that argumentation schemes do definitely have a logical aspect, expressing a kind of validity, though (as their footnote makes clear) not any kind of validity recognized in the usual formal logic of propositions and quantifiers.

The problem then is to understand generally how argumentation schemes can be seen as being a part of some framework of logical reasoning so that they can be seen as "binding," or as possessing or conveying some kind of validity, when used properly in argumentation.

In everyday conversation, the glue binding a set of premises to a conclusion is practical reasoning.

Case 1.2:   I want to get to the station to catch the train to Groningen.
                     Therefore, I must run.

In this kind of inference, the premise states a goal, and there is a nonexplicit premise stating that running, in this case, is the means of achieving the goal. The conclusion connects the two premises together, stating that the agent must (if he wants to attain the goal) carry out the indicated action.

Clearly this type of reasoning has an argumentation scheme. One premise defines or describes a goal. The other premise describes a means of achieving the goal. The conclusion directs the agent towards action to carry out the means.[6]

But this type of reasoning is so common and distinctive, having many variants and subspecies of argumentation, that it is misleading to call it an argumentation scheme. Better to call it a type of reasoning that can be used in argumentation in different types of dialogue (as in Walton, *What Reas.*, 1990).

PRACTICAL REASONING

The analysis of argumentation schemes is very much affected by the recognition of practical reasoning as a distinctive type of reasoning, as distinguished from what might be called theoretical or discursive reasoning. Practical reasoning (Walton, *Pract. Reas.*, 1990) is a kind of goal-directed, knowledge-based reasoning that is directed to choosing a prudent course of action for an agent that is aware of its present circumstances. In a practical inference, the conclusion is an imperative that directs the agent to a prudent course of action. The premises describe the agent's goals and knowledge in a given situation, especially practical knowledge of ways and means.

Discursive reasoning, by contrast, has a cognitive orientation, weighing reasons for and against the truth or falsity of a proposition. Logic, in the past, has usually dealt with discursive reasoning as the only important kind of reasoning to be evaluated, and ignored practical reasoning. However, when one turns to study argumentation in everyday conversation, it appears that practical reasoning is the medium of many of the most commonly used argumentation schemes. This hypothesis is well confirmed in chapter three, where many of the argumentation schemes are shown to be special forms of practical reasoning.

Practical reasoning is a goal-directed sequence of linked practical inferences that seeks out a prudent line of conduct for an agent in a set of particular circumstances known by the agent. Where a is an agent, A is an action, and G a goal, the two basic types of practical inferences are respectively, the *necessary condition scheme* and the *sufficient condition scheme* (Walton, *Pract. Reas.*, 1990; see also Schellens, 1987).

G is a goal for a
Doing A is necessary for a to carry out G
Therefore, a ought to do A

G is a goal for a
Doing A is sufficient for a to carry out G
Therefore, a ought to do A

The second premise, in both types of inferences, is to be understood as relative to what a knows or reasonably takes to be the case, as far as he grasps the particular circumstances in the given case. These circumstances can change, and practical

---

[6] See Clarke (1985), Audi (1989), and Walton (*Pract. Reas.*, 1990).

reasoning is therefore to be understood as a dynamic kind of reasoning that needs to be corrected or updated as new information comes in.

The concepts of necessary and sufficient conditions incorporated in the second premise need to be understood as typically flexible rather than strict relationships. Both need to be judged in relation to the given knowledge base of the agent, subject to exceptions and overriding circumstances that can come to light in a particular case. These are very special kinds of conditionals that have a special kind of logic in their own right, analyzed later.

The conclusion of a practical inference guides an agent to a prudent course of action, subject to the conditions set in the premises. The conclusion is a practical imperative directing the prudentially wise to do something, given the circumstances, as the agent sees them, expressed in the premises. If the agent is committed to the premises, then the agent ought (prudentially) to be committed to the course of action which is directed by the conclusion. Otherwise, the set of commitments is pragmatically inconsistent (Walton, *Arg. Pos.*, 1985).

As argumentation, practical reasoning is used in a context of dialogue. Most commonly, practical reasoning is used in deliberations, but it is also often used in advice-solicitation dialogues, and in critical discussions. Four kinds of critical questions function alongside a practical inference as a means of indicating a proper weight of commitment to be assigned to the conclusion in a given context of dialogue.

Q1:   Are there alternative ways (other than A) of realizing G?
Q2:   Is it possible for a to do A?
Q3:   Does a have goals other than G that should be taken into account?
Q4:   Are there other consequences of bringing about A that should be taken into account?

In weighing these critical questions against a practical inference in a given case, in a context of dialogue, burden of proof plays an important role. If the premises of a practical inference are well-supported as reasonable commitments for an agent, a weight of presumption is thrown against a respondent who questions the practical validity of the practical inference in the given situation. To shift the burden back onto the proponent, the respondent must pose one or more of these appropriate critical questions. Thus practical reasoning has a kind of validity that should be judged in relation to the requirements of burden of proof in a given situation.

The kind of analysis of practical reasoning briefly outlined previously and further developed and elaborated in Walton (*Pract. Reas.*, 1990) makes room for the pragmatic view of presumption of the sort advocated by Perelman and Olbrechts-Tyteca (1969), Ullman-Margalit (1983), and Clarke (1989). Presumption can be justified in reasoning, on a practical basis, on the grounds that it can enable the line of reasoning to go ahead, even in the absence of absolute knowledge of what will happen in a particular situation where some commitment to action or inaction needs to be made. Guidance toward a prudent course of action typically necessitates operating on presumptions that could turn out to be wrong, and drawing conclusions (tentatively) from these presumptions by practical inferences, even if such reasoning is a kind of careful guesswork.

Practical reasoning is typically based on rough and ready generalizations drawn from practical skills, common experiences, or mastery of a craft. These generalizations are often too rough to admit of quantification, and they also tend to be subject to exceptions and irregularities.

PLAUSIBLE REASONING

The argumentation schemes identified in chapter three all have one thing in common. They are presumptive and plausibilistic in nature, meaning that if the premises are true (or acceptable), then the conclusion does not follow deductively or inductively, but only as a reasonable presumption in given circumstances of a case, subject to retraction if those circumstances should change. Moreover, such changes do not tend to be quantifiable as probabilities (except perhaps very roughly), because hard or objective evidence to back them up is not available. Instead, the basis of their support is subjective (i.e., based on a source, signs or other not-very-reliable indicators that are inherently open to critical doubt).

Drawing conclusions from premises using these argumentation schemes is a kind of presumptive guesswork, where one participant in a dialogue presumes that the other is speaking in accord with the Gricean maxim of cooperativeness appropriate for the type of dialogue they are engaged in. Understandably, logicians in the past have been suspicious of this kind of inference as being a valid, genuine, or reliable kind of reasoning. And it surely must be conceded, in favor of these reservations, that this type of presumptive argumentation is often subject to failure and default, even to fallacies, and that as a species of reasoning it is not highly reliable. It is best seen as a defeasible guide to prudent action in a case where better evidence (that might enable deductive or inductive reasoning to be used) is not available. You could call presumptive reasoning a kind of lack of knowledge inference, or argumentation from ignorance, to be used when a decision is practically necessary or useful, even if uncertainty prevails (Walton, *Arg. Ig.*, 1995).

In looking for a logic behind these argumentation schemes, conventional expectations would suggest looking for a formal calculus (like propositional calculus, in deductive logic) that would enable us to calculate some numerical degrees of confidence for the inferences from premises to conclusions. In fact, Rescher (1976; 1977) already constructed a logic of plausible reasoning of this kind.

However, here we take quite a different approach, by postulating that the validity or correctness of an argumentation scheme, as used in a given case, depends on the context of dialogue appropriate for that case. On our analysis, each argumentation scheme has a set of critical questions attached to it. The use or function of the argumentation scheme is to shift a burden or weight of presumption to the other side in a dialogue (Walton, *Plaus. Arg.*, 1992). The asking of an appropriate critical question, one that matches the argumentation scheme, shifts the weight of presumption back to the other side, in turn. The basis for evaluation of the argumentation then is to be sought in the burden of proof, the obligations of each party to prove, disprove, or question some particular proposition, as set in the opening stages of the dialogue. This initial confrontation, in conjunction with the argumentation schemes used at any particular stage of the argumentation in the dialogue, determine the evaluation of the argument as strong, weak, open to doubt, fallacious, and so forth. This way of evaluating an argument is dialectical in the sense that it depends on the prior sequence of exchanges in a dialogue, on the type of dialogue, and on the initial problem the participants have set out to solve or resolve.

In this framework, attaching some numerical values, truth-values, or whatever, to the propositions is not, by itself, much help. The locus of evaluation is elsewhere. You need to look at the argument in context, especially in relation to the discussion that has preceded it in the dialogue. The argumentation schemes and the matching critical questions set out a profile of dialogue–a question-reply sequence of exchanges–that defines what is correct or appropriate at any given point, in relation to the exchanges that surround it.

ARGUMENTATION SCHEMES AND THEMES

According to this new approach, any claim that a fallacy has been committed must be evaluated in relation to the text of discourse available in a given case. The first task is to locate the argument (i.e., generally a set of premises and a conclusion, that supposedly contains the fallacy). Such an argument will always occur in a context of dialogue, according to the new theory. Much of the work of analysis and evaluation of the allegedly fallacious argument will involve placing that argument in a context of dialogue.

When dealing with fallacies, there are generally three parts or aspects of a given argument to be concerned with. First, one needs to identify the argumentation scheme, or form of the argument. For example, if it is a deductive argument the form could be that of *modus ponens*. Or if it is an argument from consequences, the argumentation scheme is of the type for argumentation from consequences (see chapter 3).

Evaluating the argument at this first level, it can be criticized on two grounds. First, it may be an invalid argument, or otherwise fail to conform to the requirements appropriate for that type of argumentation scheme. Second, one or more of the premises can be criticized on the grounds that it has been inadequately supported.

The second aspect of an argument to be considered is that of relevance. Even if the argument is a good one at this first level, it still could fail to be relevant. But what do we mean here by 'relevant'? It has been argued elsewhere (Walton, *Prag. Theory,* 1995), that relevance, in this sense, is dialectical relevance, meaning that an argument is relevant if it fulfills its proper function in the given context of dialogue.

At the first level of criticism, one is mainly concerned with the premises and conclusion of the argument–what might be called its inferential structure and content. This could be called a *local* level of analysis, because the concern is with the premises and conclusion of a single argument, as opposed to considering the broader use of the inference in a context of dialogue.

With some kinds of fallacies, of the kind called errors of reasoning (Walton, *Prag. Theory,* 1995), there is no need to go beyond this first level of analysis. However, with the sophistical tactics type of fallacies, two more levels are necessary to evaluate. The third level is global.

The third level of criticism requires studying the use of an argument in a broad context of dialogue. At this level, we need to ask what type of dialogue the argument is supposed to be taking place within, and what stage of the dialogue it is in. This is called the *dialectical* level of analysis, because it pertains to how the argumentation was used in a context of dialogue to contribute to the goal of that type of dialogue. For most of the major informal fallacies, this third level of analysis is crucial. With respect to the three major informal fallacies chiefly studied in this book, it is shown that this dialectical level of analysis is absolutely crucial.

Typically, at the second level, in order to evaluate an argument as correct or fallacious, in addition to seeing whether it meets the requirements of its appropriate argumentation scheme, we also need to see how it is used over a larger segment of the dialogue, in the sequence of question-reply argumentation. To do this, we need to reconstruct a profile of dialogue in which the argumentation should properly be used, and contrast this with the actual sequence that took place. This task involves the application of a normative model of dialogue to a text of discourse given in the actual case to be analyzed (as far as it can be reconstructed). Good examples are the profiles of dialogue used to analyze the fallacy of many questions in Walton (*Quest. Reply,* 1989) and the profiles of dialogue used to analyze the fallacy of begging the question in Walton (*Begg. Quest.,* 1991).

As contrasted with an argumentation scheme, which is a local inference used at one point or stage of a dialogue an *argumentation theme* is a sequence of argumentation modelled in a profile of dialogue which reveals how the argument was used in a protracted manner over an extended stretch of dialogue.

For each argumentation scheme, there is a matching set of critical questions appropriate for that scheme. To ask an appropriate critical question in a dialogue shifts the burden of proof back onto the side of the proponent of the original argument to reply to this question successfully. For each use of an argumentation scheme by a proponent of an argument in a dialogue, typically there arises a whole sequence of questions and replies from the response of the respondent, and the subsequent replies of the proponent. This sequence of connected arguments, questions and replies, is called the argumentation theme.

By studying the argumentation theme in a given case, much can be revealed about the critical attitudes of the proponent and the respondent. For example, we can ask whether the proponent is putting forward the argumentation in a way that shows that he or she is observing the Gricean maxims of honesty, cooperativeness, relevance, and so forth, or whether he or she is not really open to paying due accord to the evidence put forward by the other side, but merely engaging in eristic dialogue or quarrelling. Such a judgment is generally best made not at too localized a level, on the basis of a single inference or putting forward of an argumentation scheme, but rather on the basis of performance over a longer, protracted sequence of dialogue exchanges.

Where a major informal fallacy has occurred in a given case, in some instances the error can be revealed, analyzed, and evaluated at the local level as an error of reasoning. We might look at the argumentation scheme, for example, and point out that one of the premises has not been adequately supported. The problem here may simply be an error or oversight, but if it is a serious enough one, we may rightly say that a fallacy was committed.

However, in other cases, things may not be this simple, because the fallacy can only be documented and proved by bringing forward textual evidence to show that the arguer's use of the argumentation theme over a protracted sequence of dialogue reveals an uncooperative, tricky or deceptive use of argumentation. Such a use of sophistical tactics can be evaluated as fallacious to the extent that it blocks the legitimate goals of the dialogue that the participants in argumentation are supposed to be engaged in (Walton, *Prag. Theory,* 1995).

In this type of case, you have to take a broader, pragmatic view of the concept of fallacy that takes the dialectical context of an argument into account. Instead of just looking at the argument at the local or micro level, you need to evaluate the larger context of dialogue in which the argument was used (Walton, *Prag. Theory,* 1995).

Clearly then, identifying the various argumentation schemes will not, by itself, solve all the problems of analyzing the various informal fallacies. But identifying the argumentation schemes, and showing how they can be used, in some cases, as reasonable arguments, is a first and essential step in studying the fallacies. Once we see how argumentation schemes can be used rightly to yield correct (if presumptive) arguments in some cases, we can work from there to study the different ways they are abused, in different contexts of dialogue, to generate fallacies.

The purpose of this book, however, is not to analyze the fallacies. The purpose is to analyze argumentation schemes. But we pick several major informal fallacies that are especially vital in relation to the study of argumentation schemes, and show the connection between the fallacy and the argumentation scheme in these cases.

CHAPTER TWO

PRESUMPTIVE REASONING

In this chapter, a pragmatic analysis of the concept of presumption is put forward that reveals the essential function and operation of presumption in argumentation. The focus of the chapter is on presumptive reasoning, on how presumptions are brought forward in arguments as kinds of premises, and as kinds of inferences that link premises to conclusions in a context of argumentative dialogue.

Consider, for example, a very ordinary example of presumptive reasoning.

Case 2.1:   John's hat is not on the peg.
Therefore, John has left the house.

This inference is warranted by an unexpressed premise, a nonexplicit presumption that functions as a major premise of a conditional form: If John's hat is not on the peg, then (we can normally expect), he has left the house. The argumentation scheme is that of argument from sign, a species of defeasible inference subject to rebuttal in the presence of any contrary relevant evidence that becomes available (see chapter 3). Most likely, this conditional would be based (in a given case) on experience that John normally, or by habit, wears his hat whenever he leaves the house.

In Case 2.1, the key premise is a presumption that is not explicitly stated–the proposition that John normally wears his hat when he leaves the house. This nonexplicit presumption licences the speaker, and any hearer, to draw the conclusion explicitly stated by the speaker–John has left the house.

Thus in this case, presumptive reasoning works as an inference through which a conclusion is drawn. But the case reveals an important distinction between explicit and nonexplicit presumptions. In the case of nonexplicit presumptions, they come to be accepted by the parties in the discussion, even though they may never be explicitly stated by any one of these parties during the discussion. The digging out of such presumptions has often been regarded as an important function of philosophy as a discipline.

In this case, the kind of inference involved is better described as implicature rather than implication, in the sense of conversational implicature described by Grice (1975). The conclusion is defeasibly drawn rather than being strictly implied by the premises.

Although presumptive reasoning is very important in philosophy, it has tended to be neglected by logicians. Although philosophers are familiar with defeasible reasoning, there would appear to be no very influential or well-developed theories of presumption.[1]

Very recently, however, computer science has taken an intense interest in so-called "default reasoning," referring to arguments based on typical instances, subject to default in special cases. This subject has come to be of practical importance in designing "inference engines" to control information retrieval in dealing with large databases. It is also important, for essentially similar reasons, in designing practical robots.

According to Pollock (1991), there are two schools of thought, a *semantical school* that bases the theory of defeasible (default) reasoning on formal semantics, and a *procedural school* that proposes analyzing defeasible reasoning by showing "how it works." The theory proposed in this chapter falls into the second procedural (pragmatic) category. A theory showing how presumption functions as a type of speech act put forward in argumentative dialogue is set out. The goal of the analysis is not to aid research in artificial intelligence specifically, but more generally, to provide a concept of presumption that is useful for the evaluation of argumentation in everyday conversations, and especially for the analysis and evaluation of informal fallacies.

Presumption is shown, in the analysis given, to be a distinctive kind of speech act halfway between assertion and mere assumption (supposition). The distinction between these three important types of speech act is analyzed within a theory of dialogue (Hamblin, 1970; Barth & Krabbe, 1982), or conversation (Grice, 1975), in which there are two participants, usually called a proponent and a respondent, who take turns reasoning with each other. In such a dialogue, different types of speech acts are employed by the participants, in their moves, in a goal-directed sequence of exchanges (Walton, *Prag. Theory,* 1995; Walton and Krabbe, 1995).

Searle (1969) made no room specifically for presumptions in his taxonomy of speech acts. But presumably, they came under the heading of *assertives,* the point of the members of this class being "to commit the speaker (in varying degrees) to something's being the case" (p. 12). Much depends here, however, on what you mean by "commitment." Presumption requires a notion of provisional commitment, not characterized by an obligation to defend the proposition in question, if challenged.

Vanderveken (1990) did not mention presumption either, in his classification of assertives. However, he did leave a little room for possibly including presumption in or around his categories of "suggest," "guess," and "hypothesize." Although it is misleading to call presumption an "assertive" speech act, that is where it fits in, according to the current taxonomies of speech acts.

One puzzling question concerning presumptions is the nature of their relation to evidence in argumentation. It seems that presumptions can go forward in an argument without being based on evidence sufficient to prove them. This appears to make them suspicious, from a logical point of view.[2] If they can outrange

---

[1] The main exceptions are noted later.

[2] This type of suspicion lies at the basis of Plato's highly successful and historically influential denunciation of the sophists as purveyors of "mere opinion."

evidence, does it not mean that argumentation based on them can become rampant, even empty speculation–mere conjecture, perhaps masquerading as argumentation that compels rational acceptance?

Moreover if critical discussion, as a type of dialogue, is typically built on presumptions–*prima facie* cases and plausible assumptions that are generally accepted but cannot be definitively proved–does it not suggest that critical discussion does not ever really prove anything? Does this not confirm our worst suspicions about the subjective character of critical discussion as a way of proving something using evidence, or arguing from verified facts? These very general questions and worries are at the heart of our concern with the concept of presumption in this chapter. It is shown that presumptive reasoning is a distinctive kind of reasoning in its own right, one that has a valuable pragmatic function in argumentation.

RECEIVED VIEWS OF PRESUMPTION

According to Lewis and Short (1969) the meaning of *praesumptio* (the Latin root term of the English word "presumption") is "a taking up and answering in advance, an anticipation of possible or suspected objections" (p. 1433). This explication of the Latin term is very revealing, because it is premised on the key concepts of (i) a sequence of questions and answers in an extended chain of argumentation running through an ongoing dialogue, (ii) an order in the sequence, and (iii) a set of "possible or suspected objections" or critical questions put forward by a respondent, at some appropriate point in the sequence of dialogue to match an argument or speech act put forward by a proponent. The phrase *in advance* is very important here.

The idea seems to be that a presumption does meet a burden of proof, but in a manner different from an assertion or argument that is nonpresumptive. The presumption somehow takes up its meeting of this burden before any actual objection is made to it in a dialogue. How this is done, or why it is useful, is not made clear, however.

Whately (1846; 1963) described presumption using the metaphor of preoccupation of a ground, based on the idea of two parties alternately occupying and contesting a piece of terrain–it seems to be a kind of military metaphor suggesting a two-party adversarial exchange or relationship. The one party occupies the ground until the other can bring forward a sufficient weight or force to dislodge it, and then the second party occupies the ground.

This engaging metaphor was backed up by Whately by phrasing it in terms of burden of proof, a concept already recognized in legal argumentation. Whately wrote that when a presumption exists in favor of the proponent of an argument, "the burden of proof lies on the side of him who would dispute it" (p. 170). For example, in a criminal trial, there is a "presumption of innocence" (p. 171) until guilt is established by the trial.

Although Whately's account succeeded in linking the concept of presumption with its partner concept of burden of proof, he left open basic questions about the exact nature of this relationship and how it works in practice.

A continuing controversy (Reinard, 1991) is whether presumption is relevant only at the beginning of a discussion, or whether it continues to be important throughout the continuance of the sequence of argumentation in the dialogue. The same kind of controversy surrounds the notion of burden of proof. Is it set at the initial stage of a dialogue once and for all, until the issue is resolved or the dialogue ends, or does it vary (shifting back and forth) as the dialogue proceeds? Indeed, given the lack of any rigorous analytical explication of the concepts of presumption and burden of proof, it is hard to distinguish between the two notions, or to show clearly where the difference lies.

Whately also brought forward the idea that there is a legitimate weight of presumption in favor of existing institutions and practices, for example, the Anglican Church. Naturally, this idea turned out to be very controversial. However, Whately's idea was backed up by an analysis of presumption offered by Perelman and Olbrechts-Tyteca (1969) which linked it with degree of risk in practical reasoning designed to conclude towards a prudent course of action. According to Perelman and Olbrechts-Tyteca, current or traditional institutions and accepted practices have a presumption in their favor because we have an idea of what to expect from accepting them. Their likely consequences or potential side effects are known better than those of a system or practice that is yet untried. This suggestion tied presumption into practical reasoning under uncertainty in concluding toward a prudent course of action, a conceptual tie-up also later advocated by Clarke (1989). The idea is that some presumptions at least can be justified on a practical basis because our practical knowledge of their expected consequences makes them a safer basis for prudential action.

This pragmatic view of presumption was developed into a fuller analysis of presumptive reasoning by Ullman-Margalit (1983). According to this analysis, a presumptive inference from one proposition, A, to another proposition, B, is based on a rule of the following form: given that A is the case, you (the rule subject) shall proceed as if B were true, unless or until you have sufficient reason to believe that B is not the case (p. 147). This rule is not meant by Ullman-Margalit to make any claim on its subject's "cognitive or epistemic systems" which involves a commitment to, or guarantee of the truth value of the derived presumption B. The analysis is meant as a pragmatic explication of presumption in the sense that it entitles one only to hold that B is true "for the purpose of concluding one's practical deliberation on the impending issue . . ." (p. 149). In this analysis, presumption is understood as based on a kind of practical inference which sanctions a pragmatic passage from one proposition to another in the context of some overarching practical deliberation or discussion on an issue regarding some contemplated course of action or policy. This pragmatic type of analysis suggested by Perelman and Olbrechts-Tyteca, Ullman-Margalit, and Clarke sees it as a species of practical reasoning of the kind outlined in chapter one.

INTRODUCTION TO NONMONOTONIC REASONING

Classical deductive logic has the property of *monotonicity,* meaning that if you have a valid argument, no matter how many new premises you add (even to the point where they form an inconsistent set), the argument still remains valid. However, practical reasoning tends to be nonmonotonic, because if new information comes in which changes the circumstances of a given situation, the rational conclusion may be to opt for a different course of action which takes this updating of information into account. Practical reasoning is dynamic or variable in a sense in which the reasoning modelled by classical deductive logic is static or "fixed."

Nonmonotonic reasoning is currently an intense topic of interest in artificial intelligence, where the following example of an argument is often cited (Reiter, 1987).

Case 2.2:   Birds fly.
　　　　　　 Tweety is a bird.
　　　　　　 Therefore, Tweety flies.

The problem concerns the interpretation of the first (major) premise. To make the argument deductively valid, you need to construe this premise as a universal (strict) conditional of the form, "For all x, if x is a bird then x flies." But what if x is a penguin, a type of bird that does not fly? The conclusion "Tweety flies" is false, but the second premise is true, therefore the major premise must be false, assuming the argument is deductively valid.

But this interpretation is problematic, because the major premise, in reality, still seems to be true, if interpreted in a less strict way. The major premise does not seem plausibly interpreted in this case as a universal conditional that asserts that all birds (without exception) fly. As Reiter said, a more natural reading of this premise is one that allows for possible exceptions, and allows for the possibility that Tweety could be an exceptional type of bird with respect to the property of flying, that is, "Normally, birds fly" or "If x is a typical bird, then we can assume by default that x flies." What is meant here by *default* is that in the absence of evidence that Tweety is atypical, we can provisionally (subject to correction) assume that Tweety flies. Thus the inference is *defeasible,* or subject to default, in the sense that it only goes forward provisionally, subject to defeat or rebuttal, should information come in showing that Tweety is not typical.

Presenting an interesting example, Reiter (1987) linked default reasoning to what is called the *closed world assumption* in computer science, the assumption stating that all relevant, positive information has been presented in an argument or presentation of a case. This assumption licences any respondent to infer that if a proposition is not explicitly stated, its negation may be assumed to hold.

Case 2.3:   To see why negative information poses a problem, consider
                 the simple example of a database for an airline flight schedule
                 representing flight numbers and the city pairs they connect.
                 We certainly would not want to include in this database all
                 flights and the city pairs they do *not* connect, which clearly
                 would be an overwhelming amount of information. For
                 example, Air Canada flight 103 does not connect London with
                 Paris, or Toronto with Montreal, or Moose Jaw with Athens,
                 or . . . .[3]

The basic principle behind this way of presenting the information, according to
Reiter is that there is far too much negative information to present explicitly. So
this negative information is presented indirectly by licencing the respondent to
draw conclusions by default reasoning.

It is very interesting to note that Reiter's presentation of the problem of
nonmonotonic reasoning in computer science reveals an important link with the
literature on informal fallacies. For it is clear that Case 2.3 is an excellent
example of the use of the *argumentum ad ignorantiam* as a type of inference.
Although this type of argument has traditionally been treated in logic textbooks
as a fallacy, the kind of case cited by Reiter suggests that it also has correct uses
as a reasonable type of default argumentation.

Reiter (1987) presented a survey of the range of different formal (deductive
and inductive) systems that have been advanced in artificial intelligence studies to
solve the problem posed by nonmonotonic reasoning. However, he concluded that
the solution would not appear to be found in any single deductive or inductive
system of logic, but rather in implicit conventions "of cooperative communication of information where it is understood by all participants that the informant
is conveying all of the relevant information" (p. 180). In such an interactive
framework of communication, any relevant item of information not conveyed is,
by default, assumed to be false.

Another example Reiter gave, interestingly, links it with yet a further traditional informal fallacy, the fallacy of many questions (complex question).

Case 2.4:   For example, if someone were to tell you that John has not
                 stopped beating the rug, you would justifiably infer that John
                 was beating the rug despite the fact that the original statement
                 might be true precisely because John never was beating the
                 rug to begin with. The point is that if this were the case, your
                 informant should have told you. Since she didn't, convention
                 dictates the appropriateness of your conclusion, despite its
                 defeasibility. (p. 180)

---

[3] Reiter (1987).

Another type of case of default reasoning cited by Reiter is the use of pictures and diagrams where the contention is that an entity is not present if it is not depicted in the diagram or picture. Reiter commented that statistical reasoning does not seem to account for this kind of inference, because it is difficult to imagine "what it could mean to assign a probability to the failure of a circuit diagram to depict a device's power supply, or what advantages there could possibly be in doing so" (p. 180). The conclusion to be drawn from these cases then is that the understanding of nonmonotonic reasoning is not to be sought in deductive or inductive formal systems of inference, but in a more broadly pragmatic account of how conventions function in licencing one participant to draw legitimate inferences in cooperative communication with another participant who conveys information, both directly and indirectly, through a dialogue.

Case 2.4 links several factors together in a way that reveals the fundamental importance of presumptive reasoning in argumentation. First, it shows that the fallacy of many questions is linked to the argument from ignorance. To understand how the rug-beating question functions as a fallacy, you have to see the underlying inference as the drawing of a conclusion from something unsaid. If something is not specifically stated as an item in a knowledge base as true (false), then we go ahead and presume it must be false (true).

Second, Case 2.4 shows how such presumptive arguments from ignorance are involved in argumentation at the metalogical level in conventions of successful communication between two or more participants in argumentation. At this level, Gricean maxims of communication[4] both govern presumptions, and are at the same time, themselves kinds of presumptions that typically licence inferences on a basis of what is left unsaid in a discussion. To understand how presumptive reasoning works, we need to ascend to a higher level of seeing how it is used in dialogue.

BURDEN OF PROOF

A *dialogue* is an orderly sequence of exchanges between two participants where each participant has a goal and the dialogue, as a whole, has a goal. In some main types of dialogues that are especially important as contexts of argumentation, the goal of one or both participants is to prove that a proposition is true.

The critical discussion is a dialogue of this type. The goal of a critical discussion (van Eemeren & Grootendorst, 1984) is to resolve a conflict of opinions. In a simple critical discussion, the goal of one participant is to prove that his or her thesis (point of view) is true (right), and the goal of the other participant is to raise doubts (critical questions). In a compound critical discussion, both participants have a thesis to be proved, and the one thesis is the opposite of the other.

---

[4] These are the Gricean cooperative principles of conversation requiring honesty, sincerity, relevance, and informativeness by participants. See Grice (1975).

Other types of dialogues, outlined in Walton (*Inf. Log.*, 1989, p. 10; *Prag. Theory*, 1995, chapter 4) include the information-seeking dialogue, where the goal is for information to be transmitted from one participant to the other, and the negotiation dialogue, where the goal is for the parties to "make a deal" by dividing up some goods or interests that are in short supply.

The concept of an obligation applies to all types of dialogue. The obligation is the function the participant has to perform, according to the rules of the dialogue, in order to fulfill his goal in the dialogue. Burden of proof is a sub-category of obligation. In a type of dialogue, called a *probative dialogue,* where the goal of a participant is to prove (or disprove) something, the participant's obligation is matched with a *weight,* a rough rating (heavy, medium, or light) which is an estimate of how difficult or easy it is to prove that particular proposition in the given context of dialogue.

Burden of proof can be thought of as a balance in a compound critical discussion. Where the burden of the one side is relatively light, the burden of the other side will be matchingly heavy (and vice versa), at the beginning (opening stage) of the dialogue.[5]

A critical discussion (van Eemeren & Grootendorst, 1984) has four stages: the opening stage, the confrontation stage, the argumentation stage, and the closing stage. The global (technical) burden of proof is set in the confrontation stage, and fixed for the duration of the discussion, through to the closing stage. However the local burden of proof (burden of proceedings) varies during the course of the discussion, depending on the type of speech act put forward by a participant at a particular move, and the state of the commitment-set at that move. The commitment-set of a participant (Hamblin, 1970; Walton & Krabbe, 1995) varies during the sequence of the dialogue.

The argumentation stage of a dialogue is best thought of as a sequence of connected subarguments, as pictured in Fig. 2.1.

Burden of proof, at the local level, depends not only on the argumentation scheme (type of argument) which has been put forward at that move, but also on the sequence of argumentation the proponent has put forward at prior moves. Depending on the strength of a participant's sequence of argumentation at a particular point in the sequence of a dialogue, the burden of proof can shift toward the other participant, meaning that he or she must reply with a correspondingly strongly argument if the participant is to successfully fulfill his or her obligation in the dialogue.

Burden of proof is an important and useful idea where conclusive resolution of a disputed issue by appeal to decisive evidence (knowledge) is not practical or possible. The problem, in such a case, is that the argumentation could go on and on and never reach a resolution. Burden of proof is a practical solution to this problem which works by setting a required weight of strength of argumentation as sufficient to prove (disprove) the contention, and thereby close the dialogue off from further argumentation.

---

[5] Walton (1988; *Plaus. Arg.,* 1992).

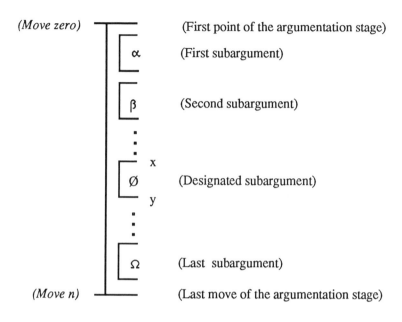

Fig. 2.1. Subarguments (Rounds) in the Argumentation Stage of a Dialogue.

At the global level, burden of proof can be set in various ways–by preponderance of evidence, by convincing evidence, or beyond reasonable doubt, for example–on a scale of increasing heaviness of the burden. At the local level,[6] some ways of apportioning burden of proof are relatively clear, for example, "He who asserts must prove." In the case of speech acts other than assertions, (e.g., questions), the apportionment of the burden may depend on many factors, like the type of question, in judging whether the asker or respondent is committed to presuppositions of the question.

But the most fundamental problem, for this chapter, is how the speech act of presumption is related to, or determined by the burden of proof. Traditionally, these two notions have been thought of as partners, but the exact nature of their relationship has never been clearly defined. Indeed, presumption and burden of proof are often confused, or treated as the same thing. Can we help to clarify this situation?

The way to begin is to observe that presumptive reasoning often plays an important role in argumentation at a local level of a dialogue, represented by

---

[6] See level ∅ of the designated subargument in Fig. 2.1.

subargument Ø in Fig. 2.1. At this level, for example, there may be a weight of presumption in favor of a particular proposition that is brought forward in a dialogue, even if hard evidence, of the sort normally required to meet a burden of proof in that type of dialogue, is not forthcoming. Presumption seems to function as a way of absolving or excusing a subargument from the usual demands of burden of proof.

COMMITMENT AND BURDEN SHIFTING

In refining Hamblin's notion of commitment in dialogue, we have to make two important distinctions between kinds of commitments. First, we need to distinguish between concessions and substantive commitments. A *substantive commitment* is a proposition that a participant in dialogue is obliged to defend, or retract, if challenged by the other party to give reasons to support it. In a word, it has a burden of proof attached to it. This is the type of commitment to a proposition that goes along with having asserted it in a dialogue. A *concession* is a commitment where there is no such obligation to defend, if challenged. Concessions are assumptions agreed to "for the sake of argument." By nature, they are temporary, and do not necessarily represent an arguer's position in a dialogue.[7]

Second, we need to distinguish between explicit commitments and implicit commitments. The commitment-set of each participant in a dialogue is divided into two sides, a *light side,* a set of propositions known, or on view, to all the participants, and a *dark side,* a set of propositions not known to, or visible to, some or all of the participants. This dark side set represents the implicit commitments of a participant in a dialogue. These are propositions that the participant is committed to, but has not explicitly agreed to, or otherwise given a clear indication in the dialogue of any commitment to them.[8] They have to be guessed, or plausibly conjectured from what we know about the nature of the participant's explicit commitments, as they have become apparent in the dialogue. For example, if George has been consistently socialist in a dialogue, so far, and shows plenty of evidence of being a committed socialist, we can make plausible conjectures about his commitments on an issue on which he has, so far in the dialogue, expressed no explicit opinions, for example, on how to finance the postal service. Although he has not explicitly committed himself to the proposition that the postal service should be funded by the government, and we do not know that he is committed to this proposition on the evidence of the dialogue, still, we can conjecture that he is likely to be committed to it, as a plausible guess, based on what we know of his position so far.[9]

The games CAVE and CAVE+ in Walton (*Quest. Reply,* 1989) have this dark-side commitment feature, and the reader who wishes a fuller exposition of how the rules of a dialogue incorporate this notion can find some answers there.

---

[7] The account of commitment outlined derives from a joint research project undertaken at NIAS with Erik Krabbe, now published as Walton & Krabbe, *Commitment in Dialogue* (1995).

[8] See Walton & Krabbe (1995).

[9] See Walton & Krabbe (1995).

Suffice it to note here that many of an arguer's commitments in argumentation are not explicitly stated, or agreed to as such, in a dialogue, and therefore have to be inferred or conjectured, on a provisional or presumptive basis. Otherwise, we could not make sense of ordinary argumentation in everyday conversations based on unexpressed premises and other kinds of important but unstated presumptions.

Given these distinctions then, how can we give a clear and useful account of the distinction between presumption and burden of proof? What is the essential difference between these two concepts?

Presumption is clearly connected to burden of proof in argumentation, but how? To begin with, we should note the difference between pure supposition and assertion as kinds of speech acts. Assertion always carries with it a burden of proof, because assertion implies substantive commitment to the proposition asserted. Supposition (or assumption) however, requires only the agreement of the respondent, and carries with it no burden of proof on either side. Presumption, as a speech act, is halfway between mere supposition and assertion. Presumption essentially means that the proponent of the proposition in question does not have a burden of proof, only a burden to disprove contrary evidence, should it arise in the future sequence of dialogue. The burden here has three important character- istics—it is a future, conditional, and negative burden of proof. It could perhaps be called a burden to rebut, in appropriate circumstances.

Presumption is functionally opposed to burden of proof, meaning that presumption removes or absolves one side from the burden, and shifts the burden to the other side. In this respect, presumption functions as a speech act in dialogue as a switching of roles of the two participants (Walton, *Plaus. Arg.*, 1992, chapter 2). Fallacies can arise, however, because this shifting back and forth can be tricky (Walton, *Prag. Theory*, 1995).

One fallacy that can be explained in relation to this shifting of the burden of proof from one party to the other in a dialogue is *petitio principii*, the fallacy of circular reasoning or "begging the question." If the proponent of a thesis A in a critical discussion has the burden of proving A, but then puts A forward as a presumption in the discussion, the argument is circular. The proponent is "begging the question" in the sense that he or she is begging the respondent to accept, as a presumption, that is, without proof, a proposition that the respondent is obliged to prove. This type of move is dialectically incoherent, in the sense that the arguer asks to be granted, without having to prove it, a proposition the arguer is supposed to be proving.

The fallacy of begging the question is actually much more complicated than this simple sketch of it indicates, when it comes to the interpretation and evalu- ation of particular cases.[10] But even this bare conceptual sketch of the basis of the fallacy shows that burden of proof is different from presumption. The existence of the fallacy of begging the question as a fallacy proves that there is a difference, in general, between burden of proof and presumption. The fallacy is precisely the fusing (or confusing) of the difference between these two things.

---

[10] See Walton (*Begg. Quest.*, 1991).

Whately (1846; 1963) astutely saw how failure to be attuned to shifts in a burden of proof in argumentation can be disastrous in allowing one party to unfairly get the best of another in an exchange. Ignorance of such matters can be a major tactical failure in argumentation. Whately compared it to the case of troops in a fort who are strong enough to defend it against all attacks, but foolishly sally forth to engage the enemy in the field, and are defeated. Whately asked us to imagine a case where a person who, confronted with an unsupported accusation, tries to prove his or her own innocence by collecting all the facts he or she can muster, instead of defying the accuser to prove the charge. Such a reply would be ineffective, and even rouse a strong suspicion of guilt by appearing too defensive. The attacked person has overlooked the strongest weapon of defence–the burden of proof. The problem is that the attacker falsely appears to have the weight of presumption on his or her side, to the extent that the underlying shift in the burden of proof has gone unnoticed.

It is this kind of tricky, unperceived, and unlicenced shift in a burden of proof in a speech act of presumption in dialogue that underlies the working mechanism behind other fallacies as well, like the *ad ignorantiam* and the fallacy of many questions, as we have seen. In the next section, a set of speech act conditions defining the movement and sequencing in the functioning of presumption in dialogue are given. This set of conditions shows how the back and forth shifting of presumption should work as a speech act in any sequence of argumentative dialogue generally. In conjunction with the requirements for a particular type of dialogue in a given case, this set of conditions can be used as a general framework for evaluating presumptive reasoning.

SPEECH ACT CONDITIONS DEFINING PRESUMPTION

In the speech act analysis of presumption given by the 12 conditions that follow, presumption is understood as a kind of speech act that is halfway between assertion and mere assumption. An assertion normally carries with itself in argumentation a burden of proof: "He who asserts must prove!" By contrast, if a participant in argumentation puts forward a mere assumption, he or she (or anyone in the dialogue) is free to retract it at any subsequent point in the dialogue without having to give evidence or reasons that would refute it. Assumptions are freely undertaken and can freely be rejected in a dialogue.

Presumptions are between these other two types of speech acts somewhere. A presumption is a proposition put in place as a commitment tentatively in argu- mentation to facilitate the goals of a dialogue. Presumptions are often put forward for practical reasons, to enable the dialogue or an action to go ahead, even if there is a lack of hard evidence that would confirm or refute the proposition in question definitively, one way or the other.

The key thing about the speech act of presumption in argumentation, according to the analysis given later, is that it reverses the burden of proof in a dialogue. More generally speaking, presumption reverses the roles of the two participants in argumentation. Normally, the burden to prove is on the one who asserts proposition *A* in argumentation, as something he or she is committed to in the dialogue. However, when a presumption is brought forward by a proponent, the burden is on the respondent to refute it, or otherwise it goes into place as a commitment.

The basic idea is that a dialogue is an extended (global) sequence of exchanges of speech acts that has a goal-directed over-all structure. But within this global structure there are "rounds" or subarguments that are woven together into the larger fabric of the dialogue. For example, a dialogue could be a critical discussion of whether the practice of tipping is generally a good thing or not, and a subargument within the larger dialogue could be a discussion of whether or not tipping creates some problems for fairly assessing income tax (Walton, *Plaus. Arg.*, 1992).

The idea is that a presumption stays in place for a certain number of moves in a dialogue, but is not a permanent or nonretractable commitment for either party that must stay in place for the whole duration of the dialogue. Typically, a presumption stays in place long enough for the participants to finish the round of argumentation in which they are currently engaged. In order to be useful, presumptions must have a certain amount of "sticking power," but by their nature, they are tentative and subject to later retraction. This analysis of presumption has been given as a set of four speech act conditions in Walton (*Plaus. Arg.*, 1992). The version that follows is a slightly simplified recounting of the four conditions.

In the analysis that follows, we speak of the subargument as a "round," a sequence of argumentation that can be isolated as having a structure (premises, conclusions, inferences) of its own. This round provides a useful place, a localized setting, where a presumption can be set in place, during the opening moves of the round. We call the actual point at which a presumption is brought forward for consideration "move *x*." The round also has a duration, lasting to a move or point *y*, where the presumption can be given up or cancelled.

I.   *Preparatory Conditions*
1.   There is a context of dialogue that involves two participants, a proponent and a respondent.
2.   The dialogue provides a context within which a sequence of reasoning could go forward with a proposition *A* as a useful assumption in the sequence.

II. *Placement Conditions*
1.   At some point *x* in the sequence of dialogue, *A* is brought forward by the proponent, either as a proposition the proponent explicitly asks the respondent to accept for the sake of argument, or as a nonexplicit assumption that is part of the proponent's sequence of reasoning.
2.   The respondent has an opportunity at *x* to reject *A*.
3.   If the respondent fails to reject *A* at *x*, then *A* becomes a commitment of both parties during the subsequent sequence of dialogue.

III. *Retraction Conditions*

1. If, at some subsequent point y in the dialogue $(x < y)$, any party wants to rebut A as a presumption, then that party can do so, provided he or she can give a good reason for doing so. Giving a good reason means showing that the circumstances of the particular case are exceptional, or that new evidence has come in that falsifies the presumption.

2. Once having accepted A at x however, the respondent is obliged to let the presumption A stay in place during the dialogue for a sufficient time to allow the proponent to use it for purposes of argumentation (unless a good reason for rebuttal under clause 1 can be given).

IV. *Burden Conditions*

1. Generally, at point x, the burden of showing that A has some practical value as a useful presumption in a sequence of argumentation is on the proponent who proposes to use A as a presumption in his or her argument.

2. Past point x in the dialogue, once A is in place as a working presumption (either explicitly or implicitly) the burden is on the respondent to rebut the presumption by giving a good reason for rejecting it.

These essential conditions for the speech act of presumption in dialogue make it clear that the key idea is the shifting of the burden of rebuttal. At a particular point in the dialogue, the participants switch roles. The burden was first on the proponent, but then at this particular point, the burden of providing a good reason shifts to the respondent.

The basic way that a presumption operates in a dialogue is to give the argument some provisional basis for going ahead, even in the absence of firm premises known to be true. Once the presumption is lodged into place, the respondent is obliged temporarily to leave it in place for a while, giving the proponent a fair chance to draw conclusions using it as a premise. How firm a weight of commitment is put into place in such a lodging depends on the type of dialogue, and other global factors like the burden of proof, as well as local requirements defined by the type of argumentation scheme used at the local level. But quite generally, in any of the contexts of dialogue suitable as frameworks for argumentation as considered previously, this set of speech act conditions for presumption shows how the shifting back and forth of presumptive argumentation should work. Thus it provides a general normative framework for the use of presumptive reasoning in dialogue which can help in the determination of certain kinds of argumentation as fallacious or nonfallacious.

PRESUMPTIONS AND PRESUPPOSITIONS

Presumption is a notion that is fundamental to philosophy as a subject, but has generally been ignored as a concept for serious investigation. In contrast, presupposition is a concept that has been studied in great intensity by both philosophers and linguists, resulting in a prolific variety of different theories, summarized by Levinson (1983). Both concepts can be put to use for varying purposes, and there is some flexibility in how they can be interpreted. Consequently, it is not easy to tell the two apart, or to firmly fix their key differences. It seems that, in many cases, they refer to roughly the same thing. Given the existing literature, it is especially hard to say what presupposition is, briefly, with much confidence.

However, in the following, a brief sketch is given of what is taken to be the key differences between the concept of presumption that is the target of analysis for this chapter, and the broad notion of presupposition that seems–if not very clearly–to have emerged as a technical term in linguistics and the philosophy of language.

Presupposition relates to a specific type of speech act and the appropriate type of response when that type of speech act is used in a dialogue. It is not so much a question of burden of proof, or of bringing forward evidence, but of what happens to the respondent's commitments when he or she gives the normal or appropriate type of response in a dialogue. For example, the concept of a presupposition of a question can be defined pragmatically as follows. A presupposition of a question asked by a proponent in dialogue with a respondent is any proposition the respondent becomes committed to in giving any direct answer to the question. For example, a presupposition of "Have you stopped cheating on your income tax?" is the proposition "You (the respondent) have cheated on your income tax." It is a presupposition because no matter which direct answer the respondent gives, the preferred answer (yes), or the nonpreferred answer (no), he or she becomes committed to that proposition (Walton, *Inf. Log.*, 1989, chapter 1).

The proposition that the respondent has cheated on his or her income tax could also be described as a presumption of the proponent's question, meaning that one the respondent commits to it by giving a direct answer, a burden is put on the respondent to then disprove it, if he or she decides to no longer accept it. And in general, presuppositions can often be described or explained as presumptions. But there is a key difference. When you describe a proposition as a presupposition, the essential thing is not the burden of proof, or the shifting of it from one party to the other, as it is in a presumption.

Presupposition has to do with the order in which a sequence of propositions put forward by a proponent in a dialogue are taken on as commitments by a respondent. With the income tax question, the problem is that asking it in a dialogue, in such a way that a direct answer can be given, presumes (prior to this, in the logical sequence of dialogue) that the respondent has already committed himself or herself to the proposition that he or she has cheated on his or her income tax. But this may or may not be the case.

If it is the case, there may be no problem. But if it is not the case in the real context of dialogue in a given, particular instance of the asking of this question, there could be a serious problem. The fallacy of many questions (complex question) could have been committed.

Of course, the respondent can always reply: "Your question has a false presupposition–I have never cheated on my income tax!" In other words, the respondent could refuse to give a direct answer by questioning, or objecting to the question. In most ordinary contexts of conversation, fortunately, this option is available.

But if there is textual evidence from the context of dialogue that the proponent is adopting a tactic of trying to seal off this option, or badger the respondent into not taking advantage of it, this is precisely the type of context where the charge of committing the fallacy of many questions is appropriate.

In many cases of everyday conversation, for example in asking directions, the proponent is operating on the presumption that the proposition advanced by the respondent is right or reliable. But the proponent is not thereby (necessarily) presupposing that the answer will be right. Nor is it a presupposition of the question "Which way to room C300?" that the answer given by the respondent is right. The proponent waits until the answer is given, and then if it seems reasonable, and there is no reason to question it, or think it is wrong, he or she goes ahead and presumes that it is (plausibly) right. This shows a difference between presumption and presupposition, because the questioner is not presupposing that the answer is right, in asking the question.

The question has presuppositions, it is true. For example, the question presupposes that room C300 exists, that there is a way to get there, and so forth. These can also be described as presumptions inherent in the asking of the question. But although the questioner presumes that the answer given is correct or reliable, it is not (necessarily) the case that the questioner, or the question, presupposes that the answer given is correct or reliable. That would only be the case if the proponent (questioner) had some reason, to which he or she was committed previously, that this particular respondent was a particularly reliable source, who could be trusted to give a correct answer to this question–for example, if he had been told previously this person was a security officer who was expert in his knowledge of all the corridors and rooms in this building. Here, the very strong presumption of correctness, in advance, could be described as a presupposition.

With regard to the notion of presupposition, it is important to distinguish (1) what the question presupposes, as opposed to (2) what asking the question presupposes, and (3) what the questioner presupposes, in asking that question. In keeping with the orientation of the traditional literature, we have concentrated on (1). But perhaps you could say that (3) comes closest to the idea of presumption.

TESTIMONY, PRESUMPTION, AND FALLACIES

Quite commonly we accept propositions on the basis of having been told they are true by someone we think is an authority (e.g., an expert), or is in a special position to know about this sort of proposition. It is quite common to do this for practical purposes, as a basis for action. Acceptance in such a case is tentative, subject to counter-indications, and is given even in the absence of hard evidence (based on knowledge, rather than just testimony and trust).

Case 2.5:   I am going to a lecture in an unfamiliar building and ask a passerby, "Which way to room C300?" He replies, "Turn left at the next corner, then right, and go straight to the end of the building, past the Dean's Office."

In this case, I have no reason to disbelieve the passerby, and go ahead on the presumption that what he says is right. Of course, he could be trying to deceive me, but if I have no reason to think that is the case, I reasonably presume that his directions are right.

Another type of case (Clarke, 1989) illustrates that we tend to give a greater weight of presumption to the say so of someone who is in a special position of authority.

Case 2.6:   The policeman tells me that the road ahead is blocked by a collapsed bridge; I accept what he tells me as true and take a detour. (p. 10)

According to Clarke, in such a case, the presumption is accepted "in the absence of grounds for doubt," even though it is "not directly confirmed relative to one's own experience" (p. 10). The testimony is accepted on trust, as a provisional basis for action.

These cases reveal links between presumption and two of the major informal fallacies. The *argumentum ad verecundiam* (argument to modesty or respect) is the use of an appeal to authority (often expertise) to convince someone to accept a conclusion. Such appeals are often quite reasonable in argumentation.

Case 2.7:   Bob and Helen are having a critical discussion on the issue of abortion, and the question arises of whether many abortions are carried out in the third or latest stage of pregnancy. Helen cites the medical statistics on this question, attributing them to a doctor who is head of a medical research institute on reproductive medicine.

Much depends here on how Helen uses this appeal in her argument but, in principle, her use of appeal to expert authority in the previous case could be quite reasonable.

Such authority-based arguments, of course, can also be abused, and quite justifiably be labeled as fallacious in other cases. The "authority" cited could be an expert in the wrong field, not an expert at all, or the proponent could try to stifle any attempt to question the expert's credentials, and so forth. See Walton (*Inf. Log.*, 1989, chapter 7).

But even when they are nonfallacious, as used in a dialogue, appeals to authority are generally weak, tentative, presumptive, subjective, and testimony-based arguments. They are inherently subject to critical questioning, or even rebuttal, on various grounds–especially on grounds relating to the reliability of the source cited.

Another major informal fallacy involved is the *argumentum ad ignorantiam* (argument to ignorance) that takes the form: proposition A is not known to be true (false), therefore A is false (true). This type of argumentation is evidently connected in an intimate and important way to presumptive reasoning, a kind of reasoning that goes forward precisely in a kind of situation where there is absence of knowledge. In general, in presumptive reasoning, you accept a proposition A as true (false) provided that you do not have any hard evidence (knowledge) that the proposition is false (true). Presumption is best seen not as a substitute for knowledge, but as a way of going forward tentatively (provisionally, subject to correction) in argumentation, in the absence of knowledge that is available within the practical constraints given, in relation to the problem or dialogue.

In the standard treatment of the logic textbooks, it is often stated or presumed that all arguments from ignorance are fallacious. For example, Copi and Cohen (1990) wrote that the argument from ignorance is "the mistake that is committed whenever it is argued that a proposition is true simply on the basis that it has not been proved false, or that it is false because it has not been proved true." They add that such fallacious appeals to ignorance are most common in developing science or pseudo-science contexts, it would seem, where absence of knowledge is preponderant over knowledge.

Copi and Cohen conceded that "appeal to ignorance" is "appropriate" in the context of a criminal trial, where "an accused person is assumed innocent until proved guilty." They comment:

> But *this* appeal to ignorance succeeds only where innocence must be assumed in the absence of proof to the contrary; in other contexts such an appeal is indeed an argument *ad ignorantiam*. (p. 94)

It is not too clear exactly what they mean to say here. What they say is that in this special context, the appeal to ignorance is not really an argument *ad ignorantiam* (and hence, not a fallacy), because "innocence must be assumed in the absence of proof to the contrary." But why is that? It seems that, they are saying, it is not a fallacious argument from ignorance because, somehow the appeal to ignorance is legitimated by the appropriateness of the act of making an assumption. But why should the making of an assumption somehow legitimize the appeal to ignorance in this special case, excluding the argument from being an *argumentum ad ignorantiam*? A problem is posed, because the argument from ignorance is connected to the notion of an assumption, but in an unclear way that would undoubtedly prove puzzling to students using this textbook.

There are plenty of other cases, however, that suggest that *argumentum ad ignorantiam* is often a reasonable (nonfallacious) type of argument.[11]

Case 2.8:   An expert on the South American economy is asked whether rubber is a major product of Guyana. She knows that rubber is a major product of Peru and Columbia, and knows enough about Guyana to confidently presume that rubber is not a major product there. She replies: "Rubber is not a major product of Guyana, at least to my knowledge."[12]

In this case, the expert has used a *modus tollens* inference of the following form.

If rubber were a major product of Guyana, I would know that it is.
I do not know this.
Therefore (presumably), rubber is not a major product of Guyana.

As a kind of presumptive reasoning, such an *argumentum ad ignorantiam* seems quite reasonable. It is a defeasible (default) argument, but that (by itself) should not make it fallacious.

One could argue that the argument in Case 2.8 is not really an argument from ignorance, because it is, at least partly, based on the expert's knowledge, not her ignorance. One might cite Case 2.1 as comparable. The observer in that case can presumably observe directly that John's hat is not on the peg. Therefore, the observer is not arguing from ignorance, but from knowledge backed up by empirical evidence. One might therefore argue that this case is not an *argumentum ad ignorantiam.*

But such an argument is not as strong in Case 2.8, because the expert did not in fact have any positive or negative knowledge that Guyana is definitely a major rubber producer or not in her memory. She just inferred that Guyana is not a major rubber producer on the basis of not having any definite knowledge that this country is a major rubber producer.

It seems then that the *argumentum ad ignorantiam* is sometimes a reasonable kind of argumentation, and when it is, it is because it is somehow based on presumptive reasoning–an inference based on a presumption about what one would know if it were the case. Identifying the argumentation schemes for this type of argumentation is the subject of chapter four.

---

[11] Recall Case 2.3 as well.

[12] Collins, Warnock, Aiello, and Miller (1975, p. 398).

INTRODUCTION TO THE FALLACY OF *SECUNDUM QUID*

According to Hamblin (1970), the fallacy of *secundum quid,* meaning "in a certain respect" (*para to pe,* in Greek) refers to neglect of qualifications to a term or a generalization. More explicitly, quoting from a textbook account cited by Hamblin, ". . . this fallacy consists of using a proposition, which has a qualified meaning, as though it applied in all circumstances and without restriction" (p. 30). A popular example is the following case.

Case 2.9:   Everyone has the right to his own property. Therefore, even though Jones has been declared insane, you had no right to take away his weapon.[13]

The fallacy of *secundum quid* in such a case evidently lies in the failure of the argument to take into account that there are legitimate kinds of exceptions to the generalization about the right to property, and that the case in point is one of these exceptional cases.

This account of the fallacy seems straightforward enough, at least up to a point, but the problem is that the textbooks use a confusing variety of different terms to refer to the same, or what appear to be similar, or closely related errors.

Copi and Cohen (1990) identify two fallacies that have to do with neglect of qualifications in arguing from a generalization to a particular case, or vice versa.

> In political and moral argument, and in most affairs of importance in community life, we rely upon statements of how things generally are, how people generally behave, and the like. But, even when general claims are entirely plausible, we must be careful not to apply them to particular cases too rigidly. Circumstances alter cases; a generalization that is true by and large may not apply in a given case, for good reasons having to do with the special (or "accidental") circumstances of that case. When we apply a generalization to individual cases that it does not properly govern, we commit the *fallacy of Accident.* When we do the reverse, and carelessly or by design, apply a principle that is true of a particular case to the great run of cases, we commit the *fallacy of Converse Accident.* (p. 100)

The kind of problem or error pointed out by this pair of fallacies appears to be essentially the same as the error in Case 2.9, identified by other texts as the fallacy of *secundum quid.* Still more confusingly, other textbooks label the kind of error Copi and Cohen call "converse accident" as the fallacy of over-generalization (glittering generality). All in all, the bewildering variety of different labels for what seems to be the same kind of fallacy (or the same family of fallacies) is a

---

[13] Engel (1976, p. 66).

serious problem for informal logic, with regard to the identification and analysis of the type of error at stake here.

If we are to retain a traditional term for this fallacy, *secundum quid* is probably better than "accident" (and/or "converse accident"), because the latter terms are bound to the Aristotelian notion of essential versus accidental properties.[14] This doctrine is unfamiliar and abstruse to modern readers (and students), and it is less than helpful to have to explain the origin of the term to such an audience or readership, especially given that the Aristotelian doctrine appears to have little or nothing to do with what is mainly important about this fallacy. We propose calling it the fallacy of *secundum quid* or, in English, *the fallacy of neglect of qualifications,* or alternatively *overlooking special circumstances.*

The basic problem with someone who commits this kind of fallacy is an attitude of over-rigidity, a kind of dogmatic attitude that fails to be flexible enough to permit the arising of appropriate critical questions about the special circumstances of a particular case. The fallacy rests on a confusion, or inappropriate shift between the following two types of generalizations:

> STRICT CONDITIONAL: $(\forall x)\ (Fx \supset Gx)$: For all x, if x has property F, then x has property G.

> DEFAULT CONDITIONAL: For a typical x, if x has property F, then we can presume, subject to default in nontypical cases, that x has property G.

The strict conditional of classical deductive logic has the property that if it is true that x has F, but false that x has G, then the whole conditional, $(\forall x)\ (Fx \supset Gx)$ is false. In other words, one instance of $F_a \wedge \neg G_a$ overturns (conclusively defeats) the conditional generalization. This property does not work for the default (defeasible) conditional. It only works in the case where the individual a is typical with respect to properties F and G. But one has to be open-minded (not rigid) here, because there is the open possibility, which we may discover in the future, that a is not typical in some significant way.

Default conditionals are inherently pragmatic because they must be evaluated in relation to a given type of dialogue, and the goals for that type of dialogue, which impose practical requirements on commitments in argumentation, including prior requirements of global burden of proof. As Rescher (1977) put it, the kind of conditional involved here is "provisoed" to how things go "normally" or "naturally," subject to dialectical countermoves that could possibly defeat it in the future course of a disputation. Rescher concluded that the logic of this defeasible type of conditional has to be evaluated in relation to a sequencing of moves and countermoves in an organized argumentative exchange of disputation.

The kind of exceptive argumentation or defeasible reasoning involved in the *secundum quid,* modelled using the default conditional as a major premise, it

---

[14] Hamblin (1970, pp. 28-31) and Walton (*Sec. Quid.,* 1990).

seems, can be reasonable in some cases, fallacious in others. The problem then is one of evaluation, and a pragmatic framework for working towards a solution based on argumentation schemes is given in chapter five.

THE PRACTICAL NATURE OF PRESUMPTION

Presumption, as characterized in this chapter, following the analysis of Walton, *Plaus. Arg.,* 1992, is an essentially pragmatic notion which enables a discussion or action to go ahead on a rational, even if provisional basis, where access to evidence that would definitively resolve a question is lacking. For even if the evidence is insufficient, there may be enough of it to indicate the wisdom of a provisional course of action, in given circumstances. Such a procedure can be rationally justified, if, for practical but good reasons, a burden of proof can be set to tilt the resolution of the issue in one direction or the other.

For example, in a potentially hazardous situation, it may be prudentially wise to tilt the burden of proof in the direction of safety. The principle behind this way of proceeding is called *tutiorism,* sticking to the safest known way of proceeding where there is doubt, or lack of knowledge on how best to proceed in a given set of circumstances. The maxim is to "err on the side of safety," where doubt creates the potential for danger.

A simple example is the accepted procedure for handling weapons on a firing range. The principle is always to assume a weapon is loaded (or at least, to act on that presumption by forbearing from waving it around, or pointing it at someone), unless you are sure that it is not loaded. The test of whether you are sure of this is that you have, just before, inspected the chamber and perceived clearly that it is empty.

The *ad ignorantiam* nature of this type of presumptive reasoning is quite clear. If you do not know the weapon is unloaded, then you infer that it is loaded. Or at least, you operate on this presumption, by acting as though it is a loaded weapon (Walton, *Arg. Ig.,* 1995).

The same kind of example shows also, however, how tied to the specifics of a context or situation this kind of reasoning is. Suppose you are a soldier in wartime getting ready to defend your position against an imminent enemy assault. Here, reasoning again on practical grounds of safety or self-preservation, you act on the presumption that your weapon may be empty, by checking to see that it is not empty. It is the same kind of *ad ignorantiam* inference as the one in the firing range case, but turned around in this new situation to reason in the opposite direction.

Presumptive reasoning is a lot more common in everyday life than you might think until you begin to reflect on it. It has many uses, and many practical justifications. One of the most common uses is to facilitate practical actions in situations when a commitment must be acted upon or implemented, even in the absence of hard evidence sufficient to resolve an issue in time to be of use. Practical reasoning, in such cases, often rests on general presumptions based on routine or customary ways of doing something. Such practices are often justified because they have been found to be successful in the past by practitioners skilled in this type of task.

It is quite common for presumptions to be based on expert opinion where the person who acts on the presumption–not being an expert–is not in a position to verify the proposition by basing it on hard evidence within the field of expertise in question. Such second-hand knowledge is, from the point of view of the user, really based on presumption.

Customs, fashions, and popularly accepted ways of doing things, are another important source of presumptions. With many choices of how to do things in life, in the absence of knowledge that one way of doing something is any better or more harmful than another, people often tend to act on the presumption that the way to do something is the popularly accepted way of doing it.

Manners and conventions of polite behavior are sources of presumptions that enable business and social activities to proceed smoothly, expedited by tolerance and cooperation. These are the sorts of nonexplicit presumptions that we take for granted so often in daily, practical affairs, without really thinking about how important they are.

The following case is a good example of how a nonexplicit presumption functions as part of a sequence of practical reasoning in the context of a discussion of a practical problem.

Case 2.10:   Bob is an astronaut in orbit in a space capsule, and he is suffering from acute life-threatening symptoms of nausea, breathing difficulty, and dizziness. He has a certain medication, M, aboard the capsule, which he could take, unless he has a rare genetic condition, X, which would make this medication fatal for him to take. Bob's physician says to Bob's mother, Alice, "We know that your husband, Henry, has condition X, and that condition X is genetically linked from fathers to sons, therefore we should not tell Bob to take M." Alice replies, "I have never told anyone this, but Henry is not Bob's father." Alice goes on to tell the physician the true circumstances of how Bob came to be conceived, while Henry was on military service overseas.

In this case, the whole sequence of practical reasoning initially went forward on the basis of the unstated presumption that Henry is Bob's father. Normally, we would have no reason to doubt or challenge this presumption. However, in this case, Alice brings forward new evidence relating to the special circumstances of the case. The doctor would have no reason not to accept what she says as reliable, since she is Bob's mother, and Bob's life is at stake.

We can represent, in outline, the sequence of practical reasoning involved, as follows.

1. The usual treatment for someone who has symptoms like those of Bob, is to take M.

2. The exception is the kind of case where the patient has condition X.

3. But, as far as we know, Bob does not have condition X.

4. Therefore, Bob should take M.

5. But, if Bob's father has condition X, Bob should not take M, because X is sex-linked, and taking M is fatal for patients with condition X.

6. We know that Henry has condition X.

7. And we presume, or take it for granted, that Henry is Bob's father, because Henry is the husband of Alice, and Alice is Bob's mother.

This last step in the sequence of reasoning contains a key inference explicitly represented in the following.

Henry is Alice's husband.
Bob is Alice's son.
Therefore, Henry is the father of Bob.

The physician accepted this presumptive inference, knowing that the premises are true. In the face of having no evidence to the contrary, he drew the inference (implicitly) from the premises to accepting the conclusion. However, Alice's introduction of new evidence overturned the presumptive inference from going forward in this case. Why? Because normally one presumes that a woman's husband is the father of her child, until paternity is rebutted or disproved by the circumstances known in a particular case. In this case, presuming that Alice was giving credible evidence to rebut this presumption, the conclusion of the inference has to be withdrawn.

In this case, there is a practical problem that is urgent–should Bob take M or not. The problem is argued out in a kind of expert consultation dialogue between the physician and Bob's mother. What should they do? Implicit in their reasoning was the presumption that Henry is Bob's father. Such a presumption would normally go forward unchallenged. But in this case, once rebutted, it changed the outcome of the sequence of reasoning entirely.

Nonexplicit presumptions are very common and important in everyday argumentation. To understand them more fully, the concept of commitment in dialogue is the key.

IMPLICATIONS FOR ARGUMENTATION AND FALLACIES

Much more remains to be learned about presumptive reasoning, but what we have learned in this chapter about its leading characteristics has fundamental implications for the project of analyzing informal fallacies as types of errors of reasoning, and for the project of the normative evaluation of argumentation generally. In the past, presumptive reasoning has been too often and severely condemned and neglected as inherently untrustworthy, erroneous, or even fallacious. Surprisingly, it has often been cast aside as being of little or no importance to philosophy.

Presumptive reasoning should be understood as inherently nonmonotonic, in the sense that it is always subject to revision or correction on the basis of new information that may come in at some future point. This means that nonmonotonic reasoning is often circular, in the sense that the new information introduced by the particular circumstances of a given case at issue often provides feedback, subjecting a conclusion based on presumptive inference to correction or enrichment. This circularity of reasoning is not necessarily a fallacious circularity, however.[15] In fact, it is characteristic of the self-correcting aspect of presumptive reasoning generally. Here, we have to overcome the prejudice against circular reasoning as being inherently fallacious.

In some cases of default reasoning, a list of kinds of exceptions can be well-defined. For example, in the Tweety case, we may have a list of the nonflying birds, including penguins, ostriches, and so forth. But in other cases, new information could come in that could not have been anticipated on any list of standard exceptions. Tweety may be a canary, normally a flying type of bird, but in fact, it could be that Tweety has an injured wing. Thus the presumptive conditional must generally be regarded as a open-ended generalization that is subject to unanticipated objections in a given case. Hence the job of evaluating presumptive reasoning is inherently pragmatic, in that it depends on the particular circumstances of a given case, as far as these are known, to a given point. This context-sensitivity and openness to revision is also characteristic of practical reasoning generally–a kind of reasoning that takes as its object an inherently variable situation unfolding in time.

As we have seen, there are many different kinds of basis for making presumptions, and it is also true that the evidence for judging a presumptive inference as successful (correct, justified, acceptable) or not are inherently pragmatic, fitting a context of dialogue. First, it depends on the type of dialogue involved, for example, a critical discussion. Second, it depends on the speech act. Presumption is a type of speech act, but presumptions are also put forward in questions, arguments, and other kinds of speech acts. Third, it depends on the stage of the dialogue the speech act occurs in–here we have been concentrating on the argumentation stage primarily. Fourth, it depends on the burden of proof, on the conditions for the speech act of presumption in the given context of dialogue, and generally on the obligations of the proponent and respondent of the presumption.

---

[15] See Walton (*Begg. Quest.*, 1991).

Fifth, it depends on the information given in the text of discourse of a dialogue explicitly, or on information that can be inferred by conventions of politeness and implicature from the given discourse. Thus judging presumptive reasoning often depends on expectations and conventions of politeness that are not explicitly stated in discourse.

Generally, presumptive reasoning can be seen as a forward-moving sequence in a dialogue–Fig. 2.2 (similar to the comparable figure in Walton, *Plaus. Arg.,* 1992, p. 68) outlines the sequence. At the choice point, the inference goes forward or not, subject to default. And then, even when the inference succeeds and the conclusion is drawn, that conclusion remains subject to possible future defeat by new circumstances that may arise in the future.

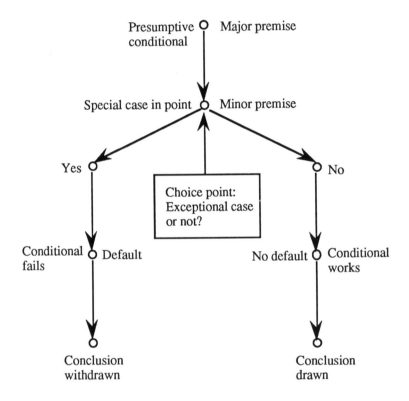

Fig. 2.2. Movement (going forward) of Presumptive Reasoning.

As portrayed here, presumptive reasoning is neither deductive nor inductive in nature, but represents a third distinct type of reasoning of the kind classified by Rescher (1976) as *plausible reasoning,* an inherently tentative kind of reasoning subject to defeat by the special circumstances (not defined inductively or statistically) of a particular case. Rescher also saw this kind of reasoning as inherently dialectical in nature, meaning that it needs to be judged in a context of dialogue. The recognition of this third type of reasoning has important and fundamental implications for the analysis of informal fallacies.

Cases 2.3 and 2.8 show how the *argumentum ad ignorantiam* can be a reasonable argument based on presumptive reasoning from data that is not known explicitly or given explicitly, in positive form, as part of a given knowledge base. The fact that a particular proposition is *not* in a knowledge base can sometimes licence a presumptive inference to a negative conclusion. We can presume that a particular proposition is false, on the grounds that it is not known to be true. As an instance of presumptive, nonmonotonic reasoning, such an inference can be reasonable. Hence, we cannot take it for granted that the *argumentum ad ignorantiam* is a fallacy.

The fallacy of many questions turns on the order in which a sequence of questions should reasonably be asked and answered in a dialogue. It is a question of the order in which a logically connected sequence of commitments should be taken on or rebutted by a respondent. The problem type of case, like "Have you stopped cheating on your income tax?" concerns a complex question that combines several commitments in the one question.[16] The problem arises when a question is posed aggressively, in a manner that incorporates a tactic of pre-empting an affirmative response to taking on a commitment that the respondent should have an opportunity to reject. The problem revealed here is that presumptions need to be put forward in an open-ended way that allows for defeasibility in the future sequence of dialogue. Closed ways of putting them forward can go against their nonmonotonic nature, which demands certain requirements on how they should be used correctly and reasonably in a context of dialogue. As Case 2.4 showed, these requirements are tied to communicative conventions of dialogue which licence presumptive inferences.

Cases 2.5, 2.6, and 2.7 show how common presumptive reasoning is in everyday conversations, persuasive arguments, and practical reasoning. Seen as an instance of presumptive inference to a defeasible conclusion, often as a provisional basis for prudent action in the absence of hard knowledge, the *argumentum ad verecundiam,* that traditional fallacy, can now be revealed as a type of argumentation that is in many cases, quite reasonable and nonfallacious. Although drawing conclusions based on testimony of a reliable source has not been given its due as a type of reasoning in traditional logic, viewed as a species of presumptive reasoning, it can be seen in a new light. From this new point of view, there is less of a tendency to reflexively condemn it as fallacious, without carefully examining the given circumstances of a particular case.

Finally, the *secundum quid* fallacy is clearly the major fallacy which directly highlights the need to see presumptive reasoning as a distinctive type of reasoning in its own right, with its own distinctively pragmatic standards and requirements. Making sense of the fallacy of *secundum quid* clearly requires

---

[16] See the account of presupposition given in Walton (*Inf. Log.,* 1989, chapter 1), in connection with question-asking fallacies.

coming to grips with case-based reasoning which is dependent on argumentation that weighs the similarity of one case to another (argument from analogy), and which takes into account shifts in the weight of presumption derived from the special features of a particular case.

Hedging (or *discounting*) as defined by Fogelin (1987), is a tactic for protecting arguments from attack by weakening one's commitment, (e.g., from "all" to "most" to "typically," or from "certainly" to "probably" to "presumably" (p. 42). In principle, hedging is legitimate in argumentation. It is not inherently fallacious. But as a critic, you have to look at each individual case carefully. In some cases, the overly defensive, evasive instances of hedging can be the opposite type of error from the fallacy of *secundum quid*. It is the opposite failure from dogmatic rigidity.

In Case 2.10, the physician would be committing the *secundum quid* fallacy if he were to persist in arguing that Bob must take medication M, because it is the prescribed treatment for patients in Bob's condition, even after it was told to him that Bob's (apparent) father had condition X. But the physician did not commit this fallacy, because he reasoned appropriately once this information came in. And then again, showing an appropriate flexibility, he changed the course of his presumptive reasoning, once Alice brought forward new information again about Bob's paternity. Now the operative presumption in the case is that Bob's father, whoever he is, presumably does not have condition X, as far as anyone privy to the discussion knows.

In this case, the physician kept changing the conclusion, and the presumptive reasoning leading to it, but this was not inappropriate or fallacious hedging. Nor was it reasoning that committed the *secundum quid* fallacy. It represented a "middle way" of reasoning appropriately in line with the known or presumed circumstances of the given case.

There is still much to learn about case-based reasoning, but it is clear that this type of reasoning is typically presumptive and practical in nature, its major faults and failures inherently dialectical in nature.

The question of how far we should admit presumptive reasoning into logic, as being a kind of reasoning that can be legitimate and correct, in at least some instances, is bound to remain controversial. Positivists, or those inclined towards a positivistic viewpoint, feel that the only kind of really good reasoning, that should be recognized or supported by logicians as respectable, is reasoning based on hard evidence, of the kind recognized in scientific methodology. Those who are inclined to evaluate reasoning from this point of view remain very suspicious about presumptive opinion-based reasoning, no matter how carefully it is pointed out that presumptions do have a genuine relationship to hard evidence–admittedly a negative, conditional relation via the *argumentum ad ignorantiam* to future evidence, should it arise in an argument. Positivists are still inclined to reject, or to be suspicious about presumptive reasoning, because the real basis of its justification is more practical than cognitive in nature.

Those of us in the field of informal logic and argumentation study, however, are increasingly inclined toward accepting presumptive reasoning, as, in principle, a legitimate kind of reasoning, even though we recognize its potential for error and abuse in fallacies, in some cases. The basic reason we are so inclined is that we can see that so much of the practical reasoning used in everyday conversations is inherently presumptive in nature. To turn our backs on this kind of reasoning any longer is simply to perpetuate our ignorance of how practical reasoning is used in everyday conversations of all sorts, including political debates, ethical disputes, legal argumentation, and even philosophical argumentation. And most importantly, the recognition and analysis of presumptive reasoning has been shown to be a required step towards the reasoned evaluation of the kinds of arguments traditionally classified as informal fallacies.

Proper evaluation of presumptive reasoning requires a flexible tolerance, a readiness to acknowledge and correct errors and biases, and finally, an appreciation of the finer shades of meaning and shifts of presumption in argumentation. The positivist point of view is more absolutistic and "black and white," tending to see presumptive reasoning as inherently sloppy, vague, or subjective, and trying to eliminate such hedging wherever possible. Unfortunately, too heavy a leaning towards the positivistic view in affairs of everyday life tends toward the kind of rigidity, prejudice, and dogmatism that does not deal very well with the exceptions and irregularities commonly encountered in practical reasoning in the real world of changing circumstances in a particular case. But this rigidity is typically the very sort of dogmatic attitude in dialogue that is associated with committing fallacies of the kind we have examined. It is hard to live with presumptive reasoning, but harder still to live without it.

CHAPTER THREE

THE ARGUMENTATION SCHEMES

In this chapter, 25 different argumentation schemes are described and analyzed. For each argumentation scheme, a matching set of critical questions is given. This pairing brings out the essentially presumptive nature of the kind of reasoning involved in the use of argumentation schemes, and at the same time reveals the pragmatic and dialectical nature of how this reasoning works. The function of each argumentation scheme is to shift a weight of presumption from one side of a dialogue to the other. The opposing arguer in the dialogue can shift this weight of presumption back to the other side again by asking any of the appropriate critical questions matching that argumentation scheme. To once again get the presumption on his or her side, the original arguer (who used the argumentation scheme in the first place) must give a satisfactory answer to that critical question.

Some of the argumentation schemes are basic or fundamental, whereas others are composites made up from these basic schemes. Where this is so, one way or the other, it has been noted in the account of the argumentation scheme given. However, no attempt has been made to classify the schemes, beyond the typology already constructed by Kienpointner (1992). Some classifications are obvious. For example, there are causal, verbal, and gradualistic schemes. However, there is no reason to think that this set of schemes is complete, or that our analysis of their structure is adequate in every respect. Therefore, the temptation to venture a new system of classification, or one different from that of Kienpointner (1992), has been resisted at this point.

Another thing these argumentation schemes have in common is that they involve the application of generalizations of an abstract sort, to a particular situation, exemplified by the particular case at issue. The generalization acts as a warrant, or as Kienpointner (1992) called it, a *Schlussregel*, to support the premise that cites the particulars of the case. Thus, these schemes involve presumptive reasoning, because the match between a generalization and a particular case is never perfect, or completely certain and absolute. To the extent that they are species of case-based reasoning,[1] these schemes embody argumentation that is defeasible, or open to retraction (default, defeat) in exceptional cases that may come to be known in the future.

Perhaps the main, arguable exception here is argument from evidence to a hypothesis, which seems to be an inductive or probabilistic, as opposed to a presumptive or plausibilistic kind of argumentation. However, it is a little early to tell. Perhaps even this type of argumentation has its presumptive aspects. And, at any rate, we include it here because it has been so often misunderstood and

---

[1] See Simpson (1985).

neglected in the past, as a distinctive type of argumentation with its own special characteristics.

Many problems and finer points of analysis remain unresolved in connection with these argumentation schemes. Where such problems exist, they have been raised and clarified, but clearly much work remains to be done in mapping the structure of argumentation schemes.

ARGUMENT FROM SIGN

Argument from sign is a familiar kind of reasoning in everyday argument. In argument from sign, a particular finding or observation x is taken as evidence of the existence of a property or event E, in a given situation.

Case 3.1:   Here are some bear tracks in the snow.
Therefore, a bear passed this way.

The particular finding of the bear tracks is taken as the sign of the presence of a bear passing through the area indicated.

The reasoning in Case 3.1 is presumptive and defeasible, for there could have been other causes of the bear tracks, for example, someone putting them there to intentionally deceive anyone seeing them. However, in the absence of some evidence to the contrary of this sort, it would be reasonable to draw the conclusion in Case 3.1.

Another aspect of argument from sign is that the confidence in the conclusion is relative to what is normally expected in the type of situation. For example, if the area in Case 3.1 is known to be populated by bears, the argument for the conclusion is strengthened.

Argument from sign can be seen as a kind of converse causal argumentation. In Case 3.1 for example, presumably we infer the presence of a bear because that is what caused the bear tracks to appear. Some also see argumentation from sign as a species of inference to the best explanation.[2] According to this analysis of Case 3.1, the conclusion is the "best explanation" of the finding cited in the premise.

Hastings (1963) identified argument from sign as a distinctive argumentation scheme, or "mode of reasoning," as he called it (pp. 55-64). According to his analysis, the argument from sign always involves a "causal or correlative relation" expressed as a "conditional of probability" (p. 59). He cited the following example that is rephrased in Case 3.2.

Case 3.2:   The Korean elections in 1948 and 1950 were free and fair. Free elections in a country indicate there is no police state. Therefore, Korea is not a police state. (p. 55)

---

[2] See Lipton (1991).

According to the analysis of this case given by Hastings, we can use a variable A to stand for "Free elections" and another to stand for "No police state," and then we can see that the inference in Case 3.2 has a structure comparable to that of *modus ponens:* If A then B; A, therefore B. However, the conditional or "if-then" in the major premise is not a "hook" or strict conditional, of the kind familiar in deductive logic. Hastings describes it instead as a "causal relation" or "conditional of probability."

In evaluating arguments from sign, Hastings postulated two critical questions that should be asked:

1. What is the strength of the correlation of the sign with the event signified?

2. Are there other events that would more reliably account for the sign?

With respect to the first question, Hastings postulated the principle that the stronger the causal relation or association between the two events, the stronger is the argument from sign. With respect to the second question, Hastings postulated the principle that other causes for the sign must be unlikely for the sign reasoning to be plausible.

More complex cases of argumentation from sign are found in what might be called *evidence accumulating arguments,* arguments that proceed through a sequence of signs, each of which only gives a small weight of presumption for the conclusion, but taken together, the whole sequence builds up to quite a plausible argument for the conclusion. The following classic case is from the Sherlock Holmes story, *A Study in Scarlet.* Dr. Watson, looking for rooms in London, has just been introduced to Sherlock Holmes. As a result of the meeting, Holmes arrived at the conclusion that Watson had just returned from Afghanistan. How did Holmes arrive at this clever conclusion, without having been told anything about Dr. Watson's recent travels or background? According to his own account, his train of reasoning was based on the following argumentation from Doyle (1932).

Case 3.3:   Here is a gentleman of a medical type, but with the air of a military man. Clearly an army doctor, then. He has just come from the tropics, for his face is dark, and that is not the natural tint of his skin, for his wrists are fair. He has undergone hardship and sickness, as his haggard face says clearly. His left arm has been injured. He holds it in a stiff and unnatural manner. Where in the tropics could an English army doctor have seen much hardship and got his arm wounded? Clearly in Afghanistan. (p. 11)

Holmes' reasoning takes the form of a sequence of inferences based on signs which he observes, for example, "His face is dark." From these signs he draws conclusions, for example, "He has just come from the tropics." As more and more signs are brought in, and more inferences drawn from them, the case builds up. Once enough evidence has accumulated, the conclusion becomes "obvious"– Watson has recently been in Afghanistan.

Clearly this argumentation is presumptive in nature, Holmes is really making a guess. But given the buildup of suggestive evidence, his guess is a plausible one, and it turns out to be right. Each sign gives a little bit of evidence. But the accumulation of the sequence of reasoning based on many signs yields a fair weight of presumption in favor of the conclusion conjectured.

However, in many cases, argument from sign is a simple, one-step kind of inference where some empirical observation is made, and interpreted as a sign or symptom, licencing the drawing of a presumptive conclusion. What makes a finding a sign, enabling the drawing of a conclusion from it seems hard to say. In many cases, there is a causal or explanatory link between the two things, but not in all cases. Common cases are the following.

Case 3.4:   Bob is covered with red spots.
               Therefore, Bob has the measles.

Case 3.5:   The barometer just dropped.
               Therefore, we will have a storm.

Case 3.6:   Bob is biting his nails.
               Therefore, Bob is worried about something.

These inferences have the following general form, where A is a proposition describing a finding or observation; and B is another proposition, a conclusion drawn on the basis of what has been observed.

A is true in this situation.

B is generally indicated as true when its sign, A, is true, in this kind of situation.

Therefore, B is true in this situation.

This type of inference is our first approximation of the argumentation scheme for the argument from sign. Argument from sign is based on a known correlation or association between two propositions A and B that is not absolute, but more suggestive (presumptive) in nature.

ARGUMENT FROM EXAMPLE

According to Hastings (1963) argument from example is the most common type of reasoning in debating. The most important characteristic is "not the number of items used, but their typicality" (p. 25). Argument from example is usually used to support a generalization of some kind, and hence Hastings called this kind of argument "argument from example to a descriptive generalization."

One type of critical response to use of the argument from example is to present a counterexample–another example that falsifies or refutes the given generalization. As Hastings pointed out, the response to this reply is for the proponent of the original generalization to qualify it with terms like "usually," "sometimes," "rarely," and so forth.

Argument from example is an inherently weak form of argumentation that does not confirm a claim conclusively, or even with probability. It gives only a small weight of presumption in favor of the claim, shifting a burden of proof in favor of it, subject to critical questioning. Five critical questions matching the use of the argument from example are given. Three of these critical questions (2, 3, and 4) are given by Hastings (1963).

1. **Is the proposition presented by the example in fact true?** This question asks whether the example is a true report of reality.

2. **Does the example support the general claim it is supposed to be an instance of?** This question asks whether the example is really an instance of the generalization it was brought forward to support.

3. **Is the example typical of the kinds of cases that the generalization ranges over?** If the example can be shown to be an exception or atypical case, its support for the generalization may be nullified.

4. **How strong is the generalization?** If the generalization holds only for a narrow range of cases, it is not very reliable. In such cases, the argument may hold, but may be weak.

5. **Were there special circumstances present in the example that would impair its generalizability?** Presumptive generalizations are inherently defeasible, or subject to exceptions. One can always examine a cited example to look for indications that special circumstances are present in it.

Argument from example is inherently presumptive in nature, and hence it is always susceptible to the *secundum quid* fallacy of neglect of qualifications. Generalizations based on cited examples should always be seen as inherently subject to qualifications to the effect that they hold "normally" or "typically." This means that any cited instance or example could turn out to be atypical in certain respects, or that future instances could come to be known that are atypical, that is, do not support the generalization.

One must be careful in identifying argument from example in a given case, because the citing of an example is also used in explanations and other speech acts that are not arguments. Not every use of an example in everyday conversation can be cited as an instance of argument from example.

Was the example given to prove a point, or merely to illustrate it? This is a crucial question if the offering of a single example is alleged to be a hasty generalization. For if the example was only part of an elucidation, a pedagogical dialogue to illustrate or explain something, it could be quite inappropriate to criticize it as a hasty generalization, a failure to prove a generalization. For it could be that it was not meant to prove the generalization at all. In such a case, hasty generalization would be a pseudo-fallacy, or a species of false (inappropriate) charge of fallacy (see chapter 5).

According to Beardsley (1950), a single incident may be part of an anecdote designed to help an addressee understand or remember a point, instead of being meant to prove the point. Here we need to be careful to distinguish between two different kinds of speech act–illustrating a generalization versus proving it. But, in practice, it can be easy to confuse these two verbal performances.

Perelman and Olbrechts-Tyteca (1969) pointed out the distinction between illustration and example: "Whereas an example is designed to establish a rule, the role of illustration is to strengthen adherence to a known and accepted rule, by providing particular instances which clarify the general statement" (p. 357). Illustration and example have different functions in discourse.

Argument from precedent also seems similar to argument from example, but the functions of these two kinds of argumentation are different. In argument from precedent, a particular case is shown to make a change in a given rule necessary, or to require adding a new rule to cover this case. But in argument from example, the particular case cited is meant to give some evidence in favor of the given generalization.

A version of negative argumentation from example is characteristic of the concept of falsification of hypotheses in science, stressed by Popper (1963). However, an invalidating case does not always result in rejection of a law. Perelman and Olbrechts-Tyteca (1969) noted that a law can be retained, in such a case, by restricting its field of application. The technique used here is to admit certain kinds of exceptions to a law or generalization, postulating the generalization as being subject to exceptions, as opposed to being a strict or absolute law. To treat all generalizations as invariably strict, ignoring legitimate exceptions, is associated with the *secundum quid* fallacy.

The conclusion of an argument from example is a generalization that can take any one of three forms. A *universal* or *strict* generalization has the form "For all x, if x has property F then x has property G (without exception)." A *probabilistic generalization* takes the form that most, many, or a certain percentage of things that have property F are likely to also have property G. A *presumptive (defeasible) generalization* states that typically or normally (subject to exceptional cases) if x has F then x will also have G.

Whichever of these three forms the argument from example takes, generally the argumentation scheme has the following structure.

In this particular case, the individual a has property F and also property G.

a is typical of things that have F and may or may not also have G.

Therefore, generally, if x has property F, then x also has property G.

This type of argumentation is generally quite weak, in the sense that the establishing of the premise only gives a small weight of support to the conclusion. However, that weight tends to be increased to the extent that the case cited is known to be typical or widespread, as a type of instance of the generalization. Support is also increased to the extent that the generalization in the conclusion tends to be less strict and more presumptive in nature.

Argumentation from example can sometimes be quite tricky to evaluate, and its strength in a given case depends very much on the type of generalization that is supposed to be involved. It may be unclear, in everyday conversation, what type of generalization is meant.

If the argument in question is meant to prove an unlimited generalization, then generalizing from only a single instance is an extremely weak form of argument. It gives almost no proof at all.

However, if the argument in question is meant to prove a limited generalization of the defeasible or plausible type, it may, in some cases, be quite a strong argument to shift a burden of proof. If it is clear that the example cited is a typical case of the generalization in question, and if the generalization is of the form, "Typically, cases of F are also cases of G," then the example may be quite a strong argument in favor of proving the generalization as an acceptable proposition.

These problems of evaluation are taken up in more detail in chapter five, where the fallacy of hasty generalization is analyzed.

Argument from example is the basis of all case-based reasoning, a kind of reasoning that proceeds by drawing inferences from one case that is similar to another in certain respects. Thus case-based reasoning depends on the use of argument from analogy. Any two cases will be dissimilar in certain respects, if they are similar in certain respects, provided they are two different cases. Hence case-based reasoning is always defeasible in nature, because the number of respects in which two cases can be found similar, or dissimilar, is unlimited.

According to the analysis of case-based reasoning given in Simpson (1985), this kind of reasoning involves the recognition of a pattern of similarity between a current case and a preceding set of cases in memory. Simpson's method of using this kind of reasoning to solve problems of dispute mediation uses trial and error, along with feedback. The reasoner compares a dispute to a previous dispute that had a known solution, and tries to apply the method used in that previous solution to the current problem.

In a critical discussion where there is a conflict of opinions on a proposition, giving an example of a case where that proposition is true (or false) varies greatly with respect to whether it is a strong or weak argument, depending on the generality of that proposition. If it is an existential proposition of the form "Some F are G," one example proves it (conclusively). If it is a universal generalization of the form "All *F* are *G*," one example gives it only a weak (presumptive) basis of support.

ARGUMENT FROM VERBAL CLASSIFICATION

This kind of argumentation takes a particular case, or single instance, and concludes that it has a particular property, on the grounds of a verbal classification of the instance as generally having such a property. For example, it might be said that Ross Perot is rich, on the grounds that anyone who has assets of more than 3 billion dollars can be classified as rich. This general type of argumentation scheme is categorized under *Einordnungschemata,* or classifying schemes by Kienpointner (1992).

Verbal classifications of empirical concepts, like "rich," tend to be vague. They admit of clear cases, where there is no room for doubt whether the instance fits the classification. But they also admit of borderline or vague cases, where there is no nonarbitrary way of making such a decision without adding qualifications. Hence the argument from classification is generally a presumptive and defeasible kind of argumentation.

Hastings (1963) called this type of argumentation "argument from criteria to a verbal classification," giving the following example.

Case 3.7:   In voluntary health insurance you generally get a poor return for your money because overhead and profits of the insurance company eat up huge chunks of the premiums you pay. On individual policies these companies spend for overhead and profits an average of about 60% of what you pay them and only about 40 cents of your premium dollar goes for benefits to policyholders. Obviously such insurance is a mighty poor buy. (p. 36)

The argument in this case could be described as the following sequence of reasoning.

Premise: There is a 40% return on health insurance.

Warrant: 40% can be classified as a poor return.

Qualifier: Unless other companies can do no better.

Conclusion: 40% is a poor return.

The warrant is a generalization, subject to exceptions of the kind cited in the qualifier. The basis of the inference is the statement of classification made in the warrant.

According to Hastings, the verification of the warrant is expected to come from common knowledge shared by the speaker and audience. The audience is expected to have enough experience with business to know or accept the idea that a 40% return would clearly be considered "poor" by conventionally accepted standards of the time.

This kind of argumentation is frequently used in eristic dialogue where one side verbally classifies the point of view of the other side in a negative way, using negative or "vituperative" terminology to describe it.

Case 3.8:   Your point of view is heresy.
                Therefore, your point of view is wrong.

One danger inherent in the use of this type of argumentation is the fallacy of begging the question. If no evidence is given for the premise which can be backed up independently of the conclusion, the argument in Case 3.8 could be circular. In other words, the proponent may be claiming both that Bob's point of view is wrong because it is heresy, and that Bob's point of view is heresy (only) because it is wrong. This type of argumentation can be fallacious if it is an attempt to evade fulfilling the burden of proof to support the premise (without already assuming the acceptance of the conclusion).

Another danger inherent in the use of the argument from verbal classification is that the dialogue can reduce to a quarrel, where each side classifies the point of view of the other side as "heresy." This kind of stalemate is a failure of communication that can block further (legitimate) argumentation needed to resolve the original conflict of opinions.

The argumentation scheme for the argument from verbal classification is the following:

a has a particular property F.

For all x, if x has property F, then x can be classified as having property G.

Therefore, a has property G.

The critical questions matching this argumentation scheme are the following.

1. **Does a definitely have F, or is there room for doubt?**

2. **Can the verbal classification (in the second premise) be said to hold strongly, or is it one of those weak classifications that is subject to doubt?**

Both these questions pertain to the degree of strength that any verbal classification will have, due to the vagueness of the property used as a classifier. For example, in the Ross Perot example previously mentioned, the term "rich" is vague. If someone has assets of over 3 billion dollars, we can definitely say that this individual is rich. But what if her total assets were 1 million dollars? Some would not say that such a person is rich. Others would classify her as rich. In such a case then, the classification does not hold strongly. At best, it is a weak classification, and subject to legitimate doubts.

When use of argument from a verbal classification is attacked (see the sections on argument from vagueness of a verbal classification and argument from arbitrariness of a verbal classification later), the dialogue takes a turn toward discussion of the terms used in the argumentation, and there is a distinctive shift in the type of dialogues involved. In Walton and Krabbe (1995) this shift is called a "tightening up" and is described as a shift from a permissive type of dialogue to a rigorous type of dialogue. In some cases, such a shift can represent a deterioration of productive dialogue into a kind of "logic-chopping." But in other cases, clarification of terminology in a dialogue can be helpful–an improvement.

ARGUMENT FROM COMMITMENT

In this type of argumentation, the proponent claims that the respondent is, or should be committed to some particular position on an issue, and then claims that the respondent should also be committed to a particular action, or line of conduct, on the grounds that the position implies (by practical reasoning) the action, in the given circumstances. A simple example is the following.

Case 3.9:   **Bob:**   Ed, you are a communist, aren't you?

            Ed: Of course. You know that.

            Bob: Well, then you should be on the side of the union in this recent labor dispute.

If Ed denies that he is on the side of the union in the dispute, then he will have to explain why. Otherwise, it will appear that he is practically inconsistent in claiming that he is a communist, but that he is also against the union side in this case.

The argument from commitment, is the basis of, and, in some instances, leads to the circumstantial *ad hominem* argument. For example, in Case 3.9, Bob might follow up Ed's denial that he is on the side of the union in this case by replying: "You are not on the side of the union, and yet you say you are a communist. Come on, Ed. You can't have it both ways!" Here Bob is implying that Ed is being inconsistent, suggesting that communism is a pro-union commitment, so that for an avowed communist to be against a union raises a presumption of inconsistency. See Krabbe (1990) on inconsistent commitment and commitment to inconsistencies, and also Walton and Krabbe (1995) on retraction of commitment.

Typically, the circumstantial *ad hominem* argument is used to negatively criticize an opponent's argument, often by suggesting that the opponent is not sincerely taking part in a critical discussion, as shown by the clash between his professed argument and the real commitment on an issue. As used previously, however, it may be more an attempt by Bob to get Ed to profess the union side in the dispute, rather than to attack him very strongly. In some cases, the *ad hominem* argument is quite a strong attack however, suggesting that the attacked party is dishonest, illogical, or confused. This type of attack on a person's integrity, character, or ability for logical reasoning often shades into the personal, or so-called "abusive" type of *ad hominem* argumentation.

The argumentation scheme for the argument from commitment is the following.

a is committed to proposition *A* (generally, or in virtue of what she said in the past).

Therefore, in this case, *a* should support *A*.

The critical questions matching this argumentation scheme are the following.

1. **Is *a* really committed to *A*, and if so, what evidence supports the claim that she is so committed?**

2. **If the evidence for commitment is indirect or weak, could there also be contrary evidence, or at least room for the rebuttal that this case is an exception?**

3. **Is the proposition *A*, as cited in the premise, identical to the proposition *A* as cited in the conclusion? If not, what exactly is the nature of the relationship between the two propositions?**

With respect to the first critical question, it should be noted that very often in this kind of argumentation, the attribution of commitment is made, not in virtue of what *a* said in the past, but in virtue of something *a* was reported to have done. From such a practice, it is then inferred that *a* must be committed to some proposition that describes such a practice. Note however, that this is a weak kind of argument, subject to interpretations, implication, and qualifications. Hence, it is important to cite the actual evidence alleged as the basis of an imputed commitment, and to assess what that evidence may be taken to imply or suggest, in context.

Hamblin (1970) thought of commitments in dialogue as statements that can be attributed to an arguer in virtue of the moves made by that arguer in a game of dialogue with rules that define the incurring of commitments for each type of move. From this point of view, a commitment is a statement that clearly goes on record, so that a participant in dialogue can be held by the requirements of consistency to what was previously said or committed to in a dialogue. However, a practical problem in the analysis of argumentative discourse is that not only explicit statements, but also actions or even personal circumstances can sometimes be taken rightly as reasonable indicators of commitment in a dialogue.

Actions speak louder than words it is said. But do a person's actions really indicate specific commitments more definitely or strongly than what the person says? The answer is that, in some cases, they do, but having conceded the point, one is confronted with the problem of interpreting a person's actions to fairly extract the commitments expressed by them. The danger of doing this incorrectly or unfairly is the risk of committing a strawman error or fallacy of distorting an arguer's position.

On the other hand, the argument from commitment is such an extraordinarily powerful tactic to use in dialogue, not only because it is an allegation based on an arguer's prior commitments, but also because actions and personal circumstances are important practical indexes of personal commitment in everyday argumentation. If you really want to know what a person is deeply committed to in his or her heart, then look to the person's personal actions more than what the person actually says. This piece of advice is often a good practical maxim, even if it can go wrong in some cases. What is suggested then as a general tactic of argumentation is that careful juxtaposition of a person's words and deeds together can often bear informative scrutiny, in building a case to assess his commitment, and also the worth of the argument. This tactical advice is especially appropriate when one is uncertain whether the argument is good in itself, yet one has to take a practical decision based on the presumptive worth of the argument. This situation is, of course, a common one when advice is given or taken on practical problems in everyday dialogue.

Another reason that the argument from commitment is interesting and practically useful to know about pertains to the fact that many presumptions are associated with a group or professional position, and that position may strongly bind the arguer to certain propositions.

But in practical terms, a general commitment might not apply in a clearly defined way to a specific situation or issue. In other words, an arguer's commitment-set of propositions may not be fully known, either to his critic or to himself or herself. The set of an arguer's commitments, therefore, may not be in full view of the participants in the argument. Only through further dialogue might the specific commitments of that arguer be revealed. The context of dialogue is crucial here (see Walton and Krabbe (1995) on dark-side (nonexplicit) commitments).

In practical terms, therefore, the analysis arising out of the use of the argument from commitment requires further specifications of an arguer's set of commitments. The arguer's personal actions, circumstances, or affiliations may commit that person to a certain position. But this position may not be perfectly spelled out yet in relation to the argument. Even so, the argument from commitment is often a powerful tactic of attack that shifts the burden of proof onto the arguer to defend or further clarify the position by answering critical questions, if the argument is to remain presumptively plausible.

A rational arguer should generally stick to his or her commitments, but must also be prepared to retract or revise commitments in some cases. Hence the argument from commitment is a defeasible type of argumentation, best seen as one that shifts a burden of proof in a dialogue.

Later, we see that argument from commitment is quite a fundamental type of argumentation that is a basic component of many other familiar and common types of argumentation in everyday conversations. Curiously however, argument from commitment has rarely, if ever, been explicitly recognized or analyzed as a distinctive species of reasoned argumentation in logic.

CIRCUMSTANTIAL ARGUMENT AGAINST THE PERSON

As noted previously, the circumstantial *ad hominem* argument (argument against the person) is a special type of argument from commitment where an arguer's circumstances are cited as revealing his or her commitment, which is claimed to be contrary to his or her own argument. Typically, the inconsistency alleged is of a pragmatic nature–a practical conflict between the personal actions, affiliations, or implications of these, and the proposition advocated as conclusion of the person's argument that is advocated. It is a clash of alleged commitments. The charge, "You don't practice what you preach!" is characteristic of this type of argumentation.

The classic case is the following example from Walton (*Inf. Log.*, 1989).

Case 3.10: **Parent:** There is strong evidence of a link between smoking and chronic obstructive lung disease. Smoking is also associated with many other serious disorders. Smoking is unhealthy. So you should not smoke.

  Child: But you smoke yourself. So much for your argument against smoking. (pp. 141-142)

This case has now been much discussed and analyzed–see Walton (*Arg. Pos.*, 1985) especially. The main point to note here is that the child's questioning of the parent's argument by citing the presumption of practical inconsistency suggested by the parent's personal actions can be a reasonable argument if it is meant only to shift a burden of proof (presumptively) against the parent's side of the dialogue. If interpreted as an absolutistic argument claiming to show that the proposition "Smoking is unhealthy" is false, it would be a fallacious circumstantial *ad hominem* argument. As with all cases of argument from commitment, much depends on how you interpret the text, and a conditional evaluation of the argument is often best.

The argumentation scheme for the circumstantial argument against the person (circumstantial *ad hominem* argument) is the following.

If x claims that everyone (including x) ought to act in accord with or support proposition A, then x is, or should be, committed to A.

a claims that everyone (including a) ought to act in accord with or support proposition A.

It is indicated by a's personal circumstances that a is not committed to A.

Therefore, a is inconsistent in a's commitments, and there should be a weight of presumption against a's argument for a's claim.

In this type of argument, a negative kind of attack on an arguer's sincerity in entering into a cooperative dialogue, the upshot is that the arguer is inconsistent. If the arguer knows he or she is inconsistent, then the arguer is dishonest, and therefore not credible as a cooperative dialogue partner. If the arguer doesn't know he or she is inconsistent, then the arguer is confused, or illogical, and must sort this out by answering the charge, or concede that his or her argumentation is not coherent.

The critical questions matching the circumstantial argument against the person are the following:

1. **Does a claim that everyone (including a) ought to act in accord with or support A?**

2. **What is the evidence from a's personal circumstances indicating he or she is not committed to A?**

3. **Does it follow from an affirmative answer to question 1 that a is, or should be committed to A?**

What a critic has to show, to back up a circumstantial argument against the person is that there is a real conflict of commitments in the given case. Often, however, such attacks are based more on suggestion and innuendo than any real evidence.

The practical problem with the analysis of realistic cases of the argument against the person is that commitments as propositions, in many cases, are not clearly stated in such a way that they can be read off from the personal circumstances of the arguer who is criticized. One practical type of problem has to do with actions. We may know what the actions of an arguer are, but it may not be so easy to determine, in a particular case, what those actions imply. In Case 3.10, we saw that the parent smoked. But what commitments may be taken for this action to imply? Does it mean that the parent is personally committed to the advocacy of smoking as a practice? Perhaps not, but the circumstantial criticism suggests that the parent may be. Do actions speak louder than words? Sometimes they do, but in this case there is certainly room for a reply by the parent. In any event, the personal criticism put forward by the child is strong enough to shift the burden of proof onto the parent to defend or clarify his or her position.

Another instance of this practical problem arises through the fact that in many arguments the position of the arguer is not fully known to the critic, or perhaps even to the arguer himself. If someone is criticized by an argument against the person on the ground that this person is an admitted Catholic or communist, or belongs to some other group or organization, that person's personal position on an issue in a given case need not be exactly identical to the group position in every respect. There is room for exceptions, and arguable deviations.

In some of the more tricky cases, the circumstantial *ad hominem* criticism has to do with professional commitments or group affiliations, as the following case from Walton (*Arg. Pos.*, 1985) illustrates.

Case 3.11:   You, a practicing Catholic agreed to have an abortion. You don't practice what you preach! (p. 281)

In this case, the burden of justification seems thrust on this woman to justify her position or special circumstances. But the problem for the critic is to make clear enough what the Catholic position on abortion is, or is supposed to be, to see whether the claim of a pragmatic inconsistency is genuine.

This type of case shows that it is the arguer's position, or personal set of commitments as expressed through the argument, that is at issue in *ad hominem* disputes. But articulating this position clearly enough to judge its applicability to the arguer's specific argument under criticism may involve much serious dialogue. Indeed, the success of such dialogue may be, to a significant extent, measured by the extent it serves to reveal the arguer's internal position in relation to the issue. The positive value of *ad hominem* argumentation has been brought out by Johnstone (1978).

But spelling out one's specific commitments as a Catholic on any particular issue of contention itself may not be a trivial or straightforward job (see Cuomo, 1984). Also, the "poisoning the well" criticism often associated with this type of case, to the effect that a committed Catholic (for example) cannot be an unbiased arguer, shows how closely the circumstantial *ad hominem* can be connected to the argument from bias.

The circumstantial *ad hominem* argument is basically a questioning of the arguer's position by alleging plausible evidence of a pragmatic inconsistency in that arguer's commitments. There is a logical basis for this type of argument because of the concept of inconsistency which is the basis of the allegation. However, the argument is called circumstantial because the inconsistency is pragmatic rather than purely logical in nature–it is the arguer's circumstances, as interpreted from the situation, that are alleged to be inconsistent with the arguer's statements. This type of *ad hominem* argument can be reasonable in some cases because inconsistency of an arguer's position should reasonably be open to criticism of questioning. But it should be put forward (and evaluated) on a basis of burden of proof, rather than being based on direct scientific knowledge or demonstration. For example, in the smoking case, the child may not be in a position to assess the scientific accuracy of the parent's claims about the medical hazards of smoking. In this type of situation of ignorance however, decisions of a practical or personal nature often have to be made because the action, (e.g., smoking or not smoking), pertains to one's own personal life. Issues of this sort are commonly practices or ways of life that we either accept or don't accept, based on presumption rather than on some conclusive reasoning. Challenging these presumptions are often enough to unseat them.

ARGUMENT FROM POSITION TO KNOW

One familiar kind of argumentation occurs in a dialogue situation where one party has reason to presume that another party has access to information or knowledge that the first party does not have direct access to. Therefore, when the second party gives his or her opinion, the first party treats the statement given as having a weight of presumption in favor of its being true, and may recommend it to others on that basis (as in Case 2.5).

For example, suppose that two tourists are lost in a city they have never been to before, and they ask a shopkeeper the location of the Central Station.

Case 3.12:   **First Tourist:**   Could you tell me where the Central Station is?

Shopkeeper: It is across that bridge, one kilometer south.

First Tourist: Thank you [To second tourist]. OK. Let's head for the bridge. Or do you want to stop for a coffee first?

Here, the first tourist presumes that the shopkeeper is familiar with the city, and therefore recommends to the second tourist that they act on the information given.

Another very common kind of argumentation from position to know is that of argument from testimony. For example, if a witness is known to have seen some event that took place, his or her statement concerning the particulars of the event may be taken as having a weight of presumption in favor of it. The argumentation scheme for the argument from position to know is the following.

a is in a position to know whether A is true (false).

a asserts that A is true (false).

Therefore, a is true (false).

The critical questions matching this argumentation scheme are:

1. **Is *a* in a position to know whether *A* is true (false)?**

2. **Is *a* an honest (trustworthy, reliable) source?**

3. **Did *a* assert that *A* is true (false)?**

The second question obviously relates to *ad hominem* generally, based on the question of the arguer's integrity or seriousness in entering into a conversation. The third question relates to the exact wording of what *a* said, or was alleged to have said–for example, whether *a* was quoted directly is a question of importance. In many cases, care must be taken because the proposition *A* in the conclusion is not what *a* exactly (directly) said. Instead, it is often an inference derived from what was said. This use of implicature or suggested inference is characteristic of innuendo, and presumptive conclusions put forward on the basis of rumor and gossip.

The argumentation scheme for the argument from position to know is often the basis for lack-of-knowledge inferences (arguments from ignorance), and is also the basis of the use of testimony in argumentation in dialogue, for example in a trial (Walton, *Arg. Ig.*, 1995). What makes testimony a distinctive type of evidence is that the witness swears to tell the truth.

The third critical question is crucial in many cases, because a source may not have been directly or exactly quoted as saying *A*. It may often be that *A* has been inferred, by the arguer using the argument from position to know, from some collection of statements that *a* made. Here we have to be careful to ask whether *a* was quoted directly, or whether the opinion attributed to *A* was derived from something else *a* said. Matters of quotation of a source are generally very important in assessing the worth of an argument from position to know.

Also very important generally is the naming of the source. The value and worth of argumentation from position to know is much more reliable and useful if the name, and even the address of the source is given. Attribution of sources by opaque phrases like, "according to an insider," or "according to normally reliable sources" is of dubious value if the source cannot be identified or verified. Arguments from position to know of this type are double-sourced, because you are depending on the reliability of the source of the report who is claiming that *his* source is reliable.

The argument from position to know is based on the Gricean maxims of communication to the effect that the speaker is making a sincere and honest attempt to enter into a conversation where he or she is communicating information that the hearer wants to know about. A dialogue structure of communication is presupposed as a context of discussion for evaluating the worth of an argument from position to know in a given case.

In the context of legal trial, the presumption of the honesty and sincerity of the witness is made explicit in the oath that the source is asked to give. But the veracity of the witness can also be tested by the questioning of the opposed attorney in cross-examination. If there is a known bias or previous record of dishonesty which would be relevant, the questioning attorney is supposed to bring this out. Done successfully, such an attack can discredit the testimony of a witness.

Generally, the argument from position to know should be seen as a presumptive type of argumentation that shifts a burden of proof back and forth between two opposed sides in a dialogue. Such an argument is successful or correct if it tilts a balance or weight of plausibility to support one side where there is a conflict of opinions between two sides of an issue. This kind of argument is never "final," but carries a weight of plausibility that is enough to overcome doubts.

The key characteristic of all source-based argumentation that separates it from other types of argumentation is that there are three participants involved in the context of dialogue.

1. The *proponent* is the person who is using an argument for a purpose in a context of dialogue, (e.g., to convince a respondent in a critical discussion that a proposition is true).

2. The *respondent* is the recipient of the argument, the person the argument is directed to by the proponent.

3. The *source* is a third party upon whose assertions or support the argument used by the proponent is based.

Typically, in this arrangement, the respondent questions, or has an attitude of doubt about the conclusion of the argument put forward by the proponent. The proponent's goal is to remove this doubt by bringing forward an argument that will convince the respondent that the conclusion is true. In a source-based argument, the proponent uses an argument that has at least one premise based on the "say so" of a third-party source who vouches for the truth of the premise. The argument depends essentially on the standing or reliability of the source.

The participation of the source in the dialogue is of a different kind from that of the proponent and the respondent. The proponent and the respondent are both directly involved in a dialogue with each other. The source is external to this dialogue. The source stands in a dialogue (dialectical) relationship to the proponent. The context of dialogue here is often of an implicit or derived nature. When the proponent uses a source-based argument in a dialogue with a respondent, the proponent in effect alleges that he or she has consulted the source in some way. This means that there exists, at least an implicit dialogue relationship between the proponent and the source. It does not mean that the proponent has actually talked to the source. The proponent may, for example, be citing a written source he or she has not actually talked to. It means, rather that what the source has asserted, allegedly, is open to challenge and critical questioning.

ARGUMENT FROM EXPERT OPINION

One very special type of argument from position to know is an especially distinctive and important type of argumentation in its own right. An expert in a particular domain of knowledge is in a special position to know about propositions in that domain, and therefore the expert's opinion on some proposition of this kind generally has a weight of presumption in its favor.

One of the most common kinds of situation in which this type of argumentation is used is in a critical discussion between two parties, where one attempts to support one of his or her contentions to the other by saying: "This proposition is said to be true by an expert (or the experts)." In such a case, there are really two layers of dialogue involved. First, there is the critical discussion between the two parties. Then there is an expert consultation dialogue (a kind of information-seeking or advice-seeking dialogue) brought in by the one party in the first dialogue.

Hamblin (1970) proposed a deductive form of the argument from expert opinion (E represents an expert source of knowledge).

Everything E says is true.

E says A is true.

Therefore, A is true.

This proposed scheme is not a very realistic representation however, for it assumes E is omniscient (not a characteristic of any actual expert).

A problem arises for this scheme in the case where one expert, E_1 says A is true, and another expert, E_2, says *not-A* is true. It follows, by the application of the scheme, both that A is true, and also that *not-A* is true (a contradiction). Because such a result is unacceptable, it follows that the argumentation scheme for argument from expert opinion is not deductive in nature (at least in the form cited by Hamblin).

Salmon (1964) proposed an inductive form of the argument from expertise.

Most statements made by E are true.

A is a statement made by E.

Therefore (probably), A is true.

This account, however, runs into the same kind of problem, because of the negation rule in the probability calculus. According to this rule, the probability of a proposition *not-A* is to be calculated as 1 minus the probability of A. In a case where one expert makes the statement A, and another makes the statement *not-A*, it follows that A is probably true, and also that *not-A* is probably true. However, such a situation is not possible in the probability calculus. Hence the argumentation scheme for argument from expert opinion is not inductive in nature.

According to Rescher (1976), there is a third kind of reasoning, called plausible reasoning, and one characteristic of it is that it has a negation rule that is different from that of deductive logic or the probability calculus. According to Rescher, plausible reasoning is inherently presumptive, dialectical, and defeasible in nature. Consistently with Rescher's approach, an argumentation scheme for the argument from expert opinion was formulated in Walton (*Inf. Log.*, 1989). *D* is a domain of knowledge or expert opinion.

E is an expert in domain *D*.

E asserts that *A* is known to be true.

A is within *D*.

Therefore, *A* may (plausibly) be taken to be true.

The five critical questions matching this argumentation scheme, as given in Walton (*Inf. Log.*, 1989) can be concisely summarized as follows.

1. **Is *E* a genuine expert in *D*?**

2. **Did *E* really assert *A*?**

3. **Is *A* relevant to domain *D*?**

4. **Is *A* consistent with what other experts in *D* say?**

5. **Is *A* consistent with known evidence in *D*?**

The argument from expert opinion, so conceived, is an inherently presumptive type of argumentation that, when used correctly, shifts a burden of proof from a proponent to a respondent in a dialogue. However, the asking of any one of the appropriate critical questions previously mentioned shifts the burden of proof back onto the proponent's side again.

The argument from expert opinion can be a fallacy (called *argumentum ad verecundiam*, argument to modesty or respect) where the proponent tries to cut off the possibility of the respondent's asking of any or all of these critical questions by suggesting that, in so doing, the respondent would show insufficient respect for an expert's opinion.

It has been shown in Walton (*Inf. Log.*, 1989, chapter 7) however, that many appeals to expert opinion in everyday conversation are weak, or insufficiently supported, but not so bad that they deserve to be called fallacious.

Practical problems in using the argument from expert opinion often arise from the quoting or reporting of the opinion from some second-hand source.

Hence in judging the second premise of the argumentation scheme of the argument from expert opinion, four critical subquestions, cited by DeMorgan (1847) should be kept in mind.

1. **Is the expert's pronouncement directly quoted? If not, is a reference to the original source given? Can it be checked?**

2. **If the expert advice is not quoted, does it look like important information or qualifications may have been left out?**

3. **If more than one expert source has been cited, is each authority quoted separately? Could there be disagreements among the cited authorities?**

4. **Is what the authority said clear? Are there technical terms used that are not explained clearly? If the advice is in layman's terms, could this be an indication that it has been translated from some other form of expression given by the expert?**

With respect to answering the first critical question (of the original set of five, mentioned earlier), it is important to note that many such appeals are vague, and the name of the alleged expert(s) may not even be mentioned.

What is especially important to note here is that a juxtaposition of two distinct types of dialogue may be involved in the use of source-based argumentation. For example, suppose the proponent and the respondent are engaged in a critical discussion on the issue of whether or not abortion is morally acceptable as a practice. To back up one of the subarguments, suppose the proponent of one side of the issue cites an expert opinion, say, the opinion of a physician on whether a fetus could survive at some particular state of pregnancy of the mother. In this type of case, the dialogue between the proponent and the respondent is a critical discussion. However, in citing the physician's opinion on a particular point that is supposedly relevant in the critical discussion, the proponent is alleging that he or she and the source (the physician) stand to each other in the relationship or structure of an information-seeking type of dialogue of the type studied in Hintikka (1981) and Hintikka and Saarinen (1979). The proponent is claiming to consult the expert opinion of the physician, in other words, as an authoritative source to back up his or her argument in the critical discussion. The proponent need not have actually talked to the physician but he has the word or the opinion of the physician that has been brought forward and announced in some form.

One problem with a good deal of source-based argumentation is that the source is not even explicitly named or identified. For example, arguments may be based on the following kinds of claims: "According to experts . . . ," "according to reliable sources . . . ," "according to insider reports . . . ," and so forth. The problem with these cases is that unless a specific person or institution is mentioned, no real verification of the claim is possible. It is just this kind of abuse (and other errors in the use of expert opinions) that is often covered in informal logic under the *argumentum ad verecundiam*. According to Imwinkelried (1981; 1986), expert testimony is increasingly being misused in the courts, and the mismanagement of this kind of argumentation is a serious legal problem of growing magnitude.

ARGUMENT FROM EVIDENCE TO A HYPOTHESIS

In argument from evidence to a hypothesis, a conditional or hypothetical prediction of the form "If A is true, then B will be true too" is put forward. The A-proposition is called the hypothesis, and the B-proposition (the consequent of the conditional) represents some empirical or circumstantial evidence that can be observed or reported, so that it can definitely be proved to be true or false.

This type of argumentation is typical of experimental verification or falsification of a hypothesis in scientific reasoning.

Argument from evidence to a hypothesis takes two basic forms, or argumentation schemes, one of which is positive and the other negative. The positive form, called *argument from verification of a hypothesis,* has the following argumentation scheme.

If A (a hypothesis) is true, then B (a proposition reporting an event) will be observed to be true.

B has been observed to be true, in a given instance.

Therefore, A is true.

An example is the following case from Salmon (1984).

Case 3.13:   The prevailing sixteenth-century view of the arrangement of the sun, the earth, and other planets had been proposed 1,400 years earlier by Ptolemy, a Greek astronomer who worked in Alexandria. The Ptolemaic system was *geocentric,* placing our immobile earth at the center of the universe with the other planets and the sun revolving around it. Although the orbits of celestial bodies were very complicated to compute, this system permitted astronomers to make quite accurate predictions of the positions of these bodies over the centuries.

In 1543, Copernicus, a Polish astronomer, proposed a new planetary system that avoided many of the complexities of the Ptolemaic system. The Copernican system was not based on any new observations. By placing the sun at the center with the planets, including the earth, revolving around the sun, the *heliocentric* Copernican system postulated more regular (nearly circular) orbits and accounted for the same observations as the Ptolemaic system, but employed less complicated mathematical calculations of the paths of celestial bodies.

About 50 years after the work of Copernicus was published, a Danish astronomer, Tycho Brahe, introduced still another planetary system in which the earth was motionless, the sun orbited the earth, and the other planets orbited the sun. The Tychonic system had the same mathematical advantages as the Copernican system–postulating simpler orbits with easier calculations than the Ptolemaic system–and it was in accord with all observational evidence.

All three of these planetary systems were proposed before 1609, the year the telescope was invented. Galileo did not invent the telescope, but he built one that same year and was the first to use the telescope for astronomical observations. Soon after Galileo built his instrument, one of his students suggested to him that if the Copernican system was correct, then Venus, which is between the sun and the earth, should show a full range of phases–from almost dark to crescent to nearly full–similar to the phases of the moon. Galileo turned his telescope on Venus, and, over a period of several months, he was able to observe the full set of phases. Galileo interpreted these data as evidence that the Copernican (heliocentric) system was correct–that the apparently immobile earth actually revolved around the sun. (p. 171)

According to the analysis of the argumentation implicit in this case given by Salmon, Galileo's reasoning has the following form.

If the Copernican system is correct, then Venus will show phases.

Venus shows phases.

Therefore, the Copernican system is correct.

This argument is a case of argument from evidence to a hypothesis. Paradoxically, as noted by Salmon (1984), an argument of this type has the form of *affirming the consequent*, the deductively invalid form of reasoning, 'If A then B; B; therefore A.' Looked at from this point of view, it may appear that the argument from verification is a fallacy.

What this overlooks is that argumentation from verification is not deductively valid. Nor is it meant to be a deductive argument of any sort, or a conclusive argument generally. Despite the conclusive appearance of the argument in Case 3.13, generally this type of argumentation is of a probabilistic, or in many cases only of a presumptive nature. Generally, that is, the truth of the observation sentence, in a given case, does not confirm the hypothesis beyond doubt, or conclusively. Instead, more and more positive findings tend to *confirm* the hypothesis, in the sense of making it more probable.

The negative form, called *argument from falsification of a hypothesis,* has the following argumentation scheme.

If *A* (a hypothesis) is true, then *B* (a proposition reporting an event) will be observed to be true.

B has been observed to be false, in a given instance.

Therefore, *A* is false.

An example is the following case.

Case 3.14:   If this solution is an acid, this litmus paper will turn red.

The litmus paper did not turn red (when immersed).

Therefore, this solution is not an acid.

This type of argument has the form of *modus tollens,* a valid form of reasoning in deductive logic. In contrast to the argument from verification, the argument from falsification is conclusive, in the sense that the hypothesis is refuted by even one negative instance.

This asymmetry between these two types of argumentation was emphasized by Popper (1963), who saw falsification as the kind of reasoning characteristic of scientific method, precisely because of its conclusive character.

Argument from evidence to a hypothesis seems to resemble argument from consequences, and also argument from sign. All three types of reasoning have a "backwards" direction that takes the form of affirming the consequent. They all reason from the consequent back to the antecedent of a hypothetical, and could all therefore be described as species of consequential reasoning, but each is nevertheless a distinctive type of argumentation in its own right.

Argument from evidence to a hypothesis has to do with truth and falsity of the propositions involved, and is therefore different from argument from consequences, which has to do with the value (goodness or badness) of outcomes and proposed actions. You could say that argument from consequences is practical, whereas argument from evidence to a hypothesis is discursive in nature, having to do with the truth or falsity of propositions *per se,* rather than on how one should act on them, or because of what one knows about them. Argument from sign also tends to be discursive in nature (although it can be combined with practical reasoning, in many cases). What makes it distinct from argument from evidence to a hypothesis is its presumptive nature. Signs can be interpreted in many ways, and mean different things in different circumstances. Hence argument from sign is variable and defeasible in a way that argument from evidence to hypothesis is not. In argument from sign, the conditional says that if *A* is true, in a certain type of situation, then you can *normally* expect *B* to be true too (subject to exceptions).

None of these three types of consequential reasoning have been very well recognized as correct or legitimate forms of argument by traditional logic. Perhaps the reason is that, as forms of affirming the consequent, they have typically been suspected as being fallacious. Aristotle, perhaps setting the trend, classified *consequent* as a fallacious form of reasoning–see his account of the fallacy of the consequent in *De Sophisticis Elenchis* (167b2 - 167b12). This account was based on a valid point, but unfortunately, Aristotle's analysis of this fallacy is not very clear, and may have suggested to readers that all consequential reasoning is fallacious.

The critical questions for the argument from evidence to a hypothesis are the following:

1. **Is it the case that if *A* is true then *B* is true?**

2. **Has *B* been observed to be true (false)?**

3. **Could there be some reason why *B* is true, other than its being because of *A* being true?**

The third critical question inquires into the nature of the connection between A and B, which, in scientific testing of a hypothesis, requires some sort of lawlike or causal linkage.

Argument from evidence to a hypothesis, as noted earlier, is quite close to argument from sign, in some respects. In some cases, it is difficult to tell whether argumentation is of the one type or the other. The following case is a good example.

Case 3.15:   If this solution is acid, this litmus paper will turn red.

The litmus paper turned red.

Therefore, this solution is an acid.

This case is a deductively invalid argument (of the form affirming the consequent). But it could also be interpreted as a reasonable kind of argumentation, if not seen as deductive in nature. But is it, so interpreted, a case of argument from sign, or a case of argument from evidence to a hypothesis? It seems more intuitively plausible to classify it as a case of argument from sign, perhaps because we know that litmus paper is a standard test used to indicate whether a liquid is an acid or a base. But on the other hand, it is not immediately obvious why this case should not be counted as an instance of argument from evidence to a hypothesis.

It could be that argument from evidence to a hypothesis is best seen in many cases as a species of argument from consequences. Later, argument from consequences has been described as a kind of practical reasoning that has to do with evaluating a course of action as prudent or imprudent on the basis of it projecting favorable or unfavorable consequences for an agent. However, it is possible that argument from consequences could also have a discursive argumentation scheme based on a major premise of the following form: If hypothesis H is a true proposition, then a proposition T describing a *test event,* some observable event that is a consequence of H, will also be true. In this type of argumentation, the occurrence of T counts toward the establishing of H as an acceptable hypothesis. According to this interpretation, a hypothesis grows more and more acceptable in a process of evolutionary acceptance in a scientific inquiry as it passes more and more empirical, and at the same time becomes more qualified and sophisticated conceptually.

Admittedly, however, such an analysis of argument from evidence to a hypothesis is novel and speculative.

ARGUMENT FROM CORRELATION TO CAUSE

Argument from correlation to cause infers a causal connection between two events from a premise describing a positive correlation between them. In the argumentation scheme for this type of argument, the variables A and B stand for propositions (Walton, *Inf. Log.,* 1989), but we generally think of them as propositions that describe events that can be observed.

There is a positive correlation between A and B.

Therefore, A causes B.

Whether there is a correlation between two events, and how frequent this correlation is, are questions of probability and inductive reasoning. Therefore argument from correlation to cause is often thought of as an inductive type of argumentation. However, according to the analysis in Walton (*Inf. Log.,* 1989) causality is a *field-dependent* relation, meaning that it is assumed that, for the relation to hold, the situation given is stable or normal, in the sense that other intervening variables are excluded or held constant. It follows that causal arguments are presumptive and defeasible, and that they are based on plausibility rather than probability.

It has often been presumed in the past that the fallacy of *post hoc ergo propter hoc* is identical to the argument from correlation to cause. However, this is a simplistic (and incorrect) view of the matter. Quite often, arguments fitting this argumentation scheme are presumptively correct. However, this type of argumentation tends to be very weak in many cases, because other factors are overlooked. These other factors can be listed in the form of seven critical questions matching the argumentation scheme for the argument from correlation to cause (*Inf. Log.*, Walton, 1989).

1. Is there a positive correlation between *A* and *B*?

2. Are there a significant number of instances of the positive correlation between *A* and *B*?

3. Is there good evidence that the causal relationship goes from *A* to *B*, and not just from *B* to *A*?

4. Can it be ruled out that the correlation between *A* and *B* is accounted for by some third factor (a common cause) that causes both *A* and *B*?

5. If there are intervening variables, can it be shown that the causal relationship between *A* and *B* is indirect (mediated through other causes)?

6. If the correlation fails to hold outside a certain range of causes, then can the limits of this range be clearly indicated?

7. Can it be shown that the increase or change in *B* is not solely due to the way *B* is defined, the way entities are classified as belonging to the class of *B*s, or changing standards, over time, of the way *B*s are defined or classified?

Very often, the argument from correlation to cause is a weak argument because it overlooks or fails to account for one or more of these seven critical questions, in a given case. Even so, the argument might still be a reasonable one in that case, because the critical question could possibly be answered with further investigation of the case. In such a case, it is an exaggeration to say that the argument is fallacious. What we should say is that it only has a small weight of presumption in its favor, which can only be increased by giving a satisfactory answer to this critical question.

An example is the following case from Walton (*Inf. Log.*, 1989), where reports cited beneficial effects of owning a pet. It was claimed that people who owned dogs, for example, showed evidence of having better than average qualities, like self-reliance, tolerance, and good social skills. The conclusion implied was that pet ownership is the cause of these improved social qualities.

Case 3.16:   At a conference on the bond between humans and pets in Boston in 1986, researchers reported that pets can lower blood

> pressure in humans, improve the survival odds of heart patients, and even penetrate the isolation of autistic children. According to a report in *Newsweek* researchers at the conference reported on the beneficial effects of pet companionship. Studies showed that women who had owned dogs as children scored higher on self-reliance, sociability, and tolerance tests than petless women. Men who had owned a dog "felt a greater sense of personal worth and of belonging and had better social skills." Children with pets also showed greater empathy. (pp. 226-227)

We can assume that these studies were based on good correlations found by the researchers. But can we conclude that a causal relationship has been shown? The problem is that such a claim is dubious, because some key critical questions have not been answered.

One question is whether people who acquire pets in the first place tend to be the kind of people who have better than average social qualities. Another question is whether the effects could be due to other variables that go along with pet ownership. For example, any change in routine or diversion (whether it is a pet or not) could make for changes in social interactions that would lead to better social skills. Until these questions from Case 3.16 are answered, the argument from correlation to cause remains weak, or open to question. That does not mean, however (by itself) that the argument in this case is totally worthless, or fallacious.

ARGUMENT FROM CAUSE TO EFFECT

The argument from cause to effect takes the form of a prediction or warning that one type of event tends to cause another. It is a species of what Kienpointner (1992) called *Kausalschemata*. Postulating that if one type of event occurs, or were to occur in a given, particular case, then it is predicted the other (the effect) would also occur (or will occur). The argumentation scheme for this type of argument is the following:

> Generally, if *A* occurs, then *B* will (or might) occur.
>
> In this case, *A* occurs (or might occur).
>
> Therefore, in this case, *B* will occur (or might occur).

The bridging principle or warrant in the major premise can be variable in strength. In a strong attribution of causality, it might be said that if *A* occurs, then *B* will definitely occur. In a weaker form, it might be said that if *A* occurs, then there is a danger that *B* might occur.

This type of argumentation was analyzed by Hastings (1963), who gave the following example.

Case 3.17:   We contend, thirdly that recognition of Communist China would harm our relations in Asia, not improve them, simply because we will once more be retreating in the face of a communist bluff. We have said, we're going to defend Formosa against Communist Chinese attack; and now if we abandon the island of Formosa, the effect on the Asians, I am sure, would be quite startling. But more important than that is the promise that for the past five years we have maintained that the United States will not recognize Communist China so long as Communist China violates international law and refuses to accept her international obligations. At this time Communist China is holding American prisoners of war as spies, one of the grossest violations of international law one can find in the books. Would it be wise for this country, at this time especially, to recognize this government when they continue to violate international law? We consider, then, that this effect on the Asians would be to decrease our prestige in Asia. [Dennis Holt, cited in Windes and Kruger (1961, p. 187)].

The argument from cause to effect in this case can be summed up as follows.

Causal Generalization: When nations do not remain consistent in their policies, their prestige drops.

Case Premise: Recognition of Communist China means not remaining consistent in our policies.

Conclusion: Recognition of Communist China means that our prestige is likely to drop.

Matching the argumentation scheme for the argument from cause to effect, Hastings (1963) cited three types of critical questions (altered in number, phrasing and emphasis).

1. **How strong is the causal generalization (if it is true at all)?**

2. **Is the evidence cited (if there is any) strong enough to warrant the generalization as stated?**

3. **Are there other factors that would or will interfere with or counteract the production of the effect in this case?**

In Case 3.17, the first critical question asks whether the causal generalization, that not remaining consistent in policies results in drop in prestige, is strong (or true). The second critical question asks for evidence cited, if any, to back up this claim. The third critical question asks whether other factors might come into play to prevent a drop in prestige in this case.

As Hastings noted, this case has a hypothetical aspect to it. The argument is not claiming that a drop in prestige will occur. It is only saying that a drop in prestige will occur if Communist China is recognized. Thus the argument, in this case, is the warning type that concludes (hypothetically), "If you bring about event A, then another event, B, will occur."

The argumentation in this case has the negative suggestion that we should not recognize Communist China as an implied (nonexplicit) conclusion. Seen in this light, it can be viewed as a case of argument from consequences (of the causal type). This illustrates how the causal argument from consequences is in fact a composite argumentation scheme, built up with argument from cause to effect as its central component.

There are many other kinds of causal argumentation that could also be recognized here. Argument from effect to cause is one type, and it may be a component in argument from evidence to a hypothesis, and argument from sign. At least it may play some important role in these and other argumentation schemes.

Another common kind of argumentation that is broadly causal, and also based on practical reasoning, is argument from motive, opportunity, and means to action. This kind of argumentation is described in Walton (*Pract. Reas.*, 1990) as a species of practical reasoning often used in a "backwards" sequence–given an action, an investigator tries to reconstruct a goal and set of circumstances that plausibly account for the bringing about of the action.

ARGUMENT FROM CONSEQUENCES

Argumentation is a species of practical reasoning where a contemplated policy or course of action is positively supported by citing the good consequences of it. In the negative form, a contemplated action is rejected on the grounds that it will have bad consequences. Typically, this type of argumentation is used in a deliberation or critical discussion where there is a divided opinion on a contemplated course of action–one side supporting the action, and the other opposing it, or doubting the wisdom of it.

An example is the following case, an argument that was put forward in a Supreme Court decision on the issue of mandatory retirement for university professors in Canada. Mr. Justice Gerard La Forest put forward the following argument against mandatory retirement (Motherwell and Fraser, 1990, A1).

Case 3.18:   There can be little question that, while the impact will vary
              from individual to individual, mandatory retirement results in
              serious detriment to the appellants' working lives, including

loss of protection for job security and conditions, economic loss, loss of a working environment and facilities necessary to support their work, diminished opportunity for grants, and generally seriously diminished participation in activities both within and outside the university. (p. A1)

In this argument Mr. Justice La Forest was citing bad consequences of the policy of mandatory retirement, inferring the conclusion that (at least, in the respects cited), mandatory retirement is not a policy that we should have (as required by law).

Argumentation from consequences is a very common type of argumentation, and is especially prominent in political deliberations and arguments on public policy. The decision-making method of cost-benefit analysis is based on argumentation from consequences, and can be viewed as a formalization of this type of argumentation, where quantitative values are placed on both the value and probability of each outcome. However, in many arguments in everyday conversations, it is not appropriate or helpful to assign quantitative values (or at least, very precise ones) to these variables. In such cases, argumentation from consequences is better viewed as a kind of presumptive reasoning that shifts a burden of proof in a dialogue.

The argumentation scheme for argument from consequences is the following, where A is a proposition that can be brought about or made true by an agent.

If A is brought about, then good (bad) consequences will (may plausibly) occur.

Therefore, A should (not) be brought about.

This argumentation scheme represents both the positive and negative versions of the argument from consequences.

Argument from consequences is advanced by a proponent in a dialogue with the aim of convincing a respondent. Therefore, when a consequence is said to be "good" or "bad," it is meant to be good or bad from the respondent's point of view. "Good" means contributing to the respondent's known or expressed (or likely) goals, and "bad" means going against or defeating the implementation of these goals.

The critical questions for the argumentation scheme for the argument from consequences are the following:

1. **How strong is the likelihood that these cited consequences will (may, must, etc.) occur?**

2. **If A is brought about, will (or might) these consequences occur, and what evidence supports this claim?**

3. Are there other consequences of the opposite value that should be taken into account?

Another reason why argumentation from consequences is often best treated as a presumptive and defeasible type of reasoning is that the claim made is often in the form of a warning that such-and-such consequences *might* occur. Such arguments are generally weak and presumptive in nature, but they can be reasonable in some cases, for example, on grounds of safety, where danger is involved. On the other hand, this type of argumentation also lends itself to fallacious variants that utilize tactics of intimidation or scaremongering, exploiting a respondent's insecurity or fear.

Curiously, argumentation from consequences has not been recognized in very many logic textbooks as a distinctive form of argument. And when it is recognized, there has been a strong tendency to classify it as fallacious. Examples cited are of the kind illustrated by the type of case where a literary work is condemned as a bad book because it led to bad political consequences, or perhaps acts of violence, or something of the sort. This seems to be a kind of fallacy, on the grounds that the book should be judged on its literary merits, not on consequences that the author had no control over. However, such cases are tricky to judge, because if the book was partly meant to contain a moral, or have implications for how one should live one's life, then if it did condone violence or unethical conduct, it could certainly be condemned, with justification, on grounds of its having led to such consequences.

Argumentation from consequences is therefore highly problematic, in light of its current treatment in logic textbooks. Since very little has been written on this subject, or is known about it, some attention will be paid later in trying to sort out whether and when it is fallacious or reasonable as a species of argumentation.

ARGUMENT FROM ANALOGY

Argument from analogy is used to argue from one case that is said to be similar to another, in a certain respect. It has the following argumentation scheme. The respect in which the two cases are said to be similar "in a certain respect" in the first premise, is specified in the second premise and conclusion.

Generally, case C_1 is similar to case C_2.

A is true (false) in case C_1.

Therefore, A is true (false) in case C_2.

A good example is the following case, cited in Copi and Cohen (1990).

Case 3.19:   As in prospecting for gold, a scientist may dig with skill,
                courage, energy, and intelligence just a few feet away from a
                rich vein–but always unsuccessfully. Consequently in scientific
                research the rewards for industry, perseverance, imagination, and
                intelligence are highly uncertain. (Kubie, 1954, p. 111)

In this case, scientific research is said to be similar to prospecting for gold. We
all know that generally, in the latter case, success is highly uncertain, even when
considerable perseverance is put into its pursuit. The conclusion drawn is that the
same can be said of scientific research.

The type of argumentation identified by the following pair of argumentation
schemes in Walton (*Inf. Log.*, 1989) is actually a practical reasoning variant of
the argument from analogy.

(F_1) The right thing to do in S_1 was to carry out A.
           S_2 is similar to S_1.
           Therefore, the right thing to do in S_2 is to carry out A.

(F_2) The wrong thing to do in S_0 was to carry out A.
           S_2 is similar to S_0.
           Therefore, the wrong thing to do in S_2 is to carry out A.

The basic discursive scheme of the argument from analogy is that given previously. (F_1) and (F_2) are the argumentation schemes that result when the basic
scheme is combined with practical reasoning. As opposed to the basic argumentation schemes for argument from analogy, (F_1) and (F_2) could be called the
practical variants of the scheme for argument from analogy.

An example of these practical variants is the following case, from Walton
(*Inf. Log.*, 1989).

Case 3.20:   President Reagan, in a speech for congressional funds to aid
                the Contra rebels in Nicaragua, compares the Contras to the
                American patriots who fought in the War of Independence. A
                speaker in Congress opposed to sending aid to the Contras
                compares the situation in Nicaragua to the war in Vietnam.
                (p. 256)

In this case, it is clear that the speaker, then President Reagan, was using the
argument from analogy to counsel for the course of action of intervening in
Nicaragua. The assumption in this argument is that the War of Independence was
a good thing for the U.S. The speaker in Congress was, of course, using the
negative variant (F_2) of the argument from analogy to counsel against taking

action to intervene in Nicaragua. The comparison case was that the intervention in Vietnam was a disaster for the U.S.

Hastings (1963) distinguished between the argument from comparison and the argument from analogy as two separate argumentation schemes. According to his account, in argument from analogy (as opposed to argument from comparison), "the second, analogical event is similar, not on the basis of facts or circumstances, but on the basis of abstract principles; the structure of the abstract relationships of the two events is the same" (p. 111). Hastings gave the following example of argument from analogy to illustrate his distinction.

Case 3.21:   I know that Mr. Reuther, Mr. Newsom, and all you good people listening tonight want to know why prices have continued to go up after the freeze. You and I realize that we cannot simply apply the brakes suddenly to a truck going seventy miles an hour without a smash-up. You have to apply the brakes gradually. We must be fair to three million business concerns selling more than eight million items. And we must protect 152 million American consumers. [Michael DiSalle, cited in Harding (1952, p. 287)].

In this case, the analogy is between the momentum of the economy to the momentum of a heavy truck that cannot be stopped quickly, but must be slowed gradually.

Hastings seemed to think that the argument from analogy is more controversial, and perhaps also more prone to fallacious use, than the argument from comparison. Making any kind of clean distinction between two such types of argument is hard to sustain, however, and we adopt the point of view here that both types can be called argument from analogy, and come under the argumentation scheme mentioned earlier.

The critical questions for the argument from analogy are the following:

1. Are C_1 and C_2 similar, in the respect cited?

2. Is A true (false) in C_1?

3. Are there differences between C_1 and C_2 that would tend to undermine the force of the similarity cited?

4. Is there some other case C_3 that is also similar to C_1, but in which A is false (true)?

The third critical question asks whether there is a counteranalogy available to refute the original argument from analogy. It takes ingenuity to construct such a counteranalogy, in many cases. Hence, in most cases, the first three critical questions are the most important ones.

The following case nicely illustrates how argument from analogy is characteristically used to shift a burden of proof in a critical discussion of an issue that has two sides. Here two analogies are actually used to support the one side or the other in a key respect. The dialogue is a discussion between a mother and daughter on whether it is more rewarding to have children or a career. The mother insists to her daughter that she (the daughter) was never boring, and the daughter replied as follows (Chazin, 1989).

Case 3.22:   I didn't believe her, so I insisted. "Surely children are not as stimulating as a career."

"A career is stimulating," she said. "I'm glad I had one. But a career is like an open balloon. It remains inflated only as long as you keep pumping. A child is a seed. You water it. You care for it the best you can. And then it grows all by itself into a beautiful flower." (p. 32)

In this case, the argument from analogy is very persuasive. But it is clear that it is a presumptive kind of argumentation which, if replied to adequately, could shift the weight of presumption back to the other side.

For example, the daughter could reply: "Yes, but some careers, like creative writing, also plant seeds that produce flowers by opening the minds of others to new ideas." Because analogies are generally open to being used in different ways in argumentation, the argument from analogy is defeasible and open-ended in nature, even when it is very persuasive.

ARGUMENT FROM WASTE

One interesting type of argumentation which is a subspecies of practical reasoning is the argument from waste. In this type of argumentation, the speaker is striving to carry out a goal, but finds the process very difficult, or perhaps even wonders whether it is impossible, and begins to question whether continuing is worthwhile. But then the speaker reasons, "If I stop now, all my previous efforts will be wasted. Therefore, I must continue." The argumentation scheme for the argument from waste is the following.

If a stops trying to realize A now, all a's previous efforts to realize A will be wasted.

If all a's previous attempts to realize A are wasted, that would be a bad thing.

Therefore, *a* ought to continue trying to realize *A*.

This type of argumentation has a *modus tollens* kind of practical reasoning structure.

It was analyzed by Perelman and Olbrechts-Tyteca (1969), who called it the argument of waste *(argument du gaspillage)*. Their description of it is included in the following quotation, which gives a good example of the argument.

Case 3.23:   The argument of waste consists in saying that, as one has already begun a task and made sacrifices which would be wasted if the enterprise were given up, one should continue in the same direction. This is the justification given by the banker who continues to lend to an insolvent debtor in the hope of getting him on his feet again in the long run. (p. 279)

The argument from waste almost seems like an irrational argument, but it need not be in every case. For example, suppose in the previous case that there is really some chance that continuing to support the debtor a little more might lead to his saving his business and repaying the loan. Then the argument from waste, in this case, could possibly be a good argument.

Another good example is the following.

Case 3.24:   A PhD student, Susan, has spent more than five years trying to finish her thesis, but there are problems. Her advisers keep leaving town, and delays are continued. She contemplates going to law school, where you can get a degree in a definite period. But then she thinks: "Well, I have put so much work into this thing. It would be a pity to give up now."

From this case, one can easily appreciate the psychological appeal of the argument from waste. Against the despair of possible failure, and frustration of continuing, is laid the possible waste of a lot of hard work and resources put into a project.

The broader context of practical reasoning always needs to be taken into account in evaluating the argument from waste. The basic problem is that of weighing the positive value of a goal against the cost, or negative value of achieving it. And "waste" is a negative value.

One should also remember however, in evaluating this type of argument, that the past cannot be changed. If you have already "wasted" something, and there is no recouping that loss, then it would be fallacious to include such a loss as negative value in practical reasoning on how to proceed now.

Case 3.25:   Bob invested heavily in a stock, *ConEd,* which had been
                 overvalued, but then plunged to a relatively low price. Bob
                 kept his money in *ConEd,* reasoning: "I can't afford to lose
                 this much money, so I had better keep my shares in *ConEd,*
                 in the hope of recouping some of my losses."

This could be a fallacy, however. Bob should only keep his money in *ConEd* if
he has some reason to think the value of its shares will rise again. If some stock
with better prospects is available, Bob should not stick with *ConEd,* even though
he may now not have much to lose, unless he thinks it will bounce back. He
should not leave his remaining funds in *ConEd,* purely on the grounds of the
argument from waste.

The case of Susan is somewhat comparable. Her past work is in the past, and
that cannot be changed. But it is also somewhat different. That past work could
possibly have a big future payoff for her, if she continues only a small while
longer.

Another aspect of the latter case is that Susan should try to specify her goal
more completely. Other than just the goal of completing her degree, does she
want it to get a job, for personal satisfaction, and so forth? Then she can ask:
"What is the value of completing my degree with respect to this goal, versus
spending the time required to complete my degree, versus the value of spending
that time pursuing some other means of achieving that goal?" The question here
is one of goal-specification, at least to begin with.

The following critical questions are appropriate for the argumentation scheme
for the argument from waste.

1. **Are *a*'s previous attempts to realize *A* really a negative value
to be taken into account in my practical decision on what to do
now, or are they simply past events that can no longer be
changed?**

2. **Is there sufficient reason to think that if *a* continues, *A* will
be realized? In other words, is *A* possible?**

3. **Is there good reason to think that, from this point, the value
of realizing *A* is greater than the disvalue (cost) of continuing
the process of attempting to realize *A*?**

The third question asks whether, forgetting the past, it is worthwhile, from the
point of view of the present, carrying on with the action currently being taken.

The argument from waste is somewhat comparable to the inductive error
called *the gambler's fallacy,* where the assumption is made that a run of heads (or
tails), in a fair sequence of coin-tosses, will likely reverse itself on the next toss.
This is a fallacy because, in a fair toss, by definition, the probability of heads
versus tails is the same value (.5). It is assumed that each toss is independent of
the previous one. Hence the tendency to think that if you have had a run of heads,

the next toss will be tails, is a fallacy. Yet it is difficult, psychologically, to resist drawing such an inference. It seems natural, somehow, to think that nature will correct itself, or even things out.

ARGUMENT FROM POPULARITY

This argument has a practical and a discursive form, and the former argumentation scheme can be regarded as a variant of the latter. The discursive form, called the argument from popular opinion, has the following argumentation scheme.

> If a large majority (everyone, nearly everyone, etc.) accept A as true, then there exists a (defeasible) presumption in favor of A.

> A large majority accept A as true.

> Therefore, there exists a presumption in favor of A.

This kind of argumentation is deductively invalid, and generally it is not highly reliable. Indeed, it is known to be misleading, incorrect, and even fallacious in many cases. However, interpreted as a presumptive kind of argumentation that shifts a burden of proof in a dialogue, like a critical discussion, it can, in some cases be a reasonable argument. It is often conjoined with other argumentation schemes, like argument from position to know, in order to make it more plausible in a given case. An example would be the following case.

Case 3.26:   Nearly everyone who lives in Cedar Rapids thinks that the lake is a good place to swim in the summer.

Therefore, the lake in Cedar Rapids is probably (plausibly) a good place to swim in the summer.

You can easily appreciate why the argument from popularity is often conjoined with, and partly based on the argument from position to know, judging by this case.

Another kind of argument from popular opinion concerns majority preferences in matters of public policy (Editorial, 1992).

Case 3.27:   VANCOUVER–the Vancouver aquarium will stop capturing killer whales but will continue to show them, officials said yesterday.
    Curator Dr. Murray Newman said a new policy proposes rescue programs and breeding programs among whales already in captivity as ways to stock aquariums. He also said the

aquarium will not return its current stock of killer whales and dolphins to the seas.

"The decision not to collect killer whales is a reflection of human sensitivity," Newman told a news conference in the aquarium's underground boardroom, where several times the huge whales swam by and looked in.

He said a year-long study showed the public preferred the aquarium not to collect whales.

"At the same time we feel we have a mandate to tell people about them and keep them before the public eye."

There have been three orca deaths at the Vancouver aquarium in three years. (p. A3)

In this case, the indication of public preference shifts a burden of proof when there exists a balance of considerations on both sides. On the one side, there is the mandate to show whales to the public. On the other side are the arguments of animal activists that these whales do not live a healthy life in captivity, and too often die.

The practical form of the argument from popularity is called the *argument from popular practice*. It has the following argumentation scheme.

If a large majority (everyone, nearly everyone, etc.) does *A,* or acts as though *A* is the right (or an acceptable) thing to do, then *A* is a prudent course of action.

A large majority acts as though *A* is the right thing to do.

Therefore, *A* is a prudent course of action.

A good case to illustrate this type of argumentation is the following one.

Case 3.28:   In a sailboat race, there were a lot of markers that had to be passed, and it was very easy for the participants to become disoriented and get lost. The competitors made elaborate charts before the race, and during the race spent a lot of time using a compass to try to figure out the route. The captain of one sailboat was asked what strategy he used. His reply: "Well, we try to prepare carefully by making good charts. But if you are really getting lost, you often just follow the other fellows who seem to be very successful in getting ahead.[3]

---

[3] This case was recalled by the author from a television interview. It has not been quoted verbatim, nor is the original source known.

In this case, the argument from popular practice is clearly a stop-gap (or even desperation) strategy that may be wrong, but is at least some basis for prudent action where better evidence (good charts and the like) is not available, or has gone wrong. It is clearly a kind of second-best basis of argument as a means of deciding a course. But as a presumptive basis for prudent action, where better information is not available, this type of argumentation could have practical value in deliberations.

On the other hand, of course, it is evident that arguments from popularity often go wrong, or are used badly, and the logic textbooks are full of cases of the fallacious use of argumentation of this kind. It can be a serious error to take them too seriously, or to try to portray them as being deductively valid or inductively strong.

In practice, using argumentation from popularity can be quite tricky. For example in cases of economic behavior, like stock market crashes, investors often try to act quickly to follow trends. Often, this leads to a kind of slippery slope effect of precipitating mass actions, based not on knowledge of what is really happening, but on rumors or suspicions. People often try to follow trends, because they may have some reason to think that the trend-setter knows something they do not know.

Teenagers are particularly adept at exploiting tactics of argumentation from popularity designed to exclude a parent from taking meaningful part in a dialogue when they reply to questions with arguments like, "Everybody's wearing them." or "That's not how we do things now." The latter, in particular, is a tactic to suggest that the parent is out-of-date, and therefore not in a position to know what is currently popular or acceptable.

ETHOTIC ARGUMENT

An *ethotic argument*, according to Brinton (1986) is one in which *ethos* (the character of the speaker) is used to transfer credibility (either positively or negatively) to the proposition advocated by that speaker. Brinton (1985; 1986; 1987) cited Aristotle as the source for the identification of the ethotic argument as a specific type of argumentation. In the *Rhetoric* and the *Nicomachean Ethics,* Aristotle remarked that persuasion can be achieved by a speaker's personal character, because the good person's speech is more credible, especially on a question when certainty is impossible, and opinions are divided.

The argumentation scheme for the ethotic argument, or argument from ethos, as it might equivalently be called, is the following.

If x is a person of good moral character, then what x contends (A) should be accepted (as more plausible).

a is a person of good moral character.

Therefore, what a contends (A) should be accepted (as more plausible).

In this context, "accepted as more plausible" means that the proposition A in a question should be granted a greater weight of presumption than it would normally be (as supported by other evidence).

This argumentation scheme does not apply to all contexts of dialogue equally. It is most useful, as noted previously by Aristotle, on deliberations, for example on questions of values or public interest issues, when sources giving hard evidence, and expert opinions, are divided, and do not decisively resolve the issue. In other contexts, for example in a scientific and technical discussion in physics, questions of the speaker's character would not be relevant.

The critical questions matching the argument from ethos are the following.

1. Is a a person of good moral character?

2. Is the question of a's character relevant, in the context of dialogue in the given case?

3. How strong a weight of presumption in favor of A is claimed, and is that strength warranted by the case?

With respect to the third critical question, it should be noted that this type of argumentation is presumptive in nature, and generally does not conclusively prove a conclusion. Rather, the argument from ethos normally enhances a conclusion for which there already exists some (nonethotic) evidence.

With respect to the second critical question, it should be noted that character is generally relevant in political argumentation, and especially in election campaign debating. However, notoriously, in some cases too much weight is put on character issues, instead of other kinds of argumentation.

The negative form of the argument from ethos is identical to what has been traditionally called the "abusive" (direct or personal) argument against the person *(argumentum ad hominem)* in logic textbooks. The argumentation scheme for this negative type of ethotic argument *(Gegensatzschema)* is a variant on the positive form.

If x is a person of bad moral character, then what x contends (A) should be rejected (as less plausible).

a is a person of bad moral character.

Therefore, what a contends (A) should be rejected (as less plausible).

Bad character for veracity is especially often cited in connection with the use of this argumentation scheme. The critical questions for this argumentation scheme are comparable to the ones for the positive version given above (putting "bad" for "good" in 1, and "against" in for "in favor of" in 3).

The negative argument from ethos is often abused, and classified as a fallacy, when an unwarranted leap is made from the allegation that a person has a bad character, to the conclusion that what this person contends must be false. This fallacy can take one of three forms, depending on which critical question is inadequately answered, ignored, or suppressed.

With respect to the first critical question, it should be noted that many fallacious *ad hominem* attacks are based on unsubstantiated rumor, innuendo, or gossip, instead of good evidence. With respect to the third critical question, it should be noted that claims based on negative ethotic argumentation are fallacious when the absolute conclusion is inferred that A is false (or that A is "certainly" false, etc.). This fallacy is perhaps most evident in the *poisoning the well* variant, in which it is argued that a is a liar, biased, and so forth, and therefore whatever a says, no matter how plausible or well-supported by good evidence, must be false. This type of attack is a tactic used to "shut up" an opponent, or disqualify him or her from taking any further part in a dialogue.

According to the account of legal evidence given by R. E. Degnan in the *Encyclopaedia Britannica* (1963), impeachment is the process of showing facts that reflect on the veracity of a witness, thereby authorizing rejection of his testimony, in whole or part. Four universally recognized forms of impeachment are cited as quoted.

> (1) showing that the witness has previously made statements inconsistent with those made on the stand (*i.e.,* in the box) under oath; (2) showing that the witness is biased either for or against one of the litigants; (3) showing general bad moral character of the witness; and (4) showing that his character for truth and veracity is bad. (p. 908)

This fourfold classification is actually a very nice division of the four main types of *ad hominem* argumentation. However, especially category (3) brings out the importance of negative ethotic argumentation as a component of argumentation from testimony, a species of argument from position to know. Argumentation from testimony is source-based, and therefore dependent on the cooperativeness and sincerity of a participant in dialogue. Here we allude again to the Gricean maxims of cooperative conversation.

ARGUMENT FROM BIAS

The argument from bias is a negative type of argumentation whereby a respondent in a dialogue attacks a proponent's argument by claiming that the proponent is biased. It would therefore come under the heading of what Kienpointner (1992) called *Gegensatzschemata*. The argumentation scheme for the argument from bias is the following.

> If an arguer x is biased, then it is less likely that x has taken the evidence on both sides of an issue into account in arriving at conclusion A.
>
> Arguer a is biased.

It is less likely that a has taken the evidence on both sides of this issue into account.

The use of this argumentation scheme is heavily dependent on the context of dialogue. If a dialogue is clearly and overtly of a partisan kind, for example, a sales speech to sell a product, then a certain degree of bias is normal and appropriate. We know in advance that it is a partisan argument for one side, and if that is what the speech is supposed to be, there is no deception involved. There is bias, but it is not a problem for the hearer.

However, if the dialogue is of a type that is supposed to take the evidence on both sides into account, and proceed in a neutral way (e.g. an inquiry), then bias is a problem. In such a case, the argument from bias can get a good grip, and rightly functions to throw a weight of presumption against a conclusion.

The critical questions corresponding to the argumentation scheme of the argument from bias are the following.

1. What is the context of dialogue, and in particular, is it a type of dialogue that requires a participant to take evidence on both sides of an issue into account?

2. What is the evidence for the charge that a is biased?

In many cases, it is not easy to prove bias, and the charge of bias is based only on suspicion, rather than evidence. In such cases, the use of the argument from bias can degenerate into a fallacious *ad hominem* attack.

The topic of the following case was the introduction of the NeXT computer on the market by Steve Jobs, former head of the Apple Computer Corporation. A *Newsweek* article discussed the features of the NeXT, and speculated on its prospects of success in attempting to move into the work-station market in the computer industry.[4] Discussing the pros and cons of the issue, the article makes a case that although the NeXT venture has many strikes against it, many industry analysts are enthusiastic about its prospects for success.

Inevitably, this article makes considerable use of appeals to expert opinions of leaders in the computer industry in its discussion of the topic. One expert opinion cited is that of William Gates, a successful and respected software engineer who produced operating systems for IBM, and many important applications of IBM and Apple computers. According to the article, Gates, a "virtuoso software engineer" who "dominates the industry" declined Jobs' invitation to contribute software to the NeXT project, because "there wasn't enough money in the narrow market Jobs was pursuing" (p. 51). Gates is described as the "most dour critic" of the NeXT project.

What is most interesting, however, is the way the *Newsweek* article provided a rebuttal to the reported criticism.

---

[4] See Schwartz, Rogers, and Sandza (1988).

Case 3.29:   Some industry observers suggest a dark motive for Gates' skepticism. The deal between Jobs and IBM centers on Unix—one major operating system Gates doesn't own. If the NeXT program helps Unix become a standard, Gates may lose money and power.[5] (p. 51)

Gates is cited as the critic, but his criticism is then criticized by pointing out that he stands to lose "money and power" if the system he has criticized becomes a success. The suggestion is that Gates' criticism could be biased, because of financial and other personal interests.

This allegation of bias is actually an *ad hominem* argument, because Gates' alleged argument is said to be possibly based on a "dark motive" of financial or personal interest. It is *ad hominem* because it opens Gates' personal integrity, veracity, or objectivity to critical questioning. Allegations of personal bias generally tend to have an *ad hominem* character in argumentation because they raise questions about an individual's veracity, integrity, or moral character by alleging a lack of objectivity.[6] If a person is not objective in an argument, there are two alternatives. Either the bias is intentional or unintentional. If it is intentional, then dishonesty or a "hidden agenda" is suggested. If it is unintentional, then it is suggested that the person is not astute, sophisticated, or detached enough to realize that his or her arguments are biased, and therefore that the person may not be capable of playing an intelligent part in a serious and sustained argument on a controversial topic of discussion.

Another interesting aspect of Case 3.29 is the way the criticism of Gates' objectivity is based on the attribution, "Some industry observers suggest. . . ." Who are these "industry observers?" They could be virtually anyone. They could be two persons queried on the street, who happen to have opinions on the computer industry. This way of introducing evidence by naming or indicating sources would not be allowed in a scholarly work. But it is allowed in journalism. Even so, in this case, basing an allegation of a respected expert's personal bias on a claim about what some observers suggest is skating on thin ice.

The article follows up by taking some sting out of the criticism of bias—while at the same time producing a superficial appearance of balance–by adding that, according to a named source, Gates is a smart enough businessman to produce software for NeXT, if NeXT really becomes a success. The suggestion made here is that while Gates may be negatively biased against Jobs personally, he is no fool, and if Jobs' project becomes successful, Gates may not continue to be against it.

By basing its allegation of bias on what some observers suggest, the article is being clever to appear not to make any allegations itself. At the same time, by reporting that Gates is a "good businessman," even though he is sometimes

---

[5] See Schwartz, Rogers, and Sandza (1988).

[6] According to Hinman (1982, p. 341), an *ad hominem* argument that questions an arguer's motives becomes relevant in controversies where the given evidence leaves enough room open for doubt so that the weaker *ad hominem* arguments are worth consideration.

"negative" to Jobs personally, the article cleverly presents a surface appearance of balance in looking at both sides of an issue. Despite these clever disclaimers however, the suggestions made provide plenty of innuendo to do the job of raising pointed questions in a reader's mind about the objectivity of Gates' cited criticism of the market potential of Jobs' NeXT project. Thus the allegation of bias is put forward in an ingenuous manner–it is a powerful argument put forward through the use of methods of suggestion and innuendo. Such tactics are highly effective.

Bias works through a dialectical shift. A certain level of objectivity or freedom from bias is required in a persuasion dialogue, for example. But if one participant in the persuasion dialogue speech event is revealed to be covertly engaged in negotiation dialogue (based on self-interested bargaining), the person may be criticized for bias. Such a criticism means that there has allegedly been a failure on the part of a participant in argument to keep up to an appropriate standard of objectivity for the context of dialogue in question.

Another example could be a participant's engaging too heavily in persuasion dialogue during the course of a scientific inquiry. There is nothing wrong with strenuous advocacy of one's personal point of view in a persuasion dialogue. But if the context of argument is clearly supposed to be that of a scientific inquiry, persuasion dialogue argumentation could be criticized as inappropriate on the grounds that it fails to meet high enough standards of objectivity.

In Case 3.29, the context of dialogue is somewhat complex. It is that of a journalistic report which speculates on the possible success of a new project just launched in the computer industry. Nobody knows, yet, whether the project will succeed or fail. It is a matter of opinion. So, expert opinions of those in the industry are cited by the article, in order to look at both points of view on the topic. However, neither the journalists nor the readers are presumed to be experts on this subject. The readers can draw their own conclusions based on their assessment of the opinions and facts collected and interpreted by the journalists. Naturally, in weighing these highly fallible opinions, the readers need to make up their own minds about the worth of a source, and the plausibility of the opinions ventured by that source. Considerations of respect for the credibility of authoritative sources, and the potential for bias of their opinions, rightly play a role in a reader's judgments of the preponderance of argument and evidence in drawing a conclusion on the controversy. Hence allegations of bias rightly have a place in this type of context of argumentation.

Bias is not only difficult to judge in a given case (Blair, 1988), it is even difficult to define exactly what it is. In Walton (*Bias Crit.*, 1991) bias is defined as a failure of critical doubt to function correctly in argumentation in a given context of dialogue. Critical doubt is defined as a second-level attitude one participant in a dialogue has toward the attitude of another participant. Analysis of argumentation schemes, and how they are used in dialogues, is helpful in studying and evaluating bias, if Walton (*Bias Crit.*, 1991) is right that bias is associated with certain characteristic types of failures of reasoned argumentation. In particular, bias is associated with the failure to be open to new evidence introduced into a critical discussion.

There are many kinds of bias, not all of them relevant to the critical evaluation of argumentation. However, in one sense, to say that a person is biased is to say that this person has shown an attitude that is inappropriate in a critical discussion, as evidenced by the use of argumentation. By this account, bias is dialogue-relative. The same argument could be biased in one context of dialogue (in the negative sense of showing harmful or obstructive critical bias) and not biased in another context of dialogue.

ARGUMENT FROM AN ESTABLISHED RULE

Argument from an established rule is a practical kind of argumentation that comes into play where one participant in a dialogue is attempting to persuade another participant to carry out an action, or to act in a particular way (or the rightness of either), and the other participant is resisting or questioning this persuasion. The following case is a familiar example.

Case 3.30:   **Student:**   I don't think I will be able to get my essay in on Tuesday. Would it be OK if I handed it in next week?

Professor: We all agreed at the beginning of the year that Tuesday is the deadline. That is the rule.

The professor might back up this argument by saying that it would not be fair to all the others, who have completed the assignment on time, if one student is given more time (an unfair advantage) without being penalized by getting a grade reduction.

There is an appeal to universality in the argument from an established rule. In this way, it is somewhat similar to the argument from popular practice. The argument from an established rule says that everyone in a particular group acts, or must act in a particular way, therefore it would be unfair to let any single person act in a different way by not having to follow the rule. This is somewhat like the argument from popular practice, which is based on the premise that a large majority of people act as though some particular course of action is the right thing to do. But the general thrust of these two types of argumentation is different. In the argument from popular practice, an individual looks to the universal practice of the group as a guide to action. In the argument from established rule, one party uses the rule established by the group to try to persuade the other to follow that rule.

The argumentation scheme for the argument from an established rule is the following.

For all x, if doing A is the established rule for x, then (subject to exceptional cases), x must do A (subject to penalty).

Doing A is the established rule for a.

Therefore, a must do A (subject to penalty).

An established rule is a universal practice, a code of action specifying a right thing to do in a given type of case. The term "established rule," used as opposed to the weaker term "universal practice," suggests that the prior agreement of the respondent may be used as evidence to back up the major premise.

The following critical questions match the argumentation scheme for argument from an established rule.

1. **Is "doing A" in fact what the rule states?**

2. **Does the rule "doing A" apply to this case?**

3. **Is "For all x, x must do A" the right rule, or should some other rule be the right one? Could there be more than one rule involved, with some doubt on which is the more appropriate one?**

As stated in the argumentation scheme for the argument from an established rule, the major premise is a defeasible conditional. Generally, in this type of argumentation, the argument is only meant to apply to normal, or nonexceptional cases. The most common type of response to it is to claim that one's own case is exceptional, for some reason. In many contexts of dialogue where this type of argumentation is used, in fact, known categories of exceptions to a rule will be recognized. Citing of an appropriate type of exception will therefore throw the burden of proof back onto the proponent of the argument from established rule.

The following argumentation scheme is a counterargument or refutation matching the argument from an established rule, called the *argument from an exceptional case.*

For all x, if the case of x is an exception, then the established rule does not apply to the case of x.

The case of a is an exception.

Therefore, a need not do A.

This counterargument is more than just a critical question, because (a) it requires definite evidence of a certain type to back it up, and (b) it throws a positive burden of proof back onto the other side when successfully deployed in a dialogue. Hence, it is best seen as an argumentation scheme in its own right, matching the prior argumentation scheme of the argument from established rule. Hence, it could be called a refutation scheme, or counterargument scheme.

An example would be the following continuation of the dialogue in Case 3.30.

Case 3.31:   **Student:**   But I had a bad case of the flu last week, and I have a note from my physician to prove it.

What is appealed to here is the recognized category of exception "illness" as proven by the accepted kind of evidence (note from a physician). The effect of this counterargument is to shift the burden of proof back to the other side to show why the cited claim to exceptional status is illegitimate, or to concede the point.

When the argument from an exceptional case is used, in some cases the argument will be clearly acceptable. In other cases, it will be clearly unacceptable, for example, "I had a lot of other assignments to do." And in still other cases, it will be borderline, that is, neither clearly acceptable nor clearly unacceptable. Deciding borderline cases sets precedents, and is related very closely to argumentation from precedent.

Argument from an exceptional case is also closely related to argument from analogy. Often, a case is argued to be exceptional or nonexceptional (especially in borderline cases) in virtue of its comparison with an allegedly similar case. For example, if one student successfully argues "My mother died last week," another might try the argument "My dog died last month." The professor is then put in the position of "judge" who must give a decision, one way or the other. Such a decision will then function as a known or established precedent in further argumentation.

The critical questions for the argumentation scheme for the argument from exceptional case are the following.

1. **Is the case of *a* a recognized type of exception?**

2. **If it is not a recognized case, can evidence why the established rule does not apply to it be given?**

3. **If it is a borderline case, can comparable cases be cited?**

The asking of any of these three critical questions shifts the burden of proof back onto the proponent's side.

The applicability of these two argumentation schemes to legal argumentation is clearly evident. Clearly this type of argumentation uses case-based reasoning, and the citing of particular cases is generally used to back up the use of both argumentation schemes, and to try to refute the opposing side.

ARGUMENT FROM PRECEDENT

Argument from precedent is a species of case-based reasoning where citing a particular case is used to argue for changing an existing rule, or adding a new rule to supplement existing rules. Argument from precedent is one way of responding to argument from an established rule (as an opposed refutation). The precedent slippery slope argument is one way of responding to the argument from precedent (as an opposed refutation).

An example can be given by extending Case 3.30 of argument from an established rule.

Case 3.32:   Student: Yes, but I heard that you said to Ms. Reasoner that she could hand her essay in a week late because she has another assignment due this week. I have another assignment due this week too. So I should be able to hand mine in a week late too.

The basis of this appeal is the argument from precedent, on the grounds of the similarity of one case to another. According to Golding (1984), the idea of adherence to precedent in moral and legal reasoning can be traced back historically to Aristotle's concept of justice or fairness, according to which, like cases should be treated alike.

The argument from precedent functions by shifting a burden of proof. In Case 3.32, the citing of a similar case functions as a presumptive appeal to a precedent, to plead for exemption from the established rule. The proponent of the rule needs to give some explanation or argumentation, in order to justify applying the rule to the current case, in light of the previous case cited as an opposed precedent.

The argumentation scheme for the argument from precedent is the following.

The existing rule says that for all x, if x has property F then x has property G.

But in this case C, a has property F, but does not have property G.

Therefore, the existing rule must be changed, qualified, or given up, or a new rule must be introduced to cover case C.

The critical questions matching this argumentation scheme are the following.

1. **Does the existing rule really say that for all x, if x has F then x has G?**

2. **Is case C legitimate, or can it be explained away as not really in violation of the existing rule?**

3. Is case C an already recognized type of exception that does not require any change in the existing rule?

The use of argument from precedent poses a puzzle or problem, by introducing a novel type of case that does not appear to fit the existing rules. It therefore points the way to some new development in the evolution of a set of rules, for example, by adding a new rule, or by recognizing a class of exceptions to an existing rule.

ARGUMENT FROM GRADUALISM

Argument from gradualism is a sequential argument that moves forward by a series of small steps to persuade a respondent to accept a conclusion he or she would not accept in one big step. An example is the following case.

Case 3.33:   A government knows that it needs to get an 18 percent value-added tax (VAT), sometimes also called a goods and services tax (GST) in order to deal with the deficit. However, the public would never vote for, or approve such a large tax, in one single step. Therefore, the government adopts the strategy of introducing a 3 percent VAT, and then increasing it every few years, when politically appropriate, until the 18 percent level is reached.

Perelman and Olbrechts-Tyteca (1969) called this tactic the *device of stages.*

> It is often found to be better not to confront the interlocutor with the whole interval separating the existing situation from the ultimate end, but to divide this interval into sections, with stopping points along the way indicating partial ends whose realization does not provoke such a strong opposition. Though the passage from point A to C may cause difficulties, it might happen that no objection may be seen to passing from point A to B, from which point C will appear in a quite different light. We may call this technique the *device of stages.* The structure of reality conditions the choice of these stages but never imposes it. (p. 282)

It is a good question whether this type of argumentation should be defined as a distinctive argumentation scheme, or as a tactic of argumentation that is used in conjunction with various argumentation schemes. However, sometimes, as in Case 3.33, it is used as a distinctive type of argumentation in its own right. Hence, it is appropriate to define it as a separate argumentation scheme.

The argumentation scheme for the argument from gradualism is the following.

Proposition A is true (acceptable to the respondent).

There is an intervening sequence of propositions, $B_1, B_2, \ldots, B_{n-1}, B_n$, C, such that the following conditionals are true: If A then B_1; If B_1 then B_2; $\ldots$; If B_{n-1}, then B_n; If B_n then C.

The conditional 'If A then C' is not, by itself, acceptable to the respondent (nor are shorter sequences from A to C (than the one specified in the second premise) acceptable to the respondent.

Therefore, the proposition C is true (acceptable to the respondent).

This type of argumentation is successful if and only if each small step, from A to B_1, from B_1 to B_2, and so forth, is acceptable to the respondent as an argument. And second, it is successful if and only if the entire sequence leads from A as a premise to C as the final conclusion.

THE CAUSAL SLIPPERY SLOPE ARGUMENT

The slippery slope argument is a species of argument from gradualism. At the same time, it is characteristically used in opposition to (the reality or threat of) the argument from gradualism. A slippery slope argument, (Walton, *Slip. Slope*, 1992), warns a respondent that if he or she takes a first step, this person will find himself or herself caught up in a sequence of consequences leading to a disastrous (dangerous, horrible) outcome. The conclusion is: "Respondent, do not take this first step!" In the causal variant, the sequence is causal in nature.

A classic case concerning the once fashionable controversy on the decriminalization of marijuana is taken from Johnson and Blair (1983).

Case 3.34:   The federal proposal to switch cannabis from the Narcotics Control Act to the Food and Drug Act will probably be the first step leading to the eventual legalization of this 'soft' drug. Under the drug act the possession of marijuana or hashish will be punishable with a fine rather than with a jail sentence as called for in the narcotics act.

The penalties for trafficking, importing, and cultivating the drug will still be stiff. However, it is hardly likely that judges will take as serious a view of a drug as they do of a narcotic, and in time the penalty for trafficking or importing will probably be a light fine and a ticking off by the judge. Then, in turn, the fine for possession will likely be dropped and it will be legal to have cannabis for personal use.

From there the next step is controlled manufacture and sale along the same lines as alcoholic drinks. Then the emphasis on the nature of the crime will switch to smuggling and bootlegging with the intention that the Crown gets its legitimate revenue from the sale of the drug. By that time, cannabis will probably be called joy candy or fun smoke or by some other euphemism.

If we seem to be moving too fast, remember that this is the usual way of softening up the law. We hope that when Health Minister Lalonde makes the change he will understand that he is opening the door to putting pot in every pocket. (pp. 161-162)

In their analysis of the argumentation in this case, Johnson and Blair spelled out the steps in the sequence of reasoning.

1.   Marijuana put under Food and Drug Act;

2.   Possession punished by fine rather than jail; trafficking, importing, and cultivating punished stiffly;

3.   Judges take a less serious view of offenses against this law;

4.   The penalty for trafficking and importing becomes less severe–a light fine;

5.   Penalty for simple possession dropped; legal to possess marijuana;

6.   The manufacture and sale of marijuana controlled by the government;

7.   Emphasis changes from possession and trafficking to smuggling and bootlegging;

8.   Marijuana legal and in common use.

Some of the links in this chain are obviously weaker than others. Johnson and Blair suggested that the best method of criticizing the argument, therefore, is to attack the weakest links first.

The argumentation scheme for the causal slippery slope argument is the following (Walton, *Slip. Slope,* 1992).

A_0 is up for consideration as a proposal that seems initially like something that should be brought about.

Bringing up A_0 would plausibly cause (in the given circumstances, as far as we know) A_1, which would in turn plausibly cause A_2, and so forth, through the sequence $A_2, \ldots, A_n$.

A_n is a horrible (disastrous, bad) outcome.

Therefore, A_0 should not be brought about.

The critical questions matching the argumentation scheme for the causal slippery slope argument are the following (Walton, *Slip. Slope*, 1992).

1. **Does the proponent's description of the initial action A_0 rightly express the proposal being advocated by the respondent?**

2. **Do any of the causal links in the sequence lack solid evidence to back it up as a causal claim?**

3. **Does this outcome plausibly follow from the sequence, and is it as bad as the proponent suggests?**

Generally, as with all slippery slope arguments, the key critical question concerns the chain of conditionals that make up the sequence. The evidence for the steps in this sequence is often very poor, and only meant to shift a weight of presumption by suggestion or innuendo.

In many cases, the slippery slope argument is so sketchy and weak, it is used as more of a scare tactic, (e.g., "Bad things might happen if you embark on this dangerous course"), than as an argument that is backed up by serious evidence. In these types of cases, it may be described as a fallacy. However, in principle, the causal slippery slope can be used as a correct or reasonable presumptive type of argumentation. Its correct function is as a kind of warning in advice-giving dialogue of the deliberation type, where the respondent is using practical reasoning to try to determine a prudent course of action, and the proponent of the slippery slope argument is warning against a particular action being considered by the respondent.

Johnson and Blair (1983) recognized two forms of the causal slippery slope argument, a long form and a short form. In the long form, the whole series of causal steps is included, whereas in the short form, just the first and last steps are (explicitly) given. In the following example of the short form (Johnson & Blair, 1983), Canadian unions had been complaining that foreign visitors were taking Canadian jobs, in contravention of immigration rules. In 1972, the government proposed issuing work permits to deal with the problem. However, union leaders strongly protested against this proposal, and the leader of the United Auto

Workers, Dennis McDermott, argued that such remedies would be worse than the problem they were designed to solve.

Case 3.35:   They [work permits] would run counter to our traditional freedoms and would be *the first step* toward a police state.

This case of the causal slippery slope argument is a short form type, because we are not told what all the intervening steps between "work permits" and "police state" are supposed to be. It is easy to imagine what these steps are. The issuing of work permits would obviously make it easier for the government to keep track of people, and this would increase government control, which could lead, at least potentially, towards a better ability for the government to "police" certain kinds of illegal activities. But just how this would or might lead to a "police state" seems highly questionable. The basic problem is that the purported intervening steps are simply not specified.

It is a good question whether the short form of causal slippery slope argument should be classified as inherently fallacious, or whether, in some cases, it can correctly function as a weak, but not fallacious, presumptive argument that shifts only a slight weight of presumption to the other side of a dialogue. In Walton (*Slip. Slope*, 1992), the later hypothesis is supported.

In any event, in the short form case especially, the most important emphasis in critical questioning should be directed toward filling in the missing steps in the sequence. In many cases, these steps are not explicitly given, but can be filled in (hypothetically) from the context of dialogue in the given case.

The causal slippery slope argument is not a basic argumentation scheme in its own right. It is a composite of the argument from gradualism and the argument from cause to effect. A fuller treatment of the causal slippery slope argument, and more case studies of it, can be found in Walton (*Slip. Slope*, 1992).

THE PRECEDENT SLIPPERY SLOPE ARGUMENT

The precedent slippery slope argument is a combination of the argument from precedent and the argument from gradualism. In the precedent type of slippery slope argument, one participant in a dialogue is contemplating a particular action and a second participant argues that if he or she takes this step, it will set a precedent that will lead to a series of actions that will be not good (from the point of view of the first participant). In many cases of the precedent slippery slope argument the series not only gets worse and worse, one precedent leading to another, but some particularly horrible outcome is cited as the end result.

The context of the following case was a debate on whether the practice of having religious prayers in the schools should be kept or discontinued.

Case 3.36:   One participant argued that with all the different minority
                 groups, once you accept one kind of religion as legitimate,
                 you are going to have to accept many other kinds of religious
                 groups as having a legitimate right to have prayers or reli-
                 gious services in the classroom. This participant said: "It's a
                 Pandora's box. You know that satanism is a religion too!"

From the text of this case, it is not made explicit what side of the debate this
participant was on. But it appears that the person was taking the side against the
practice of keeping prayers in the school, by arguing that if you keep this
practice, you will have to admit more and more religions to have prayers of their
own kind. The argument is that once you accept one religion (which presumably,
is the case), it will function as a precedent so that you will have to accept
another, and so on. Eventually, by this process, the argument runs, you will have
to accept (unacceptable or horrible) religions like satanism.

The particular case also has an element of argument from a verbal classification present, in defining satanism as a religion. Such an element is very common
in the use of the precedent slippery slope argument, but not essential to it.

This case is also a little bit different from the usual in that usually, the
slippery slope is a conservative type of argument that warns against changing an
existing practice, on the grounds it will lead to a dangerous outcome. In this case,
assuming that having prayers in the schools is the existing practice, the slope
argument warns against the dangers in trying to maintain this practice.

The argumentation scheme for the precedent slippery slope argument–compare
Walton (*Slip. Slope*, 1992)–is the following.

Case C_0 would set a precedent with respect to an existing rule R.

Case C_0 is similar to case C_1, that is, if C_0 is held to be an exception to
R, then C_1 must be held to be an exception too (in order to be consistent
in treating equal cases alike). A sequence of similar pairs $\{C_i, C_j\}$ binds
us by case-to-case consistency to the series, $C_0, C_1, \ldots, C_n$.

Having to accept case C_n as a precedent, or as a recognized exception to
R, would be intolerable (horrible, bad).

Therefore, admitting case C_0, or bringing it forward in the first place, is
not a good thing to do.

The precedent slippery slope argument takes the form of a warning, or practical
advice. It says: "Do not take this first step of allowing case C_0 (as a recognized
exception to a rule, or as any new step), because once you do, it will set a
precedent, and then one case will lead to another!" The warning tells you that
things will go from bad to worse, once the first step has been taken.

The critical questions for the argumentation scheme for the precedent slippery slope argument are the following.

1. **Would case C_0 set a precedent?**

2. **What is the exact sequence of intervening steps in virtue of which C_0 would lead to C_n?**

3. **What is the evidence showing why each of these intervening steps would occur?**

4. **Is C_n intolerable, and if so, why?**

5. **Which are the weakest of the intervening steps, and is the evidence backing them sufficient to warrant the strength of the claim made in the conclusion?**

In evaluating precedent slippery slope arguments, it should be noted that they come in varying degrees of strength of claim made. Sometimes the conclusion claims that the horrible outcome "must" occur, but in other cases, it is only claimed that it "may" or "might" occur. The evidence backing up the premises needs to be adequate only to support the strength of the claim made in the conclusion. Hence the wording of the claim in the given case is very important.

Other case studies of the precedent slippery slope argument can be found in Walton (*Slip. Slope,* 1992).

ARGUMENT FROM VAGUENESS OF A VERBAL CLASSIFICATION

This argument is a kind of counterargumentation used to reply to the argument from an established rule and to the argument from verbal classification. The argument from vagueness of a verbal classification claims that the rule or verbal classification in question is overly vague, and therefore cannot sustain the conclusion it was supposed to support. It is a species of refutation scheme or *Gegensatzschema*.

For example, in reply to Case 3.7, our example of the argument from verbal classification, a respondent might argue as follows.

Case 3.37: Well, the notion of "poor return" is too vague to be well-defined. What is a poor return on stocks or bonds, is not a poor return on health insurance. This concept is too vague, so you can't just say absolutely that 40% is a poor return.

To say that a term is vague is to say that it lacks sufficient precision to support a classification required to sustain an argument.

The argument from vagueness of a verbal classification is a kind of meta-argumentation, because it refers to the degree of precision of language used in an argument. Thus it makes a judgment about the fittingness of the language in relation to the context of dialogue in which the argument has been advanced.

A typical example is the following case.

Case 3.38:   Marcia and Ted are debating on the issue of abortion. Ted, who is pro-life, argues: "There can be no abortion when the fetus becomes a person." Marcia replies: "That's hopelessly vague! There is no way to exactly define when the fetus has become a 'person.' You don't have a leg to stand on there!"

What Marcia is objecting to here is that the term "person" is too vague to resolve the dispute at issue. Both sides can interpret it in such a way as to support their own arguments. Hence, introducing this vague term is of no use in contributing to the resolution of the dispute. The argument is not that the vagueness of the term "person" is a bad thing *per se,* but that this term lacks enough precision in relation to the context of dialogue for the argumentation in this particular case (according to Marcia's claim).

In the argumentation scheme for argument from the vagueness of a verbal classification given later, the variable *Arg* stands in for an instance of argument from a verbal classification, or argument from an established rule that occurred in prior dialogue.

If an argument, *Arg* occurs in a context of dialogue that requires a certain level of precision, but some property *F* that occurs in *Arg* is defined in a way that is too vague to meet the requirements of that level of precision, then *Arg* ought to be rejected as deficient.

Arg occurs in a context of dialogue that requires a certain level of precision that is appropriate for that context.

Some property *F* that occurs in *Arg* is defined in a way that is too vague to meet the requirement of the level of precision appropriate for that context.

Therefore, *Arg* ought to be rejected as deficient.

The critical questions matching the argument from vagueness of a verbal classification are the following.

1. Does the context of dialogue in which *Arg* occurs demand some particular level of precision in the key terms used?

2. **Is some property F that occurs in Arg too vague to meet the proper level or standard of precision?**

3. **Why is this degree of vagueness a problem in relation to the dialogue in which Arg was advanced?**

The argument from vagueness of a verbal criterion does not totally refute the argument against which it is directed. Instead, it shifts a weight of presumption against that argument by raising critical questions about the language or concepts used.

One typical, and also generally adequate way to reply to the argument from vagueness of a verbal classification, is to tighten up the level of precision of the vague term by offering a precise (or more precise) definition of the term. A typical way to respond to this response, in turn, is to deploy the argument from arbitrariness of a verbal criterion. In such cases, the dialogue shifts to verbal argumentation (argumentation about the meaning of terms used), as opposed to substantive argumentation about the content of the issue.

Characteristically, when there is a shift to verbal argumentation, there is an accompanying shift in the dialogue itself, to a different type of dialogue. In Walton and Krabbe (1995), this type of dialectical shift is called a "tightening up" of the dialogue, and is defined as a shift from permissive persuasion dialogue (*PPD*) to rigorous persuasion dialogue (*RPD*). In the latter type of dialogue, the rules are more strict and exact, and allow fewer options for moves, and require an arguer's commitments to be determined in a more precise and rigorous way. Such a shift is not necessarily bad, and can assist the original permissive dialogue in reaching its goal.

Argument from vagueness of a verbal classification is the basic component in the fallacy called *argument of the beard* by the logic textbooks. For example, according to Byerly (1973), this fallacy "consists in arguing from the vagueness of a distinction to the absence of any meaningful distinction" (p. 56). For example, Byerly wrote that the existence of bluish-green shades does not "imply that the colors blue and green are not really distinct hues" (p. 56). The fallacy appears to reside in arguing from the premise that some cases are vague to the conclusion that all cases are vague.

According to Moore (1967), the argument of the beard may be considered the opposite of the black-or-white fallacy, the fallacy of failing to admit the possibility of a middle ground between extremes. In the argument from the beard, "we use the middle ground, or the fact of continuous and gradual shading between two extremes, to raise doubt about the existence of real differences between such opposites as strong and weak, good and bad, and black and white" (p. 166). For example, a gray shade between black and white does not prove that there is no difference between black and white (at all, or in every case).

The term "beard" suggests the verbal slippery slope argument, and clearly the argument of the beard is a component in that argument. However, we do not try to analyze the argument of the beard here, or to explain why it is a fallacy.

ARGUMENT FROM ARBITRARINESS
OF A VERBAL CLASSIFICATION

This argument is similar to argument from vagueness of a verbal classification, except that the arbitrariness of a verbal criterion is the objection instead of its vagueness. The one argument is often used to back up the other, or in conjunction with the other. The argument from arbitrariness of a verbal classification claims that a rule or verbal classification proposed by one participant in a dialogue is arbitrary, or too arbitrary to support the argument of the other side in the dialogue.

For example, the dialogue between Ted and Marcia in the abortion case might continue as follows.

Case 3.39: **Ted:** The fetus should be considered a person through the third trimester.

Marcia: You mean to say that the day before the third trimester, the fetus is not a person. And then the first day of the third trimester, it is a person. That is an arbitrary way of drawing the line.

In this case, Ted has given a precise criterion. But Marcia still objects to his classification, now on the grounds that it is arbitrary. The suggestion is that such arbitrariness is inappropriate in this case, because there is a substantive issue being disputed, requiring a real basis for a classification affecting the issue.

The argumentation scheme for the argument from arbitrariness of a verbal classification is the following.

If an argument, *Arg* occurs in a context of dialogue that requires a nonarbitrary definition for a key property *F* that occurs in *Arg*, and *F* is defined in an arbitrary way in *Arg*, then *Arg* ought to be rejected as deficient.

Arg occurs in a context of dialogue that requires a nonarbitrary definition for a key property *F* that occurs in *Arg*.

Some property *F* that occurs in *Arg* is defined in a way that is arbitrary.

Therefore, *Arg* ought to be rejected as deficient.

The critical questions matching the argument from arbitrariness of a verbal classification are the following.

1. Does the context of dialogue in which *Arg* occurs require a nonarbitrary definition of *F*?

2. Is some property *F* that occurs in *Arg* defined in an arbitrary way?

3. Why is arbitrariness of definition a problem in the context of dialogue in which *Arg* was advanced?

In some contexts of dialogue, defining a term in an arbitrary way is appropriate and useful, in contributing to the proper resolution of the conflict or problem posed by the dialogue. However, this is not always the case. In critical discussions on controversial issues, participants generally try to define terms in a way that favors their own side. This happens because words and phrases in a natural language already have positive and negative connotations, favoring one side or the other. For this reason, there is the danger, or reality, that a term defined in an arbitrary way might favor one side too much, thereby infringing on the linguistic rights of the other side.

For example, in the abortion dispute case, no doubt one side would be happy with a definition of "person" that required the baby to be out of the womb before it could qualify as a person. And the other side would be happy with a definition that allowed a fertilized ovum in the womb to count as a person. But either definition would provide too much of a strong weight of presumption against the other side. Thus any definition of "person" in this context would be extremely controversial, and either side should have the right to object to any proposed definition. In this context, an arbitrary definition of "person" should not stand. It should be open to critical questioning by the other party as arbitrary, and for that reason, unacceptable.

THE VERBAL SLIPPERY SLOPE ARGUMENT

The verbal slippery slope argument is a composite type of argumentation that combines argument from vagueness of a verbal criterion and argument from gradualism. In a verbal slippery slope argument, one participant has used a vague term or property *F* in a dispute with another participant who exploits that vagueness by using an argument from gradualism as follows: "You accept that some individual *a* has *F*, but *a* is indistinguishable from *b*, so you must admit that *b* has *F* too (and so on for individuals *c*, *d*, and so forth, to individual *n*, each pair being so indistinguishable that if one has *F*, the other must too). Therefore, you must admit that *n* has *F*. But this is clearly unacceptable (from your point of view). Therefore you were wrong to accept the proposition that *a* has *F*, in the first place." The verbal slippery slope argument looks a lot, in its general outline, like a *reductio ad absurdum* argument. And in fact, it is very similar in form. Both start with an assumption accepted by a respondent, and then draw an implication out of that assumption that the respondent does not, or cannot accept, by a series of steps or inferences.

The verbal slippery slope argument trades on the vagueness of a key term in the respondent's argumentation. The proponent of the slope argument utilizes this vagueness to exploit the respondent's inability to "draw the line" between pairs of cases on a continuum of closely related cases.

An example of the verbal slippery slope argument can be given by continuing the debate on abortion between Marcia and Ted (Case 3.39) as follows. This case is an adaptation of one in Walton (*Slip. Slope*, 1992).

Case 3.40:   **Ted:**   Surely the baby in the womb must be defined as a person, with rights during these latter stages, because a surgeon can do intra-uterine surgery to correct the baby's heart defect, in some cases of this sort. The baby is the doctor's patient, therefore it must be a person. Moreover, in many such cases, the baby, if delivered by Caesarian section, could be supported by intensive care, without the mother's support.

Marcia: Well, yes, I think the baby is a person just before it is born, but not before that.

Ted: But where do you draw the line? If the baby is a person in these latter stages near birth, then it is also a person in the earlier stages, where it cannot survive on its own, but where it has all the same features like a heart, lungs, limbs, and so forth. I don't see any point where you can draw the line, other than by having to admit that it could be a person from the moment of conception (an absurd proposition to admit, for anyone advocating your viewpoint). I mean if it is a person on one day, then the day before, it couldn't have been that much different, so that it couldn't be a person that day. (p. 46)

In this type of argumentation, Ted is using a series of steps, each of which is a kind of *modus ponens* argument from a pair of cases, over and over again. Ted is, in effect arguing, "If the fetus is a person at stage y of its development, then it is also a person at stage x, just prior to y. But (you admit) it is a person at stage y. Therefore, it is a person at stage x." He is applying this step of inference over and over again, until eventually, he reaches a conclusion that is intolerable (unacceptable very clearly) from Marcia's point of view on the issue.

The argumentation scheme for the verbal slippery slope argument is the following. The variable F stands for a (vague) property, and the constants a_1, a_2, $\ldots, a_n$ stand for a set of individuals.

Individual a_1 has property F (as you, the respondent, concede).

For all x and y, if x has F, then if y is indistinguishable from x with respect to F, then y also has F (as you, the respondent cannot deny).

For any given pair $\{a_i, a_j\}$ of adjacent individuals in the sequence, a_1, $a_2, \ldots, a_n$, a_j is indistinguishable from a_i with respect to F.

Therefore, a_n has property F (following from the three previous premises, by a series of steps).

But a_n does not have property F (or at least, this outcome is not acceptable to you, the respondent).

Therefore, it is not true that a_1 has F (or you, the respondent, should not have accepted this proposition).

This type of argumentation works best where there is a continuum of closely related cases and a fuzzy or vague property of the kind that once you accept it as applying to the one case, you can hardly deny that it could also apply to a closely related, or similar case. Because of the vagueness, the respondent can be driven along the continuum by the proponent's use of a series of small step-arguments.

The critical questions for the verbal slippery slope argument are the following.

1. **Does a_1 have F (according to what was conceded)?**

2. **Is F really vague, in the sense that for all x and y, if x has F, then y also must be conceded to have F?**

3. **Are the pairs a_i, a_j in the continuum really indistinguishable from each other?**

4. **Is the conclusion that a_n has F truly unacceptable from my (respondent's) point of view?**

5. **Can some precise definition of F be given that will remove the vagueness, sufficiently to stop the slope?**

The usual response to a verbal slippery slope argument, if the first four critical questions can be answered adequately (showing that the slope is correctly structured and supported), is to propose a precise definition of the vague concept in question. In such a case however–see Walton (*Slip. Slope,* 1992)–a common response is to attack the precise definition as arbitrary, using argument from an arbitrary criterion.

The basic structure of the verbal slippery slope argument is expressed very well in the "heap" or *sorites* paradox, said to have been invented by Eubulides, a contemporary of Plato. If you take one grain away from a heap, it is still a heap. And each time you do so, it makes no difference, because one grain is too small to make a difference, by itself. But repeated over and over, such an argument can be shown to be absurd, for eventually, there will no longer be a heap.

This argument can be applied wherever there is a vague term, like "bald" or "short." Kneale and Kneale (1962) cited the following ancient Greek version of the *sorites* argument.

Case 3.41:   Would you say that a man was bald if he had only one hair?

Yes.

Would you say that a man was bald if he had only two hairs?

Yes.

Would you . . . , and so forth.

Then where do you draw the line?

Interestingly, this version is in the form of a dialogue.

A version similar to that of Black (1970) has a base premise, B_0, and an inductive premise, I.

Case 3.42: (B_0) Every person who is 4 feet in height is short.

(I) If you add one-tenth of an inch to a short person's height, that person is short.

(B_1) Every person who is 4 feet and one-tenth of an inch in height is short (and so on, for two-tenths, etc.).

(B_n) Therefore, every person is short.

The conclusion is clearly false. Therefore, because the argument is valid (a series of *modus ponens* steps, by transitivity of logical implication), it follows that at least one of the premises must be false. But since, apparently, all the premises are true, we have a paradox. In this sense, a paradox is a contradiction.

Many solutions–outlined by Sainsbury (1988)–to the *sorites* paradox have been offered, perhaps most notably the famous fuzzy logic of Zadeh (1987). However, looked at from a pragmatic point of view of argumentation schemes, this type of argument is not paradoxical, erroneous, contradictory, or (inherently) fallacious. It is simply a kind of argumentation that can be used by one participant in a dialogue to argue against the point of view of another participant by drawing out a presumptive contradiction in the collective commitments of that participant. In principle, it is a reasonable kind of argumentation, although it can often go wrong, or be used incorrectly to commit a fallacy.

THE FULL SLIPPERY SLOPE ARGUMENT

The full slippery slope argument is a complex network of argumentation that combines argument from gradualism and argument from popularity with the causal, precedent, and verbal slippery slope arguments. This argument claims that once a first step is taken, it will lead by small steps of a causal precedent or verbal type, to a sequence of further cases that people will come to gradually accept, until some horrible outcome finally ensues. In this type of argumentation, it is suggested that once people become comfortable with one stage of development, increasing popular acceptance will push the whole sequence along towards the final outcome.

The following example (Rachels, 1986) is a case of the full slippery slope argument against starting a policy of accepting euthanasia in any form.

Case 3.43: If voluntary euthanasia were legalized, there is good reason to believe that at a later date another bill for compulsory euthanasia would be legalized. Once the respect for human life is so low that an innocent person may be killed directly even at his own request, compulsory euthanasia will necessarily be very near. This could lead easily to killing all incurable cancer patients, the aged who are a public care, wounded soldiers, all deformed children, the mentally afflicted, and so on. Before long the danger would be at the door of every citizen.

Once a man is permitted on his own authority to kill an innocent person directly, there is no way of stopping the advancement of that wedge. There exists no longer any rational grounds for saying that the wedge can advance so far and no further. Once the exception has been made it is too late; hence the grave reason why no exception may be allowed. That is why euthanasia under any circumstances must be condemned. (p. 171)

The full slippery slope is a presumptive and defeasible kind of argumentation because it is based on a prediction, or plausible scenario, on what might happen in the future. It therefore becomes highly questionable in a given case, when phrased in terms of what "must" happen, what is "inevitable," and so forth.

However, in some cases, if phrased as a warning, in terms of what might or may happen, and each of the steps in the chain of reasoning is backed up by the required evidence, it can be a reasonable argument.

The argumentation scheme for the full slippery slope argument (adapted from the account given in Walton, *Slip. Slope,* 1992) is the following.

Case C_0 is tentatively acceptable as an initial presumption.

There exists a series of cases, $C_0, C_1, \ldots, C_{n-1}$, where each case leads to the next by a combination of causal, precedent, and/or analogy steps.

There is a climate of social opinion such that once people come to accept each step as plausible (or as accepted practice), they will then be led to accept the next step.

The penultimate step C_{n-1} leads to a horrible outcome, C_n, which is not acceptable.

Therefore, C_0 is not acceptable (contrary to the presumption of the initial premise). (pp. 199-200)

The argumentation scheme presented is sketched out in an abbreviated form, but the detailed framing of the premises and conclusion can be grasped by looking back to the argumentation schemes for the causal, verbal, and precedent slippery slope arguments.

The full slippery slope argument combines all three types of slippery slope arguments, but what makes it distinctive is its use of the public acceptance premise as the force that propels the respondent down the slope.

The critical questions for the full slippery slope argument are the following.

1. **What are the various subarguments or "links" that make up the intervening steps from C_0 to C_n?**

2. **How strongly is the conclusion phrased, that is, what is the burden of proof in the dialogue?**

3. **Is evidence given to back up each of the subarguments, and is it strong enough to meet the requirements of burden of proof?**

These are the three major considerations, but a detailed analysis could give a more finely differentiated set of critical questions for the full slippery slope argument. See Walton (*Slip. Slope,* 1992) for more case studies, and a more detailed analysis of the full slippery slope argument.

CHAPTER FOUR

ARGUMENT FROM IGNORANCE

We have seen with all the arguments associated with argumentation schemes that they are typically used in a balance of considerations type of case, where knowledge or hard information is lacking, of a kind that would enable the problem to be resolved or the dispute to be settled on that basis. In other words, these presumption-based arguments are generally arguments from ignorance. The logic of these arguments could be expressed by the phrase, "I don't know that this proposition is false, so until evidence comes in to refute it, I am entitled to provisionally assume that it is true." All of the argumentation schemes previously studied tend to take this general form. Hence, the argument from ignorance has a special status in connection with the study of argumentation schemes for presumptive reasoning.

The argument from ignorance has now been analyzed in greater depth in Walton (*Arg. Ig.*, 1995). Chapter four introduces the reader to the argument from ignorance as a distinctive type of reasoning that is commonly used in everyday conversational argumentation, showing how it fits in to the study of argumentation schemes for presumptive reasoning.

The argument from ignorance (*argumentum ad ignorantiam*) has traditionally been classified as a fallacy, but there is growing recognition that this kind of argument can be nonfallacious in some cases. This raises a question: what kind of successful or good argument is it, in these cases? In this chapter, two basic argumentation schemes to represent the form of the *argumentum ad ignorantiam* are introduced. It is argued that they are best judged as fallacious or not in a particular case, in relation to a context of use in dialogue.

FOUR CASES

The fallacy of the argument from ignorance (*argumentum ad ignorantiam*), according to Copi and Cohen (1990) is "the mistake that is committed whenever it is argued that a proposition is true simply on the basis that it has not been proved false, or that it is false because it has not been proved true" (p. 93). But is this kind of argument a fallacy? It has been argued in Woods and Walton (1978) that it is generally, even though there are some cases where it is not.

Copi and Cohen provided an example that suggests that, at least in some cases, it is not.

Case 4.1:   In some circumstances, of course, the fact that certain evidence or results have not been got, after they have been actively sought in ways calculated to reveal them, may have substantial argumentative force. New drugs being tested for safety, for example, are commonly given to mice or other rodents for prolonged periods; the absence of any toxic effect upon the rodents is taken to be evidence (although not conclusive evidence) that the drug is probably not toxic to humans. Consumer protection often relies upon evidence of this kind. In circumstances like these we rely not on ignorance but upon our knowledge, or conviction that if the result we are concerned about were likely to arise, it would have arisen in some of the test cases. This use of the inability to prove something true supposes that investigators are highly skilled, and that they very probably would have uncovered the evidence sought, had it been possible to do so. (p. 94)

But if the argument from ignorance is nonfallacious in this case, what kind of argument is it? What species of correct (good, reasonable) argument is it?

In some cases, the *argumentum ad ignorantiam* is a correct (nonfallacious) argument because we can rightly assume that our knowledge base is complete. If some proposition is not known to be in it, we can infer that this proposition must be false.

Case 4.2:   The posted train schedule says that train 12 to Amsterdam stops at Haarlem and Amsterdam Central Station.

We want to determine whether the train stops at Schipol. We can reason as follows: Since the schedule did not indicate that the train stops at Schipol, we can infer that it does not stop at Schipol. In other words, we can presume that the knowledge base is complete (epistemically closed) on the ground that if there were additional stops, they would be specified on the schedule posted. Perhaps we could even know that this knowledge base is complete, by knowing that the railway policy is to be sure that if the train stops at a particular station, the name of that station is always marked on the posted schedule. The basic principle at work here is what de Cornulier (1988) called *epistemic closure,* the principle, "If it were true, I would know it."

> *Epistemic Closure:* If one knows that it cannot be the case that *A* without his or her knowing it, then, if not-*A*, he can infer that not-*A*.

The example de Cornulier gave is the following: "If it were raining, I would know it; now, it is not the case that I know that it is raining; therefore, it is not raining" (p. 182). This principle of inference is rightly called epistemic closure because once a knowledge base is definitely closed, then if a proposition does not appear in it, we can conclude that this proposition is false.

It is a kind of inference that takes the form of an epistemic counterfactual: If *A* were true, it would be in my knowledge base; but *A* is not in my knowledge base; therefore *A* is false. It is an *ad ignorantiam* argument but, apparently a principle of epistemic reasoning that could be quite correct and reasonable in many cases of everyday argumentation.

In other cases, however, the *argumentum ad ignorantiam* can be a fallacy precisely because the knowledge base is incomplete in a relevant respect.

Case 4.3:   According to Benoit (1990), some of Aristotle's works on rhetoric (e.g., the *Synagoge Technon,* the *Gryllus,* and the *Theodecta*) are not extant: "Hence, the absence of a topic from the surviving corpus . . . is insufficient evidence that [Aristotle] failed to discuss it." (p. 25)

In this case, our list of the topics that Aristotle wrote on, in the subject of rhetoric, is incomplete. Hence, as Benoit warns, it would be an erroneous inference to conclude that Aristotle failed to discuss a topic, simply on the basis of the absence of a discussion of that topic in his known writings.

In still other cases, however, our knowledge base may be incomplete in a relevant respect, but we can still argue nonfallaciously from ignorance, on the basis of intelligent guesswork. In the following case from Collins, Warnock, Aiello, and Miller (1975), a computer program called SCHOLAR is asked whether rubber is a product of Guyana (recall Case 2.8, which was similar).

Case 4.4:   SCHOLAR does not have any specific item of knowledge saying that Guyana produces rubber or not. However, SCHOLAR does know that Peru and Colombia are the major rubber producers in South America. And SCHOLAR also knows that rubber is an important product, so if Guyana did produce rubber, SCHOLAR would presumably know it. SCHOLAR concludes: "I know enough that I am inclined to believe that rubber is not an agricultural product of Guyana." (p. 398)

In this case, SCHOLAR's nonfallacious *argumentum ad ignorantiam* is warranted by an epistemic counterfactual; if this proposition were true, I would know it. SCHOLAR argues from ignorance nonfallaciously: I do not know that this proposition is true; therefore, it is false.

In a case like this, absence of knowledge is significant because of a presumption that if a particular proposition were true, it would be known to be true. But it is a kind of shaky reasoning or guesswork. It would be incorrect to say that you *know* the proposition in question to be false (beyond doubt). Rather, you can say it is a reasonable presumption to infer, based on what you know.

ARGUMENT FROM IGNORANCE AS
PRESUMPTIVE REASONING

It would seem that in Case 4.4, and Case 4.1 as well, the argument from ignorance involves a kind of practical reasoning, of the type analyzed in Walton (*Plaus. Arg.,* 1992), that goes forward in argument as licensing a tentatively reasonable conclusion, acceptable on a basis of burden of proof. It may be useful to go ahead and licence the drug in question, in Case 4.1, for example, on the grounds that it can save lives or help in medical treatment, provided there is no evidence, that has yet arisen, to show that it is harmful to humans.

Whatever kind of reasoning this is, it is clear that it is a species of nonmonotonic reasoning (chapter 2) subject to default in the sense that if new evidence should come into consideration, in the future, that shows the conclusion to be false, it must be given up. In other words, this kind of reasoning licences an arguer to accept a proposition as true (or false) provisionally, subject conditionally to future evidence that may arise in the future investigations or argumentation (see Reiter, 1987). It is a kind of presumptive reasoning that can be correct (or at least not incorrect) in some cases.

In Case 4.1, the basis of the reasoning is the presumption that the investigators would have been likely to turn up some evidence of toxicity, if it existed, because they are skilled, and because they have done some thorough or serious investigations already. This is an expectation, an initial presumption that, in the context, allows the drawing of a presumptive conclusion of safety that in turn licences a policy or prudent course of action, in the circumstances.

Presumption, as defined in chapter two, is a speech act halfway between assertion and mere assumption or supposition in argument. The key thing about presumption as a speech act in a context of dialogue is that it reverses the initial burden of proof. In the case previously mentioned, initially the burden of proof was on the side advocating the use of the drug for treatment of human subjects, on grounds of safety, or danger to human life. Given the presumptions raised by the current level of testing and investigation of the effects of the drug, however, the argument from ignorance licences the drawing of the presumptive conclusion by reversal of this burden. Anyone who claims that the drug is too dangerous or toxic to be used on humans is now obliged to step forward and present some new evidence to this effect. Otherwise the presumptive inference (argument from ignorance) goes ahead.

How presumptive argument can be reasonable in some cases as a species of nonmonotonic reasoning is best analyzed pragmatically by understanding how the following sequence of speech acts is used to shift a burden of proof in a dialogue exchange between speech partners. Burden of proof is best visualized as a balance, which can tilt more toward one side of an argument than toward the other. In the following example, the burden of proof is heavier on the proponent's side of the argument than on the respondent's side. In this kind of case, one side is harder to argue for than the other, meaning that one side must mount a stronger case to prove its point and thereby "win" the contention at issue in the discussion.

As we saw in chapter two, in practice, presumptive arguments are based on generalizations that express normal expectations and plausibility, not necessity.

Case 4.5:   Bob and Ed waited in the duck blind, their eyes scanning the sky. A formation of ducks came into view. There were six booming reports, three from each shotgun. Four ducks tumbled towards the marsh. Bob and Ed watched as the remaining ducks flew out of range.

Reading the text of the previous discourse, it is reasonable to presume that Bob and Ed are hunting ducks. No proposition in the text explicitly states that. But it is a reasonable inference to draw. One clue is the mention of "duck blind." We know that the usual purpose of a duck blind is to conceal hunters so that they can shoot ducks from a good range without being seen too soon by the ducks.

We can also infer other reasonable presumptions from the given discourse. We can presume, for example, that Bob or Ed shot some ducks, that Bob and Ed fired their shotguns, that Bob pulled the trigger of his shotgun, and so forth. Of course, it is possible that Bob could have fired his shotgun by some method other than pulling the trigger. But pulling the trigger is the normal or usual way of firing a shotgun in this type of situation. And so it is a reasonable presumption here that Bob pulled the trigger of his shotgun.

Reasonable presumptions are characteristically based on a *script,* characterized by Schank and Abelson (1977) as a predetermined stereotyped sequence of actions that defines a well-known situation. The key thing about a script is that it is not explicitly stated information given in a text of discourse. Rather, it is information shared by the proponent and respondent of the discourse. Therefore, the respondent must infer it as a presumption from the cues given in the text.

Uses of the *argumentum ad ignorantiam* based on reasonable presumption are often based on reasonable expectations of what kind of action on the part of another person would be appropriate in a particular kind of situation, where definite knowledge of intentions is lacking. A characteristic type of situation of this sort could be represented by the following case.

Case 4.6:   Trudy phoned on Tuesday to tell Karen and Doug that they would come for dinner on Wednesday or Thursday, but a part had been ordered for their car which had not arrived, so she said that she and Anton might not be able to make it on Wednesday. Then Wednesday she phoned again to say that they could definitely not make it for dinner on Wednesday. On Thursday, Doug asked Karen, "Will Trudy and Anton be coming for dinner tonight?" Karen replied: "If we don't hear from her, then we can presume that they are coming for dinner tonight."

In this case, the truth of the proposition "We have not heard from Trudy," which expresses a lack of knowledge, activates the conclusion that Trudy and Anton are coming is a reasonable presumption. This means that it is a reasonable basis for acting on the presumption, by getting the dinner ready, for example. The presumption is that Trudy and Anton will be coming. For if their car was still not working and they could not come on Thursday, Trudy would phone to call the dinner engagement off. This is just a presumption, but should be a reasonable enough one, in these particular circumstances, to make a long-distance call (which would supply more conclusive confirmation) unnecessary.

In allowing or denying presumptions, much may depend on the seriousness of the consequences of the presumption turning out to be right or wrong. Unfortunately, presumptions are often made that should not be, because the burden of proof should be heavier.

Case 4.7:   Just after their divorce and during a struggle for child custody, a wife accuses her former husband of child abuse. Because of the seriousness of the charge, the husband's conduct is subject to deep suspicion, and he is barred from seeing the child until she reaches the age of sixteen. Because of these allegations, the husband is put on a list of child abusers and fired from his job.

A problem is that in this kind of case, because of the seriousness of the charge, and the possibility of the serious consequences if in fact the husband is guilty, there may be a presumption of guilt at the outset. Once such a charge is made, it tends to "stick," just as innuendo or gossip can thrive on presumptions made on the basis of little or no real evidence. Here the *argumentum ad ignorantiam* can be a serious problem, because a presumption of guilt may make a fair trial or inquiry into the situation even more difficult. The problem is that absence of evidence may fuel suspicion, and the person alleged to be guilty may not get a fair chance to rebut the presumption by stating the other side of the case. In such cases, the argument may not get beyond the opening stage, where a charge is made, and the attacker may try to force closure by a conclusion of guilt without both sides being heard.

Consider the case of the memo from the Supervisor of Library Circulation who wrote to all faculty of a university that some old exams would be destroyed if no response from the faculty members is received by a certain date. This case is different, presuming that if there are seriously bad consequences of disposing of the exams, the departments will have time to report their objections before the exams are destroyed. No response can then be taken to imply that the respondents do not have any objections to the proposed policy. It is being declared that anything not affirmed by the date specified will be taken to be denied, at the closure date of the inquiry proposed in the memo. See Walton (*Arg. Ig.,* 1995, Case 3.17).

Here we notice again the interesting link between the *ad ignorantiam* argument and the closure of an argument. The reasonableness of the *ad ignorantiam* argument is relative to the reasonableness of the assumption that the inquiry can be closed at the proposed stage of the argument. The gist of it is that once the inquiry is *closed,* then if a certain proposition subject to the inquiry has not been proved true, it can reasonably be declared or concluded as false, for the purposes of the inquiry.

Here too, the link between presumption and the *argumentum ad ignorantiam* becomes clearer. The function of both the *argumentum ad ignorantiam* and the concept of presumption is to shorten an inquiry by facilitating the progress of the inquiry towards a reasonable closure. Indeed, presumption is really a kind of argument from ignorance, because presumptions are only useful and necessary when an inquiry is still open and the facts are not yet, or cannot yet be determined. It is precisely in this type of situation of ignorance where it may be necessary to make a presumption in order for an inquiry to go ahead and reach provisional closure, in the absence of new facts or circumstances sufficient to re-open the inquiry.

CONTEXTS OF DIALOGUE

Persuasion dialogues, negotiations, and inquiries of the practical sort most commonly encountered in natural language contexts of argumentation, characteristically take place under conditions where factual evidence is unavailable or cannot be deployed decisively. In short, life being what it is, ignorance is the norm. Fortunately, there is a technique for contending with ignorance in interactive reasoning. It is the device of burden of proof (Walton, 1988).

One context of dialogue is that of the *inquiry,* where the goal is to prove that a particular proposition is true (or false), or that it cannot be proved true (or false) by evidence based on premises known to be true (Walton, *Prag. Theory,* 1995; Walton & Krabbe, 1995). The inquiry has a particular burden or standard of proof that has to be met for a conclusion to be proved. Once that standard is met, the inquiry is closed, and the burden of disproof is cast onto anyone who would raise questions to challenge or reopen the inquiry.

The audience-specific directedness of the persuasion dialogue contrasts with the aim of the inquiry, which is to find facts and conclusions that cannot be disputed by any reasonable audience, at the present state of knowledge. We could say that the inquiry is knowledge-oriented, whereas the persuasion dialogue is opinion-oriented. The inquiry seeks a chain of argumentation that is essentially *cumulative,* meaning that once certain facts are well-established, conclusions can also be established, based on prior facts in an orderly way. The ideal of cumulativeness implies that there should be no need for "turning back" or retraction of commitments, if the inquiry is premised on solid beginnings. The ideal is to eliminate "mere presumptions" not based on solid knowledge. By contrast, in the critical discussion, the issue is who has the strongest presumption on his side.

In Case 4.1, for example, once a new drug has been tested thoroughly enough to meet a standard considered sufficient for human safety, a decision may be made to go ahead and licence the drug for use. The inquiry is, at least provisionally, closed. But should new evidence come in from users of the drug that raise serious questions about its safety, the inquiry may be reopened.

Another context of dialogue is that of the critical discussion, where the goal is to resolve a conflict of opinions by rational argumentation. The goal of each participant is to prove his or her thesis is right, using arguments based on premises that are accepted by the other side. The thesis of this party is a proposition that conflicts with, or is opposed to, the point of view of the other party in the discussion.

Case 4.3, for example, could be in the context of a critical discussion of whether Aristotle discussed a particular topic in rhetoric. However, both parties might accept that Aristotle wrote some works on rhetoric that are not extant. Suppose one of the parties in the discussion were to try to use the argument that Aristotle failed to discuss a particular topic on the grounds that she could not find this topic in the writings of Aristotle that she analyzed. The other party could reject this argument from ignorance with justification, given that there is prior agreement, or agreement can be presumed to be reachable, on the historical finding that Aristotle may have written works on rhetoric that are not extant.

Presumably, such a historical finding would be relevant to the critical discussion because it is the result of a prior inquiry that has been widely accepted, and that the participants would not be prepared to dispute (in the context of their present discussion). In such a case, we could say that the critical discussion is functionally related to an inquiry in such a way that certain results of the inquiry can be taken as agreed-upon knowledge for the purpose of the critical discussion. Van Eemeren and Grootendorst (1984) called this aspect of a critical discussion an *intersubjective testing procedure* (ITP) where sources of knowledge (like an encyclopedia or dictionary) can be introduced into the critical discussion to provide information or knowledge acceptable to both participants. An ITP can function to tilt burden of proof in a critical discussion to one side or the other.

Whether the *argumentum ad ignorantiam* is fallacious or not, in a given case, can be seen then as depending on how it was used in the context of dialogue for that particular case. Such standards of correctness depend on an allocation of burden of proof, telling us what constitutes a successful proof for that type of dialogue in the given case. So conceived, the *argumentum ad ignorantiam* can be nonfallacious in some cases, and its being judged as correct in such cases depends on pragmatic standards of correctness of use of an argument in a context of dialogue.

The sequence of the various stages of the criminal trial in law is a good case in point. This sequence begins with an opening stage where a specific accusation is brought forward, and if it is serious enough, charges are laid. If the charge is well-founded, the second stage is to set trial. This second stage already requires some evidence against the defendant (or *prima facie* evidence). The trial is a form of dialogue with rules of procedure and rules of evidence, where the arguments for both sides are set out by questioning witnesses and other participants. As an outcome of the trial, a verdict is arrived at, which is legally binding, and closure of the dialogue is achieved. This third stage establishes the guilt or nonguilt of the defendant in relation to the charge, and that represents the conclusion of the trial.

However, in legal reasoning, the conclusion is binding, but not altogether conclusive (closed to further discussion). The process of argument may be reopened in exceptional cases, where new evidence (not already considered in the trial) has been introduced. In this type of case, the trial may be reopened. So in legal argumentation, closure of dialogue is not absolutely final. But it is relatively final, in that there must be "good grounds" for allowing an appeal.

The criminal trial is a kind of persuasion dialogue, but it involves some elements of the inquiry, especially where expert witnesses are brought in to testify. The inquiry is a more cumulative type of dialogue where the goal is to prove a proposition by inferring it from a set of facts that can be established as definitely known through the process of inquiry.

In a critical discussion, an instance of the *argumentum ad ignorantiam* should be evaluated in relation to the openness or closure of the dialogue at the particular stage of the dialogue where the *argumentum ad ignorantiam* move occurred. Similarly, in an inquiry, the strength or weakness of an *argumentum ad ignorantiam* in a particular case depends on how far along the process of inquiry may be judged to have progressed in that case.

Consider the case of the "foreign agent" from Copi (1982).

Case 4.8:   In some circumstances it can safely be assumed that if a certain event had occurred, evidence of it could be discovered by qualified investigators. In such circumstances it is perfectly reasonable to take the absence of proof of its occurrence as positive proof of its nonoccurrence. Of course, the proof here is not based on ignorance but on our knowledge that if it had occurred it would be known. For example, if a serious security investigation fails to unearth an evidence that Mr. X is a foreign agent, it would be wrong to conclude that their research has left us ignorant. It has rather established that Mr. X is not one. Failure to draw such conclusions is the other side of the bad coin of innuendo, as when one says of a man that there is "no proof" that he is a scoundrel. (p. 102)

Whether the *argumentum ad ignorantiam* is well-founded or fallacious in a particular case depends on how far along the process of inquiry has gone. If after a very thorough search that would satisfy any competent security investigator as adequate has failed to turn up any evidence at all that Mr. X is a foreign spy, it could be reasonable to conclude that it has been established that Mr. X is not a foreign spy. Suppose, however, that the security investigation has just begun, but the investigators had so far found no evidence that Mr. X was a spy. Suppose that, so far, the investigators had only had time to spend a few hours talking to Mr. X's neighbors, asking them for any indications of suspicious activities on the part of Mr. X. And suppose that none of the neighbors interviewed could give any indication that Mr. X had been behaving in a suspicious manner, as far as they could tell. In this case, it would be very risky and weak to take the absence of proof as a positive proof that Mr. X is not a foreign agent. Putting much weight on this deployment of the *argumentum ad ignorantiam* at this point in the inquiry could be a serious error in reasoning. In this context of dialogue, the use of the *argumentum ad ignorantiam* could be fallacious, because the inquiry should be treated as still open. Drawing the conclusion that Mr. X is not a foreign agent could be premature. Trusting Mr. X with critical information on matters of national security could be unwisely operating on a presumption that is not a reasonable conclusion at this point.

Theoretically, the *argumentum ad ignorantiam* could be deductively valid as a form of argument, but only on the (idealistic, in most cases) assumption that the inquiry is closed. This assumption implies that the knowledge base of the reasoner toward whom the argument is directed is complete, and that this person knows "all the facts" that can be known. It implies that this knowledge base is immune to further additions, revisions, or appeals. This strong closure assumption means, in effect, that for the purpose of the inquiry, any proposition not already in the knowledge base may be declared *false* (or known not to be true).

Such a strong closure requirement on dialogue is generally, however, a risky one, especially where the dialogue is still underway, and knowledge may be hard to come by. Indeed, in contexts of presumptive reasoning on controversial topics of discussion, the strong closure condition can be unrealistic and inappropriate to the subject-matter and context of dialogue. Hence the deductive version of the *argumentum ad ignorantiam* is, in many cases, strongly subject to evaluation as a fallacy of reasoning. And indeed, the tactic of declaring a dialogue strongly closed is often an objectionable tactic of trying to stifle further debate on an issue by presuming foreclosure of concession of one's own conclusion. The question to be asked in evaluating the *argumentum ad ignorantiam* in such a case is: When can discussion of the issue be reasonably closed, on the assumption that no further evidence will be relevant? It is where attempted closure is premature, and contrary to the agreed procedures of conducting the dialogue or inquiry, that the *argumentum ad ignorantiam* should be judged a fallacy.

In a criminal trial, the decision when closure has been reached is decided by the judge. In a committee meeting, the chairperson may have to decide when the discussion is ended and a vote should be taken. Typically however, in these kinds of cases an appeal may be made to reopen the dialogue. Generally, a dialogue is properly judged to be closed when its goal has been achieved, or when the participants have been given enough opportunity to achieve the goal, even if they have failed. In persuasion dialogue, this means that both sides have been given an adequate chance to bring out their strongest arguments, and to criticize the arguments of the other side. If, after an appropriate interval, the burden of proof has been tilted decisively to one side, the argument may be declared closed. Or, if neither side has met the burden of proof, despite good opportunities for interactive argumentation on both sides, closure may be judged appropriate on practical grounds (say, lack of further time). Much may depend, in a particular case, on the specific rules and institutional framework of the given speech event. However, closure may be relatively strong or weak, and in the latter case may be subject to reopening in a new "round of talks" on some future occasion.

In a case like the security investigation of Mr. X, closure presupposes some given standards of inquiry to determine when a professionally adequate investigation has been carried out by an agency responsible for this type of inquiry. These standards are typically not absolute, and indeed, the subject of such an inquiry may himself want to dispute closure.

A REASONABLE KIND OF ARGUMENT

In the cases studied previously, the argument appears to be a genuine *argumentum ad ignorantiam* (subject to some reservations discussed in the next section below). But it is by no means clear that either argument is fallacious. Indeed, rather than being a fallacy, it seems that this kind of argument can sometimes be correct and reasonable. And this applies not just to the "special context" of legal reasoning, but to scientific reasoning in induction and probability, and to closed world data bases. Indeed, it is often said that probability is reasoning in a situation of incomplete knowledge. If so, the *argumentum ad ignorantiam* can be not a fallacy, whether one's knowledge is complete or incomplete in a case.

It seems fair to conclude that the argument from ignorance is, in some cases, a reasonable kind of argument, and not necessarily fallacious. It is an epistemic type of argument, but in many cases the conclusion one is warranted to infer is not a knowledge claim. Instead, it is a defeasible (default) conclusion based on a sequence of presumptive reasoning. The premises in this sequence of reasoning are not known to be true (or false), but are presumed to be true (or false) on the basis of what one would normally expect the reasoner to know, given the depth of his, her, or its knowledge base, and other circumstances of the case. And, indeed, if we can accept the above analysis of presumptive reasoning as a legitimate kind of argument, used in a context of dialogue, it is possible to see how the argument from ignorance works as a species of correct argument. "Correct" here means a kind of argument that is used properly to fulfill requirements of burden of proof in a context of dialogue.

The argument goes forward tentatively on a practical basis, advocated by a proponent, subject to refutation by evidence that can be introduced by a respondent in dialogue. This kind of presumptive reasoning is best seen not as a competitor or usurper to knowledge-based reasoning, but as a useful temporary alternative, in cases where existing knowledge is not completely sufficient to resolve a practical conflict requiring an action or opinion.

WHAT COUNTS AS AN ARGUMENT FROM IGNORANCE?

Three distinctive forms of the *argumentum ad ignorantiam* as an informal fallacy are described by Woods and Walton (1978). The first form is an illicit negation shift in knowledge-based inferences of one of the following four forms, where **A** is a proposition.

(K1)   **A** is not known to be true.
Therefore, **A** is known not to be true.

(K2)   **A** is not known to be true.
Therefore, **A** is not true.

(K3)   **A** is not known not to be true.
Therefore, **A** is known to be true.

(K4)   A is not known not to be true.
       Therefore, A is true.

The *argumentum ad ignorantiam* in any one of these four forms is said to be a fallacious argument in Woods and Walton (1978) because of the unlicensed shifts of the negation operator over the "is known to be true" operator. However, this leaves the problem of determining, in a given case, when the negation shift is warranted or not.

The difficulty remaining is that even though it may be granted that (K1), (K2), (K3), and (K4) are not generally valid kinds of argument in knowledge-based reasoning, applying them to particular cases to explain why a fallacy has ostensibly occurred is problematic. First, there is the identification problem. In many cases, it is hard to know whether the situation is best described as one of ignorance–as in the premise of (K1) for example–or as positive knowledge that a proposition is false–as might be more appropriately described by the conclusion of (K1). Second, in any particular case, it may fail to be evident that the negation shift is unlicensed. Both these problems are evident in the case of Copi's foreign spy example (Case 4.8).

The second species is the inductive type of *argumentum ad ignorantiam*, which, according to Woods and Walton (1978), can take one of the following two forms (and variants thereof).

(I1)   There is no disconfirming evidence for A.
       Therefore, A is confirmed.

(I2)   There is no confirming evidence for A.
       Therefore, A is disconfirmed.

However, Woods and Walton (1978) noted that these inductive forms of the *argumentum ad ignorantiam* are not always fallacious. As arguments about unconfirmed hypotheses, such instances of argumentation from ignorance could be reasonable.

The third type of argument from ignorance is the dialectical argumentation typified by the following sequence of dialogue.

Case 4.9:   **Bob**:   Prove proposition *A* is true!
               Helen: You prove it's false!

Clearly this type of argument from ignorance relates to matters of burden of proof in a dialogue.

Before we go on to raise the question of when such arguments are correct or fallacious, a prior problem is to define them as a class or type of arguments.

There is a question about what counts as an argument from ignorance. For typically, in these cases, especially in Case 4.2, there is some existing knowledge, so the argument is not, at least completely, an argument from ignorance.

Also, a negative result, finding that something did not happen, is often described as knowledge. Again, especially in Case 4.2, the absence of a proposition could be described as a kind of knowledge that it is false. As Copi and Cohen stated, in Case 4.1: "In circumstances like these we rely not on ignorance, but upon our knowledge, or conviction, that if the result we are concerned about were likely to arise, it would have arisen in some of the test cases." Even if such a negative finding can be properly described as a kind of knowledge, in some cases, it can still be justified to classify the argument as an *argumentum ad ignorantiam* in a broad spectrum of cases in everyday argumentation, because it is based on presumption or "conviction" that goes forward in the absence of complete knowledge. Where epistemic closure is insufficient to warrant a conclusion as "known to be true," it is often practically useful and correct to draw a presumptive conclusion, not by closure but by default. It is not an argument from total ignorance, but an argument from partial ignorance, where the existing or available knowledge is insufficient to resolve the practical problem, or settle the issue beyond continuing doubts.

Using the expression *argumentum ad ignorantiam* as a name for a type of fallacy is therefore somewhat misleading. Such arguments are not fallacious simply because they are based on ignorance. A more balanced viewpoint is that they are typically based on partial ignorance. Generally they are presumptive arguments that can be used correctly and appropriately in some cases, yet can be misused in a variety of ways in other cases. However, in some cases, as in Case 4.2, they are negative epistemic arguments based on knowledge that a particular proposition is *not* in a given knowledge base.

Ignorance comes into it because the cases of presumptive inference are characteristically based on ignorance (and hence are species of arguments from ignorance) in two ways. First, they tend to be appropriately used in a kind of case where knowledge-based reasoning (hard evidence) cannot get enough of a grip, or is not available within the practical constraints needed to resolve a problem or take prudent action. Second, they involve a negative type of reasoning based on exclusion.

THE NEGATIVE LOGIC
OF *ARGUMENTUM AD IGNORANTIAM*

Both the epistemic cases and the cases of inconclusive presumptive reasoning characteristically have a "negative logic," as used in argumentation. The argument has the form: *A* is not proven true (false), therefore *A* may be presumed to be false (true). This "flip-flop" type of reasoning is, as shown previously, characteristic of how presumptive reasoning functions in a context of dialogue by reversing the roles (probative obligations) of the proponent and respondent.

Because of this negative logic, it is still worthwhile to preserve the name *argumentum ad ignorantiam* in the logic textbooks as a distinctive type of potentially erroneous or fallacious argument to be on the lookout for, because of its potential for misuse as a fallacy. It is a distinctive type of argument that can be used appropriately (correctly) in a context of dialogue, in some cases, and inappropriately (incorrectly) in other cases.

The argument from ignorance is not exclusively an inconclusive type of presumptive argument, nor is it generally equivalent to presumptive reasoning as a type of argumentation. For it is also used in knowledge-based (epistemic) reasoning. To the extent we know a knowledge-based K is closed (i.e., complete, in the sense of containing all the relevant information), we can infer that if a proposition A is not in it, then A is false. This argumentation scheme for the *argumentum ad ignorantiam* has the following form.

All the true propositions in domain D of knowledge are contained in K.

A is in D.

A is not in K.

For all A in D, A is either true or false.

Therefore, A is false.

This form of inference is deductively valid. To the extent that it can be established (and not merely presumed or assumed) that K is closed, we can conclude on the basis of what is known (and not just on the basis of presumption) that A is false. Hence, in such cases (rare though they may be, in actual practice), the *argumentum ad ignorantiam* is not a merely presumptive type of argumentation, in the sense of being inconclusive, as opposed to being based on established knowledge.

However, in many cases like Case 4.1 and Case 4.4, the argument from ignorance is a reasonable (nonfallacious) argument, but is a weaker type of inference than a deductively valid inference. It is a plausible or presumptive type of inference, in the sense of Rescher (1976), which rests on a major premise that is not strictly universal, but states how things *normally* or *usually* can be expected to go (subject to exceptions). This type of presumptive inference is a type to be identified or at least associated with the principle of epistemic closure expressed by de Cornulier (cited earlier). This second argumentation scheme for the *argumentum ad ignorantiam* has the following form.

It has not been established that all the true propositions in D are contained in K.

A is a special type of proposition such that if A were true, A would normally or usually be expected to be in K.

A is in D.

A is not in K.

For all A in D, A is either true or false.

Therefore, it is plausible to presume that A is false (subject to further investigations in D).

There may be various kinds of evidence that back up the second premise for the use of this type of inference. One is that A, if true, would be a prominent item of knowledge in a domain D, and would therefore normally be expected to be included in any reasonably comprehensive knowledge base in D. But this could vary, and would depend in a given case how deep K is with respect to D.

So conceived, the correctness of an argument from ignorance in a given case is best evaluated by pragmatic criteria, that is, relative to a background context of dialogue or inquiry. In Case 4.1, for example, an evaluation of the *argumentum ad ignorantiam* needs to take into account the matter of how far the investigation into toxicity of this drug has gone. In this context, the presumption of nontoxicity for humans will carry a heavier weight as the inquiry is more and more complete. But as long as the findings are based exclusively on tests with rodents, conclusions drawn about toxicity for humans will remain presumptive in nature. The correctness or incorrectness of the *argumentum ad ignorantiam* will depend on what stage the inquiry is in, and, if it is closed, what its findings were. This in turn, depends on the standard or burden of proof appropriate for the inquiry.

Not only is it right to say that the *argumentum ad ignorantiam* is closely linked to presumptive reasoning and burden of proof. You could even say that the very structure of the *argumentum ad ignorantiam* is an expression of how presumptive reasoning and burden of proof can function correctly in argumentation to shift a presumption to the other side in a dialogue. From a point of view of this framework and criteria, the cases of argument from ignorance found in ordinary conversations and in the logic textbooks can, in many instances, be shown to be nonfallacious.

WHEN IS IT FALLACIOUS?

The problem, once again, is that the *argumentum ad ignorantiam* pattern of moves need not always be self-evidently fallacious in a particular instance of discussion. In the dialogue sequence outlined in Case 4.9, presumably the fault lies with the respondent if he or she is committed to the truth of A, and has therefore incurred a burden of proof. If challenged, he or she is reasonably required to defend A, or give reasons for having accepted A. But suppose he or she hasn't accepted A at all, in the prior sequence of dialogue. Suppose instead that the questioner has strongly declared a commitment to the proposition that A is not true, in a manner that makes it clear that he or she is obliged to defend A if challenged. In this case, the respondent's reply is not a fallacious *argumentum ad ignorantiam* at all. Whether it is a genuine *argumentum ad ignorantiam* or not, it seems to be a reasonable (nonfallacious) move in the dialogue.

We noted earlier that inductive reasoning from a sample to a larger population can be a reasonable kind of *argumentum ad ignorantiam*. Indeed, the process of advancing a scientific hypothesis and provisionally accepting it on the grounds that no disconfirming instances of it have been found, is really a species of *argumentum ad ignorantiam*. There is nothing inherently fallacious about this kind of reasoning. When it does go wrong, and become a fallacious *argumentum ad ignorantiam*, it is because specific faults can be identified.

As indicated by the kinds of examples cited in the logic textbooks, arguments from ignorance often seem fallacious because cases like ghosts, ESP, and the like, are used where empirical verification or falsification of the premise is problematic. What sort of evidence counts for or against seeing an object that can definitely be identified as a ghost? It may be that we are ready to accept such an argument as fallacious not simply or exclusively because it is an *ad ignorantiam* argument, but because our ignorance is due to the elusive nature of the hypothesis which makes it problematic to test in a scientific inquiry.

Perhaps the problem is that a scientific inquiry requires that a hypothesis be relevant to some kind of empirical evidence. When the *argumentum ad ignorantiam* is reasonable in a scientific inquiry, it is because it is not totally based on ignorance, but also partly based on observations that do count for or against a hypothesis.

In cases of practical reasoning as a basis for action or refraining from action in a situation characterized by lack of conclusive knowledge, evidence may be incomplete. Even so, a reasonable conclusion to act or refrain may be drawn as a presumption that meets the requirements of burden of proof.

One proposal for the analysis of the fallacy of *argumentum ad ignorantiam* is offered by Robinson (1971), who conceded that this type of argument can legitimately lead to conclusions concerning matters of action and policy. Robinson contended that an *argumentum ad ignorantiam* can be fallacious, however, if it is taken to lead to a conclusion about what is true or false. Where **p** stands for a proposition, Robinson gave the following analysis to distinguish between the reasonable and fallacious instances of the *argumentum ad ignorantiam*.

> Given only that **p** has been neither proved nor disproved, it is fallacious to say "therefore **p** is true"; but it may be proper to say "therefore we act as if we knew **p** to be true." (p. 106)

This analysis is going in a good direction by suggesting that what is wrong with the *argumentum ad ignorantiam*, when it is wrong, is drawing a conclusion that is unjustifiably strong in its claim that a proposition is true, based on a premise stating that the proposition has been neither proved nor disproved.

But as an analysis of what is wrong with such an improper way of drawing a conclusion, this criterion is not helpful. For, to take a simple example, given that it has been neither proved nor disproved that this gun is loaded, it may be proper in some cases to say "therefore I act as if I knew it was loaded." But in other cases, this conclusion may be the wrong one, and it may be more reasonable to conclude, "therefore I act as if I knew it was unloaded." More correctly, I should not act as if I *knew* it was loaded (or unloaded). The conclusion I should draw is that I should presume that it is (or could be) loaded (or unloaded, depending on the case). But in any event, the problem of distinguishing between the reasonable and fallacious instances of the *argumentum ad ignorantiam* in these instances is not solved by Robinson's analysis.

What Robinson's analysis indicates, insightfully, is that we must be alert to the possibility of the occurrence of a fallacious *argumentum ad ignorantiam* precisely where there is a dialectical shift–a switch from one context of dialogue to another. For such a shift may be expected to entail a shift in the goal of the dialogue, and a shift in the burden of proof that sets the standard for meeting that goal. Where there is a shift from a context of dialogue where the goal is to establish a conclusion of truth or falsehood of a proposition, to a context of dialogue where the goal is to find a practical basis for action by drawing a conclusion that a proposition is a reasonable presumption, the situation is ripe for an erroneous *argumentum ad ignorantiam* to creep in. But the existence of this kind of shift, from one standard of argument or burden of proof to another, does not necessarily mean that a fallacy of the *argumentum ad ignorantiam* has been committed. For the fallacy can occur even within one context of dialogue, like that of practical reasoning as a basis of action, where no shift of context has taken place. Even so, drawing attention to the role of the dialectical shift is a positive step toward the analysis of the fallacy of the *argumentum ad ignorantiam*.

In a particular case, several of these factors may be indeterminate or unknown. For example, they may not be stated or implicit in the text, and the participants in the dialogue may not be available to answer these questions. In such incomplete cases, any evaluation of whether the *argumentum ad ignorantiam* is fallacious or not must remain hypothetical. But even a hypothetical answer may be useful in helping to sort out a dispute, or clarify an allegation of fallacious argumentation. Consider the following single assertion without any further details of context specified.

Case 4.10:   There is no evidence that quintozene is dangerous to human beings.

Robinson (1971) argued that this case is an instance of a fallacious *argumentum ad ignorantiam* because it is fair to infer both the tacit conclusion that quintozene is not dangerous to human beings and the tacit premise that "bad consequences have been searched for, and would have been observed if they had occurred." But is it a reasonable presumption that this pair of propositions can be added in to the proponent's argument and knowledge base? It depends on the context of dialogue.

Consider the following fragment of a dialogue sequence, where Ed has just run a small experiment to test the effects of smearing quintozene on the arms of a group of human subjects.

Case 4.11:   **Bob:**   Is there any evidence that quintozene is dangerous to human beings?
               Ed: There is no evidence that quintozene is dangerous to human beings.

In this case, it would not be justified by the evidence of the dialogue to attribute the conclusion "Quintozene is not dangerous to human beings" to Ed. Nor would it be fair to attribute to Ed the tacit assertion that any complete search for harmful consequences has been made. These attributions are simply not justified by the dialogue, as given in Case 4.11.

However, in another case, this pair of presumptions could be reasonably added. Let's say that Herman is an expert on quintozene.

Case 4.12:   **Bob:**   Is quintozene dangerous to human beings?
             Herman: There is no evidence that quintozene is dangerous
                           to human beings.

In this case, Herman is an expert, so Bob has a right to interpret his reply as a knowledge-based claim that quintozene is not dangerous, and that Herman is saying this on the basis of his knowledge of the existing state of knowledge on the harmful effects of quintozene. Moreover, since Herman has answered in the negative, Bob is entitled to infer that Herman is telling him that enough investigations into the harmful effects of quintozene have been carried out so that a burden has been met, and it is safe to conclude that quintozene is not dangerous.

RELATED FALLACIES

The *argumentum ad ignorantiam* becomes incorrect or erroneous where too much presumptive weight is claimed for the conclusion at a particular stage of a dialogue. In all the cases studied, the proponent can use the tactic of pushing ahead with the argument too fast, going from a permissible presumption to a required presumption, even if the context of dialogue does not justify this leap. There are three kinds of *ad ignorantiam* leaps that can take place.

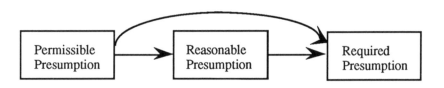

FIG. 4.1. *Ad Ignorantiam* leaps of presumption.

Advising students of argumentation how to attack or defend arguments more effectively is, of course, more a subject of rhetoric than of logic. But it is a general thesis advocated here that these subjects are not independent of each other, because arguments like the *ad ignorantiam, ad hominem,* and *ad verecundiam* tend to be more rhetorically effective when in fact they are based on strong logical structures of argumentation themselves, or are used to attack arguments that are inherently weak and open to this particular type of attack. In chapter three, the underlying structure of various argumentation types that are species of argumentation from ignorance have been revealed, and this will be used later, as a basis for giving advice on how to rightly use these types of argument as attacking and defensive tactics in argumentation. The techniques involved are powerful methods of persuasion–sometimes too powerful, for they can sometimes be used as sophistical tactics of deceit to get the upper hand in an argument (Walton, *Prag. Theory,* 1995).

The use of the appeal to expert opinion in argument can be one way of capitalizing on the relative ignorance of the person you wish to persuade. Curiously enough, the structure of the basic *ad hominem* fallacy studied in chapter three is also, essentially, an argument towards a respondent's ignorance–citing an inconsistency which makes a proponent's defence of a certain proposition open to question, the respondent concludes that this attack shows that the proposition in question is false. For example, as Copi (1986) noted, if it can be shown that a witness is a chronic liar, doubt may be thrown on the credibility of his testimony: "But if one goes on to infer that the witness's testimony establishes the *falsehood* of that to which the witness testifies, instead of concluding merely that the testimony does not establish its truth, then the reasoning is fallacious, being an *argumentum ad ignorantiam.*" Just so. In such a case, the argument is an argument towards ignorance, and at the same time it is an instance of the basic *ad hominem* fallacy. Hence the basic *ad hominem* fallacy is a special case of the fallacious argument towards ignorance *(argumentum ad ignorantiam).*

In short, both the argument from expertise and the argument against the person function as powerful and important mechanisms for producing a respondent's assent in dialogue (by a proponent of an argument) through the proponent's exploitation of the ignorance of the respondent.

FALLACIES AND BLUNDERS

At a more general level, the *ad ignorantiam* can be viewed as a fallacy when there is a shift of tactics in an argument in such a way that the proponent of the argument tries to forcefully evade fulfilling his or her obligation by attacking the opponent instead. This account of the fallacy stems from the fact that there are basically two types of tactics in an argument. One type is to try to build up your own argument, internally, by giving reasons or evidence to support your contentions. The other is to try to tear down your opponent's argument, by criticizing it, or finding weaknesses in it. The first approach is called defensive tactics, as opposed to the second approach which could be characterized as "attacking your opponent," or an offensive type of argumentation tactic. Sometimes the one type of tactic is more useful and appropriate, and sometimes the other is better.

The basic fallacy of the *argumentum ad ignorantiam* could be described as a kind of illicit shift from the defensive strategy to the offensive. It is the fallacy of attacking the other person's lack of proof instead of backing up your own argument with positive proof (as you are supposed to be doing). The underlying mechanism could be schematized, where White and Black are engaged in a persuasion dialogue. Instead of defending his or her own argument (indicated by the light arrow on the left of White), White is attacking the weakness of Black's argument (the line of attack indicated by the dark arrow).

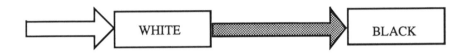

FIG. 4.2. Fallacy of *Argumentum Ad Ignorantiam.*

The dark arrow represents the line of argument White is actually pursuing, whereas the light arrow on the left represents the line of argument White is thereby neglecting.

Attacking the weak points in an opponent's argument is not an argumentation tactic that is inherently fallacious. Indeed, this tactic is a normal part of the process of criticism. Such a tactic only becomes open to criticism itself as an instance of the *ad ignorantiam* fallacy where the proponent is engaging in it in place of what should properly be engaged in, namely defending his or her own point of view with positive evidence to support it. Thus we could say that the fallacious *argumentum ad ignorantiam* is a species of offensive argumentation tactic where the attack has gone too far, in violation of proper requirements of the burden of proof in the argument. It is a species of improper attack instead of defence.

The blunder of *argumentum ad ignorantiam* is the opposite fault of defending your own position instead of questioning the weaknesses of your opponent's attacks on that position. This failure occurs where the proponent of an argument has a strong presumption already in favor of his or her side of the argument, and therefore has no need to resort to the defensive strategy of giving further evidence to support his or her side of a dispute. All the proponent needs to do is to indicate the weakness of the opponent's position in the argument. In this kind of situation, if the proponent mistakenly tries to marshall further evidence to support the case, he or she may actually weaken the persuasiveness of the argument by seeming to concede that his or her side of the argument is weaker than it really is.

In this type of situation, White (see Fig. 4.3) is the proponent of an argument that has already been backed up by plenty of positive evidence that has not been adequately challenged by Black. But White continues attempting to build up this stock of evidence by further arguments (as indicated by the darkened arrow), instead of carrying the argument forward offensively to question the weakness of Black's side.

The fault here is in trying to support your own argument instead of attacking the other person's weaknesses of argument.

FIG. 4.3. Blunder of *Argumentum Ad Ignorantiam.*

Whately (1963) warned of this very kind of blunder in argument where he described it as the bad strategy of overlooking one of your strongest arguments–the burden of proof on your side of a debate. It is like the case of "Qui s'excuse, s'accuse," where the victim of an unsupported accusation tries to take upon himself or herself the burden of his or her own innocence instead of defying the accuser to prove the charge. An unduly defensive strategy appears an admission of weakness or guilt.

But this kind of *ad ignorantiam* blunder in argument is not a fallacy. It is a weakness of argumentation tactics that weakens or undermines one's own side of an argument, not an instrument of strategy to defeat the other side of the argument. It is not contrary to rules of procedure or guidelines for reasoned, interactive dialogue. It is simply a weak use of tactics, a poor rather than tricky or deceptive use of argumentation tactics in dialogue, an argument that (unnecessarily) weakens the perpetrator's own side of the case to be disputed. It is less like unfairly or illicitly attacking your opponent than it is like shooting yourself in the foot.

The fallacy of *argumentum ad ignorantiam* and the blunder of *argumentum ad ignorantiam* are closely related as methods of argument that have gone wrong. In fact, one is the opposite tactic of the other. Each of them is a different kind of misuse of the *argumentum ad ignorantiam,* an argument mechanism that has its correct uses in interactive reasoning. Each of them is based on an inappropriate response to the circumstances of burden of proof and context of dialogue. Both are worth knowing about. But only one is a fallacy in the sense of being a systematic tactic used to violate a rule of reasonable dialogue, by attempting to trick or deceive the other party in the dialogue.

CONCLUDING REMARKS

From the cases studied in this chapter, it is possible to see that many arguments in everyday conversations (and especially many of the ones associated with the traditional informal fallacies) are species of *argumentum ad ignorantiam.* We could even say that all 25 argumentation schemes identified in chapter three are species of arguments from ignorance. What is characteristic of such argumentation is its dependence on and mirroring of the concept of the shifting of a burden of proof in presumptive reasoning as used in a dialogue. This provides its standard of correct use.

Far from being a fallacy then, the *argumentum ad ignorantiam* is often a reasonable, and also very common form of argumentation. It has its own distinctive argumentation schemes, as shown in this chapter. But it is a kind of argumentation that is a basic component of all of the types of argumentation identified in chapter three.

You could say, indeed, that presumptive argumentation generally is a species of argument from ignorance, in the sense that presumptive reasoning is useful and appropriate precisely in those cases where knowledge, in the form of so-called "hard" or "direct" evidence to prove or disprove a proposition is insufficient.

Where such knowledge is available, or can be gotten in time to be practically useful to solve a problem or resolve a dispute, it should be collected. However, in some cases, a decision or commitment is called for even in the absence of enough of such hard evidence to resolve the issue. It is in just this type of case where presumptive reasoning rightly comes into play, and with it the argument from ignorance as a useful and reasonable kind of argumentation.

Of course, it would be a fallacy to prefer presumptive reasoning to knowledge-based reasoning, in a case where the latter is available. But it is equally a fallacious move to dismiss all arguments based on ignorance as fallacious, in a wholesale fashion, where presumptive reasoning is appropriate and useful in a case (and is correctly deployed). In such cases, correct deployment of the argumentation scheme calls for a middle way.

CHAPTER FIVE

IGNORING QUALIFICATIONS

In the experience of teaching courses on informal logic and argumentation, one finds that the fault of being overly rigid and absolutistic in thinking, of being too insensitive to the defeasible nature of much ordinary reasoning, is an important type of error. In a critical discussion, it is important for an arguer to be open to refutation, to admitting his or her argument was wrong, should convincing evidence be brought forward by the opposing side. It would be nice to have a name for this general type of failure in argument, and for the subfallacies or special failures that come under it. It is a fault that can occur in connection with all of the argumentation schemes identified in chapter three.

The idea of neglecting qualifications, or legitimate exceptions to a plausible generalization in a particular case, is a clear and simple kind of failure that covers this gap. It is quite clear to students, from their personal experience, at least in general, what kind of error this is.[1]

On some accounts, the traditional informal fallacy of *secundum quid* (originally from the Aristotelian fallacy *para to pe,* meaning "in a certain respect")[2] fits this bill, referring to the fault of not paying attention to qualifications that would invalidate the use of a general proposition in a particular case. For example, in the *Dictionary of Philosophy* (Runes, 1964) we find:

> **Secundum quid:** (Lat.) Relatively, in some respect, in a qualified sense; contrasted with *simpliciter,* absolutely.–V.J.B.
> Secundum quid, or more fully, *a dicto simpliciter ad dictum secundum quid,* is any fallacy arising from the use of a general proposition without attention to tacit qualifications which would invalidate the use made of it. A.C. (p. 287)

So far, so good. But the problem comes in when we consult the logic textbooks, and see this type of error mixed in with a lot of other kinds of logical errors and faults of various kinds, under the heading of *accident, hasty generalization, converse accident, leaping to a conclusion,* and so forth.[3] The textbooks not only disagree with each other, showing a great proliferation of terms and classifications, but they introduce abstract terms like *essence* and *accident* that sound not only obscure, but also bizarre and antiquated to current students.

---

[1] Generally, the goal of instruction in informal logic should be to use, and at the same time, improve on the already existing skills of the students in argumentation, by helping them to "look twice" at arguments that should be open to critical questioning.

[2] Hamblin (1970, p. 28).

[3] Hamblin (1970, pp. 28-31, 45-47).

As someone who has been struggling to teach informal logic courses for more than 20 years, my own experience was discomforting in dealing with this particular subtopic because of the bewildering variety of terminology and different classifications of subfallacies in the textbooks. Trying to explain the historical origins of unfamiliar and puzzling terms like accident and converse accident seems a hopeless and unrewarding task, not to mention the variety of Latin terms and phrases peppered through the traditional textbook treatments. While ignoring exceptions to a rule or qualifications to a generalization did seem important failures to warn students about, nevertheless, the complications and puzzles inherent in the standard treatment suggested that it was prudent to bypass this area, restricting coverage to a brief mention of the basic fault, in simple terms.

The confusing state of the textbook treatments of *secundum quid* cannot be blamed on the textbook writers. The cases they either invented or cited from earlier traditions were often good illustrations of common and important errors of reasoning. And their comments and analyses were often helpful and revealing, sometimes even innovatively advancing well beyond any existing logical theory.

TERMINOLOGY AND CLASSIFICATION

One unfortunate aspect of this area of fallacies is the failure of agreement to arrive at any standard system of terminology and classification. In many textbooks, the umbrella term "hasty generalization" is used to cover three types of failures of argument: (1) inductive or sampling failures, like arguing from too small a sample, or an unrepresentative sample;[4] (2) presumptive failures, involving neglect of qualifications, or overlooking exceptions;[5] and (3) straightforward cases of overlooking new information in dynamic reasoning, like the raw meat case outlined later. In other textbooks, the term hasty generalization is used to refer to one or two of these failures, whereas some other term is used to refer to the other(s).[6]

Still other textbooks introduce other terminology to label these faults, or other related faults. One common label is "jumping to a conclusion."[7] This term is sometimes used, more narrowly, to refer to one or more of the three faults, listed under hasty generalization. But very often it is used in a much broader and more sweeping fashion to refer to any logically weak or insufficiently supported argument. Such a failure could refer to virtually any type of argument that is faulty because the premises fail to give enough support to the conclusion. It could be a weak (invalid) deductive argument, or a weak (insufficiently supported) inductive argument, for example.

Once the terms accident and *secundum quid* are blended into this terminological mixture, the result, in the textbook treatments, is generally confusing and disorienting. Imagine the student being introduced to this subject who begins by

---

[4] Hamblin (1970, p. 46).

[5] Hamblin (1970, p. 46), and see also the textbook treatments cited later.

[6] See also the survey in Bueno (1988), and remarks on terms.

[7] Fearnside and Holther (1959, p. 13).

consulting several different textbooks on *secundum quid* or hasty generalization. It would not be an encouraging experience. The sheer diversity of terminologies prevents one from even beginning to speak about these fallacies in a coherent and orderly way, never mind trying to build up some basic knowledge on what the fallacies are.

Surely a first step is to clearly distinguish between the inductive/ statistical failures of argument, which might perhaps more properly be called "hasty generalization," or something of the sort, and the presumptive failures of argument that have to do with neglect of qualifications.

Some textbooks treat hasty generalization exclusively as a failure of inductive generalizations which is essentially and inductive/ statistical fallacy. Fearnside and Holther (1959) defined the fallacy of *hasty generalization* as follows. For this same fault, they also use the label "jumping to conclusions," which they take to be equivalent.

> The fallacy of generalization from too few cases consists in drawing a general conclusion on the basis of an experience with particulars, which statistical science shows to be insufficient in view of the size of the unit examined, or, as pollsters say, the "population." Even where there is a lack of time or money to prepare a proper actuarial survey, there is no excuse for ignorance about the minimum size of the sample–the man who talks to a few people in his office and to his neighbors and then makes a bet on a presidential election deserves to lose the bet. (p. 13)

Under the same heading of hasty generalization, Fearnside and Holther also included sample-based inductive inferences that fail because the sample is not representative of the population from which it was selected.

In Walton (1989, *Inf. Log.*) the two criticisms of insufficient and biased statistics are treated as referring to distinctive types of errors of inductive reasoning in their own right. They are not classified under an umbrella term like hasty generalization. However, as long as the term is being used clearly and consistently, it would not appear to be objectionable to use it, or some equivalent term, for this purpose. I would prefer not to use the term jumping to a conclusion for this purpose, however, for it suggests something much too broad, as a type of failure. And indeed, it is shown later that many of the major informal fallacies can be classified under that heading, as presumptive leaps.

Another text (Salmon, 1984) treated several different fallacies under the general heading "Fallacies Associated with Inductive Generalizations," while stating "this fallacy has been called the *fallacy of insufficient statistics, hasty generalization,* or *leaping to a conclusion.*" Salmon offered two examples.

> If a friend snaps at you when you ask a question, you would be committing the fallacy of hasty generalization if you argued that this one instance of unfriendly behavior showed that he was no longer your friend. If you conclude that no one likes turnips because none of your friends do, this too would be a hasty generalization. The psychological reasons for leaping to a conclusion are fairly obvious in these cases. In the first, hurt feelings may color your judgment; in the second, personal knowledge of opinions of friends may

obscure the fact that they are only a small part of the population. To avoid this fallacy, we must dispassionately take account of the size of the sample before we draw any conclusion from it. If feelings are not the issue, and, instead, there is an inadequate amount of appropriate background information on which to judge whether a sample is large enough, we should try to acquire the information. If this is not possible, it would be advisable to suspend judgment on the conclusion. (p. 58-59)

The turnips case does seem to be an inductive failure that can be analyzed very well by pointing out that the generalization was based on too small a sample.

However, the problem is that this same kind of inductive failure is not a convincing analysis of what is wrong with the argument in the snapping friend case. Friendship is a presumption based on trust, and a basis for normal expectations on how a person will act on the presumption that he or she is your friend. However, not all situations are normal, and in some cases, a friend will behave in an unexpected way that may seem to run counter to the presumption of friendship. If a friend snaps at you, in a particular case, however, it does not necessarily signal the end of the friendship. Perhaps the case is exceptional, and there is a reason or explanation for this ostensibly unfriendly behavior. Along these lines then, a case can be made out that the failure in the snapping friend example is not an inductive fallacy of insufficient statistics, but a *secundum quid* type of failure to take exceptional circumstances into account in presumptive reasoning.[8]

Another text (Engel, 1976) seems, at least initially, to do better on the job of classification by distinguishing between two types of faults in arguments–the inductive type of failure and the presumptive type of failure of ignoring exceptions. According to Engel's account, "the *fallacy of sweeping generalization* is committed when a general rule is applied to a specific case to which the rule is not applicable because of the special features of that case" (p. 105). This type of failure appears to correspond to the *secundum quid* type of presumptive fallacy of ignoring qualifications. The examples given by Engel bear out this interpretation.

Case 5.1:   Everyone has a right to his or her own property. Therefore, even though Jones has been declared insane, you had no right to take away his weapon.

Case 5.2:   Since horseback riding is healthful exercise, Harry Brown ought to do more of it because it will be good for his heart condition.

Both are classic cases of the traditional (Aristotelian) fallacy of *secundum quid*.

---

[8] Rescher (1976) supported our presumption that presumptive reasoning is a different kind of reasoning from inductive reasoning.

Using a separate classification, Engel characterized the fallacy of hasty generalization in a way that initially makes it appear to be an inductive error of generalizing on the basis of a single instance, or too small a sample. The example given is the following case.

Case 5.3:   I had a bad time with my former husband. From that experience I've learned that all men are no good.

But the problem with this case is that it is not too clear whether the argument is supposed to be an inductive generalization, based on a sample, or a presumptive generalization, based on a (supposedly) typical case.[9]

In fact, a closer look reveals that Engel is, apparently, not making the distinction on an inductive versus presumptive basis at all, but on a basis of the direction of argumentation. In the fallacy of sweeping generalization, the argument goes from general rule to specific case. In the fallacy of hasty generalization "an isolated or exceptional case is used as the basis for a general conclusion which is unwarranted" (p. 108). Cases 5.1 and 5.2 are instances of the fallacy of sweeping generalization then, according to Engel, whereas Case 5.3 is an instance of the fallacy of hasty generalization.

This way of making the distinction turns out to be not too helpful.[10] Indeed, another example offered by Engel as a case of the fallacy of hasty generalization, is nothing of the sort. This case (Case 3.3, reprinted below), came from the Sherlock Holmes story, *A Study in Scarlet,* where Holmes is introduced to Dr. Watson for the first time, and Holmes reasons that Watson must recently have been in Afghanistan.

Case 3.3:   Here is a gentleman of a medical type, but with the air of a military man. Clearly an army doctor, then. He has just come from the tropics, for his face is dark, and that is not the natural tint of his skin, for his wrists are fair. He has undergone hardship and sickness, as his haggard face says clearly. His left arm has been injured. He holds it in a stiff and unnatural manner. Where in the tropics could an English army doctor have seen much hardship and got his arm wounded? Clearly in Afghanistan.

Engel's analysis of Case 3.3 is that Holmes is "guilty of a hasty generalization founded on insufficient evidence" (p. 110), because Watson could have had the air of being a military man without ever having been in the army, or he could have a

---

[9] This confusion is itself the basis of one variant of the *secundum quid*–see later.

[10] Bueno (1988) supports our contention and also argues (in greater detail later) that this way of making the distinction between two types of fallacy is not helpful.

tanned face while remaining in England. All these things are possible, but to cite them as evidence that Holmes has, in this case, committed a fallacy of hasty generalization is setting too high a standard for Holmes to meet. Admittedly, Holmes' conclusion was only a conjecture, a guess based on expectations and normal patterns which might not have been applicable to this particular case. But does that mean that Holmes committed a fallacy by making the guess, and advancing such a presumptive, but fallible conclusion?

The answer, judging from what we know of the (fictional) context of Case 3.3 is no. His argument was a correct use of argumentation from sign. Holmes should not, in the circumstances, be convicted of having committed a fallacy of hasty generalization. Indeed, you could say that such an accusation is itself a case of the *secundum quid* fallacy, characterized by portraying someone's argument in an overly rigid way. To say that Holmes' argument was fallacious because he could *possibly* have been mistaken is to insist, unsympathetically and unfairly, that Holmes' argument must be interpreted as a deductively valid argument, or perhaps a very strong kind of inductively strong argument, in order for it to have been successful.

But far from that, Holmes' argument was evidently meant to be a clever guess, a plausible conjecture based on presumptive reasoning. And as such, at least as far as we are told in the story, it turned out to be a good argument of the type we called argument from sign in chapter three.

Engel's treatment of Case 3.3 as a fallacious argument on grounds that it is deductively invalid shows graphically the general failure in logic textbooks to acknowledge that presumptive reasoning can be a legitimate type of argumentation in its own right. Small wonder the textbook treatments of the fallacy of *secundum quid* lack any kind of theoretical basis for arriving at an adequate understanding of this fallacy.

ACCIDENT AND CONVERSE ACCIDENT

The most widely used logic textbook, Copi and Cohen (1990), follows a common practice among many textbooks of treating what is essentially the fallacy of *secundum quid* under the heading of two fallacies, called accident and converse accident. Both fallacies are said to arise through the careless, or "deliberately deceptive" use of generalizations:

> In political and moral argument, and in most affairs of importance in community life, we rely upon statements of how things generally are, how people generally behave, and the like. But, even when general claims are entirely plausible, we must be careful not to apply them to particular cases too rigidly. Circumstances alter cases; a generalization that is true by and large may not apply in a given case, for good reasons having to do with the special (or "accidental") circumstances of that case. When we apply a generalization to individual cases that it does not properly govern, we commit the *fallacy of Accident*. When we do the reverse, and carelessly or by design, apply a principle that is true of a particular case to the great run of cases, we commit the *fallacy of Converse Accident*. (p. 100)

Copi and Cohen use several of the standard examples, in their brief (equivalent to one page) treatment, characterizing the basic fallacy as follows: "Almost every good rule has appropriate exceptions; we argue fallaciously when we reason on the supposition that some rule applies with universal force." This is in fact quite a good capsule characterization of the basic fault behind the fallacy of *secundum quid,* or ignoring exceptions.

The two questionable aspects of Copi and Cohen's otherwise helpful treatment of this fallacy are: (a) their terminology–using accident instead of ignoring qualifications–a practice that is neither historically justifiable nor helpful to students as indicative of the fault,[11] and (b) their emphasis on distinguishing between the converse and direct (nonconverse) variants of the fallacy.

The example Copi and Cohen give of the fallacy of direct accident is said to be fallacious on the grounds that it is a rule that has appropriate exceptions. The fallacy is reasoning on the supposition that the rule has universal force.

Case 5.4:   The rule that hearsay testimony may not be accepted as evidence in court is not applicable when the party whose oral communications are recorded is dead, or when the party reporting the hearsay does so in conflict with his own best interest.

But what exactly is the fallacy here? Is it the following kind of inference?

It is a rule that hearsay evidence may not be accepted as evidence in court.

This statement is hearsay evidence.

Therefore, this statement *cannot* be accepted as evidence in court (even though the person who made it is dead).

If so, the fault is an instance of the fallacy of direct accident, according to Copi and Cohen, because the inference goes from the general rule to the conclusion of a specific case.

But what is the problem in this case? Surely a significant part of the problem is that the rule in the major premise is being interpreted in too strict a way–as Copi and Cohen put it, "with universal force"–so that the legitimate exception is being (unreasonably) excluded.

If this is right, then the direct-converse distinction is really not all that significant, because it is basically the same kind of problem of ignoring qualifications to a general rule or principle that is the root fault in the converse type of case as well. The example Copi and Cohen give of the fallacy of converse accident concerns the following type of inference.

---

[11] According to Bueno (1988), this practice is followed in the Anglo-American tradition, but not in the Continental tradition of fallacies.

Case 5.5:   Drug x in dosage y has beneficial effects for the health of
                 patient z in circumstance c.

                 Therefore, plenty of drug x is good for anyone in all circum-
                 stances.

This type of inference goes from the particular premise to the generalization as a
conclusion. Hence for Copi and Cohen, it commits the fallacy of converse accident, as opposed to direct accident.

But is this distinction very significant when it comes to identifying and
analyzing the basic problem inherent in this kind of inference as a species of
fallacy? It would appear not, for the basic problem that is really all that needs to
be identified and analyzed is the ignoring of the role of exceptions, of the defeasible nature of the generalization, in so arguing.

However, if you look over some of the cases, it is not hard to appreciate why
the textbooks have found it plausible to classify between the direct and converse
categories. Cases 5.1 and 5.2 are classified as instances of sweeping generalization
by Engel, and would presumably be classified as instances of direct accident by
Copi and Cohen, because the argument goes from a general premise to a specific
conclusion that describes a single instance. In contrast, Case 5.3 is classified as
an instance of hasty generalization by Engel, just as Case 5.5 is classified as an
instance of converse accident by Copi and Cohen, because these arguments go
from a premise describing a single case to a general conclusion containing the
word "all." Whatever you call the fallacy or fallacies–*secundum quid*, accident,
hasty or sweeping generalization, and so forth–it does seem to make some sense
to observe that the inference contained in it can go either way–from the general
statement to the specific case, or vice versa.

Sometimes an inference can go both ways as well, in a given case. Suppose,
for example, it has been found, in general, that aspirin is good for patients with
heart disease, but bad for patients with stomach problems.

Case 5.6:   Taking aspirin has been good for John, who has heart disease.

                 Therefore, taking aspirin is good for anyone who has heart
                 disease.

                 Susan has heart disease and ulcers.

                 Therefore, taking aspirin will be good for Susan.

In this case, the inference from the first premise to the first conclusion was a case
of direct accident or hasty generalization (going from a single case to a generalization). But then the inference from the first conclusion, taken together as a

premise with the next premise, made up an argument that is a case of converse accident or sweeping generalization (going from a generalization to a specific conclusion).

In this case, you could say that the argument is a chain of inferences or subarguments, and the one subargument is a case of direct accident, the other a case of converse accident. But such an observation is not the main thing, or the key factor that identifies the argument, as a whole, as an instance where the fallacy of *secundum quid* (or whatever you choose to call it) has been committed. The main thing is that the argument, in general, is faulty because, or to the extent that, the susceptibility of the generalization to exceptions has been ignored or suppressed. The main thing is that the general statement that aspirin is good for people with heart disease is a defeasible presumption, a rule of thumb that is highly sensitive to certain kinds of exceptions. To draw conclusions from it, while interpreting it in a rigid or absolutistic way, could be to commit quite a serious kind of error.

The conclusion of this discussion seems to be that the direct-converse distinction does have some legitimate basis, or role to play, in the presentation of *secundum quid* (or whatever name you choose for it) as a kind of fallacy. But it would be a mistake to lay too great a stress on the direct-converse distinction as being essential, or even very important, in identifying and analyzing the fallacy. The fallacy basically involves a failure to recognize the defeasible nature of generalizations, and to draw faulty conclusions by inference using a wrongly interpreted generalization, no matter whether the generalization functions as a premise or as the conclusion of the inference.

The fallacy of *secundum quid* is associated with an attitude of rigidity or dogmatism that confuses the two different types of generalizations in a given case that are defined in chapter two, resulting in the drawing of an incorrect inference. The strict kind of generalization could also be called the *universal (absolute)* generalization, a type of generalization that does not admit of exceptions. One counter-instance falsifies (refutes) it. This type of generalization was represented in chapter two by the universal quantifier and the strict (material) conditional, in the general form: $(\forall x)(Fx) \supset Gx$, where x is an individual variable and F and G are predicate variables. The default type of generalization can also be called the *defeasible (presumptive) generalization,* a type of generalization that admits of exceptions, and is compatible with some new arguments that turn up counter-instances. This type of generalization is not strict, but is openended and tentative in nature. Later, it is shown that the formal properties of the logical reasoning involved in these two types of generalizations are different in a clearly definable way.

THE RAW MEAT EXAMPLE

A very common and typical example of the fallacy of *secundum quid* given by the logic textbooks is the following inference, with two premises: "What you bought yesterday, you eat today; you bought raw meat yesterday; therefore, you eat raw meat today." According to Hamblin (1970), this example first appeared in the 12th-century *Munich Dialectica,* and is an "interesting, and entirely typical illustration of the ossification of the traditional treatment of fallacies in modern times. . . ." Usually treated as an example of the *secundum quid* fallacy, this same inference has also been classified under the heading of the fallacy of accident by many textbooks.

For example, according to Whately (1836), the inference is an instance of the fallacy of accident *(fallacia accidentis)* because the major premise "signifies something considered simply in itself" (as to its substance merely), whereas the minor premise "implies that accidents are taken into account," in regard to "conditions and circumstances." Whately's account of what is supposedly wrong sounds like he has a point, but he has not succeeded in applying to the example in a specific enough way to be very convincing.

DeMorgan (1847) cited the same example as an instance of the fallacy of *secundum quid,* commenting that it was "raw when Reitsch mentioned it in the *Margarita Philosophica* in 1496, found in the same state by Whately in 1826," and "has remained uncooked, as fresh as ever, a prodigious time." Little appears to have changed, in this regard, since 1847. Many 20th-century texts continue to use the example, though their diagnoses of the supposed error differ.

In the form it is put in by Cohen and Nagel (1934), the fallacy of accident appears to be a failure of dynamic reasoning, in the sense that it is a failure to take new information into account. Using the raw meat example, they cited the fault as the failure to take into account "that the meat has grown older" during the inference, a fact that may have introduced significant changes.

> The *fallacy of accident* (also called *a dicto simpliciter ad dictum secundum quid).* It is illustrated by the argument: You eat today what you bought yesterday and you bought raw meat yesterday; therefore you eat raw meat today. The two assertions do imply that the meat which was raw and bought yesterday is eaten today, but not that it is eaten raw. The particular form in which we eat it is not implied in the premises. In other words, the adjective which characterizes the condition of the meat when bought does not apply necessarily to the form in which we eat it. The premises of our argument do not, for instance, preclude the fact that the meat has grown one day older between the two operations. (p. 377)

According to this account, the argument in question has the form of an inference, with two premises.

Case 5.7:   You eat today what you bought yesterday.
                     You bought raw meat yesterday.
                     Therefore, you eat raw meat today.

What is wrong with this inference? The answer is that it overlooks the possibility that new information may have come in, that is, that the condition of the meat may have been changed between the purchase and consumption stages.

In fact, this change is more than just a possibility. In the given circumstances, it is the normal practice for us to cook meat before eating it (subject, perhaps, to unusual or exceptional cases). In other words, a nonexplicitly stated third premise can plausibly be added to the inference.

Normally (subject to exceptions) meat is cooked before it is consumed.

Adding this premise, the former conclusion is rebutted or cancelled, and its opposite is derived.

Therefore, you eat cooked meat today.

Hence the original inference is faulty because it overlooked new information that came into the situation between the buying of the meat (expressed in the one premise) and the eating of the meat (expressed in the other premise). In this instance, the information was tacitly conveyed in context. The context suggests that normally the practice is to cook meat at some point between the buying stage and the eating stage.

Overlooking this covert premise could be called a kind of fallacy or failure of reasoning. However, the failure in this case is not exactly the same fault as the main type of *secundum quid* fallacy, which is to construe a defeasible statement too rigidly and overlook legitimate exceptions. In this case, the fault is to overlook a whole (defeasible) premise altogether. It is the fault of overlooking a change that has (likely) come into the situation, given presumable, normal practices known to exist in that type of situation. Here, the fault is not being overly rigid, or interpreting a defeasible statement in an (unfairly or unreasonably) rigid way. It is overlooking the whole defeasible statement altogether.

Hence, the raw meat case is clearly related to the *secundum quid* fallacy. But it is, if anything, a special case of it, and not the typical or standard type of error that characterizes this fallacy. The standard case would look something like this.

You bought raw meat yesterday.

Raw meat is always (without exception) cooked after it is bought and before it is consumed.

You eat today what you bought yesterday.

Therefore, you eat cooked meat today.

The fallacy in this type of case would occur where the proponent of the previous argument insists that the argument is deductively valid and that the premises are true, and therefore that the respondent *must* accept the conclusion. This would be a type of case where the proponent interprets the conclusion as expressing the proposition, "It is not possible that you did not eat cooked meat today." In such a case, the proponent allows the respondent no further room for asking critical questions or claiming exceptions exist in the case. The fallacy, in such a case, relates to the overly rigid (dogmatic) posture of the proponent, in not allowing for any discussion of possible exceptions or special circumstances.

In this second kind of failure, the fault is also one of overlooking or barring new (and relevant) information. But it is the way the information is excluded, by an overly rigid interpretation of the second (general) premise, that is the key fault.

The failure in the first inference was different. It was the fault of overlooking the general premise altogether, and thereby arriving at a conclusion that is the opposite of the one that should really be drawn.

The classic raw meat example, and some of the other examples used in the textbooks, do provide some good cases for discussion and analysis. The textbook treatments suggest that the fallacy of *secundum quid* is basically a very interesting and pervasive type of error of argumentation, well worth exploring. However, the textbook treatments also show basic disagreements on what the fallacy is, on how it should be named and classified, on what its relationships to neighboring fallacies are, and on how it should be analyzed as some identifiable type of argument that is incorrect.

How did the textbooks ever get into this highly confusing state of affairs? As usual with the major fallacies, finding the answer means going back to Aristotle (or perhaps even further back, as will be seen later).

ARISTOTLE'S ACCOUNT

Near the beginning of *On Sophistical Refutations,* Aristotle listed seven kinds of fallacies connected with language. The first one is called "accident," and the example Aristotle gives is puzzling: "If Corsicus is different from 'man,' he is different from himself, for he is a man." It is puzzling in the sense that it is not clear exactly what the error is, and not convincing that this is a common or important error in everyday reasoning. Aristotle's general account of this alleged fallacy is none too straightforward either.[12]

> Fallacies connected with Accident occur when it is claimed that some attribute belongs similarly to the thing and to its accident; for since the same thing has many accidents, it does not necessarily follow that all the same attributes belong to all the predicates of a thing and to that of which they are predicated (166b29 - 166b33).

This pattern might appear to fit an inference like the following: this desk is brown; brown is a color; therefore this desk is a color. But why this type of faulty inference represents some kind of tricky or common, persuasive error of argument worth designating as a fallacy is simply not obvious.

The second kind of fallacy listed by Aristotle is "those [kinds of argument] in which an expression is used absolutely, or not absolutely but qualified as to manner or place or time or relation." An example: The Ethiopian is black; the

---

[12] Bueno (1988) agrees, showing that Aristotle's account of the fallacy of accident is unclear and confusing to begin with, leading commentators to many different conflicting theories and attempted analyses.

Ethiopian has white teeth; therefore the Ethiopian is both black and not black." The problem here is that the Ethiopian is black generally, but white in one particular respect. The problem, clearly an important kind of error, lies in the failure to distinguish between a thing having a property absolutely (generally), and its having a property in one particular respect.[13]

Aristotle, much later in *On Sophistical Refutations,* clearly showed how this kind of problem is an important type of fallacy or confusion in reasoning, and distinguished between the two kinds of statements that can appear as premises or conclusion of the associated arguments. One is the general type of statement that is meant to be held or taken "absolutely," with no qualifications attached. The other is the statement that is alleged to be true only "in certain respects," that is, true in particular circumstances, relative to a particular time, place, degree, or relation, and not "absolutely" true. The problem is that if these two types of statements are confused in the same argument, a fallacy can arise–the argument can superficially appear to be valid when it really is not.

Aristotle offers many examples that clearly and convincingly represent common, important kinds of errors. One is the following: ". . . there is no reason why the same man should not be absolutely a liar yet tell the truth in some respects, or that some of a man's words should be true but he himself not be truthful." The danger here, for example, is taking the following type of argument to be generally valid or correct.

Case 5.8:   Bob is a liar.
                Bob said *A* is true.
                Therefore, *A* is false.

Or, the opposite mistake could be in taking the following kind of argument at face value.

Case 5.8a: Bob said *A*.
                A is true.
                Therefore, Bob is truthful.

The problem with the second inference is that Bob may have just hit on something true here inadvertently, yet, in general, he may be a congenital liar. Or Bob may be honest or accurate about some things, but generally unreliable and mendacious as a source. There is a different problem with the first inference. Even though Bob is generally a liar, there may be good reasons to think he has told the truth in some particular case.

---

[13] Hamblin (1970) suggested that a formal logic of the words "wholly" and "partly" is "not difficult to build." He then actually sketched out the foundations for such a logic, which would formally show Aristotle's example of the Ethiopian to be a fallacy, based on a confusion between two types of adverbial attribution.

Another interesting type of case Aristotle considers concerns a statement that is true at a general level of abstraction, but may be false when applied to a particular case.

> Is health (or wealth) a good thing? But to the fool who misuses it, it is not a good thing; it is, therefore, a good thing and not a good thing. Is health (or political power) a good thing? But there are times when it is not better than other things; therefore the same thing is both good and not good for the same man. Or is there no reason why a thing should not be absolutely good but not good for a particular person, or good for a particular person, but not good at the present moment or here? (p. 180b9-180b14)

Here, the same kind of problem is apparent. Wealth is generally a good thing. But used badly in particular circumstances by a particular person, that wealth may not be a good thing for that person.[14] Here Aristotle notes that this problem even seems to violate the law of non-contradiction: ". . . the same thing is both good and not good for the same man." He is aware it is a serious logical problem, and even a serious foundational problem that could give some at least potentially legitimate grounds for denying the law of non-contradiction.

At the very beginning of this whole passage on statements true in a particular respect, Aristotle does offer a general solution to the problem of how to deal with arguments where this type of difficulty arises. According to Aristotle's account, the problem arises where, through a kind of confusion, what appears to be a genuine refutation, is not. What he means by "refutation" is an argument that has been used by one participant in a dialogue to refute or "go against" the contention of the participant on the other side.

The problem arises, in such a context, where in the one premise of the refutation, the predicate belongs to the subject absolutely, whereas in the other premise, the predicate belongs to the subject only "in a particular respect," (i.e., nonabsolutely). So far, the problem may be simply a confusion. But it becomes a fallacy when the participant to whom the refutation was directed fails to detect the key difference between the two premises, and (erroneously) takes the argument as a real refutation, when in fact it is not. Thus the fallacy is a kind of illusion or trick.

How did Aristotle propose to deal with this kind of problem? It is quite clear from his remarks that he did, in effect, propose a kind of practical method that could be used by someone who wants to detect this type of fallacy in a given argument.

> Arguments which turn upon the use of an expression not in its proper sense but with validity in respect only of a particular thing or in a particular respect or place or degree or relation and not absolutely, must be solved by examining the conclusion in the light of its contradictory, to see if it can possibly have been affected in any of these ways. For it is impossible for

---

14 This is a typical kind of case where practical reasoning is used to infer from abstract principles to particular circumstances and vice versa. See Walton (1990, *Pract. Reas.*) for a general account of this kind of reasoning.

contraries and opposites and an affirmative and a negative to belong absolutely to the same subject; on the other hand, there is no reason why each should not belong in a particular respect or relation or manner, or one in a particular respect and the other absolutely. Thus if one belongs absolutely and the other in a particular respect, no refutation has yet been reached. This point must be examined in the conclusion by comparison with its contradictory. (180a23-180a31)

Aristotle's method is to start by examining the conclusion of the argument used as a refutation in a context of dialogue. You must "examine" the conclusion "in light of its contradictory" to see if it can be affected by this sort of problem. Is the conclusion meant to be true absolutely, or only in certain respects? Having determined this, then you have to look back at the relevant premises and ask the same question about them. If there is a disparity here–for example, if the conclusion is supposed to be true absolutely, whereas a premise required to get to this conclusion is only true in a certain respect–then the conclusion will have to be withdrawn. In such a case, the argument fails, and "no refutation has yet been reached."

Aristotle's analysis of the fallacy is excellent in two respects especially. First, it is a general analysis of the type of error involved, and not tied to any specific situation of use or calculus. He is saying that you have to look at each particular case on its merits, and scan it by first looking at the conclusion, asking: "Does the predicate belong to the subject absolutely, or only in a particular respect?" Having answered this question, next you need to scan over the premises and ask it again. Thus Aristotle's test is to take any given argument and "think twice" about it, to see if it fails because of the ambiguity between these two types of predication.

Second, Aristotle's analysis is excellent because it reveals the deep, underlying import of this fallacy for logic as a subject. Failure to recognize the fallacy means that in the practice of dealing with arguments, you could be violating the law of non-contradiction. Because, in practice, it is possible for something to have a property generally, but fail to have that property in some particular respect, the fault of not being attuned to this distinction means that you will be open to refutation on grounds of contradicting yourself in some cases.

In short, Aristotle did an excellent job of explaining what this fallacy is, by giving good examples of it, by giving a clear analysis of its theoretical basis, and by giving a practical test to detect the existence of the fallacy in particular cases.

Evidently the problem began with the later Greek commentators on Aristotle, who began to mix Aristotle's fallacies of *secundum quid* and accident together.[15] Moreover, what Aristotle wrote on the fallacy of accident was found to be highly abstruse, leading ultimately, in the middle ages, to deep metaphysical controversies on essence and accident among the leading logicians of the time.[16] The initially clear Aristotelian fallacy of *secundum quid* was mixed into this melee,

---

[15] See Ebbesen (1981); Bäck (1987); and Bueno (1988).

[16] See Ebbesen (1981); Bäck (1987); and Bueno (1988).

and the treatments of this fallacy in the textbooks never recovered from the ensuing confusion (with only a few exceptions).

HISTORICAL DEVELOPMENTS

The history of the fallacy of *secundum quid* is a tortured trail. It starts out with the clear account of a readily recognizable type of common error in everyday reasoning given by Aristotle in *On Sophistical Refutations*. From there, things went badly. In subsequent textbooks, for the next 2,000 years, this fallacy somehow got lumped in with the other Aristotelian fallacy called *accident*. Accident is not so much a fallacy in the sense of a common error of reasoning. It could perhaps better be described as a paradox or series of puzzles, a general category for a family of quite subtle types of errors or problems of reasoning. Whatever accident is, it is far from clear that it is the kind of common error of reasoning or fallacy that belongs in the standard treatment of fallacies in logic textbooks (especially textbooks meant for general reading by nonspecialists and introductory students). Even worse, the already obscure fallacy of accident became more and more convoluted and abstruse as variants, like converse accident were added, each of these variants having an impressive-sounding Latin name.

As if this wasn't bad enough, *secundum quid* was also treated, especially in the modern textbooks, as being the same as, or a subspecies of, what was described as an inductive/statistical error, the so-called fallacy of hasty generalization, also known as leaping to a conclusion, *inadequate statistics, overgeneralization,* and so forth. This further confused matters, because the original *secundum quid* fallacy, as described by Aristotle was clearly something distinctively different from the inductive error of concluding to a generalization on the basis of too small a sample (often called the fallacy of insufficient statistics).[17]

The original fallacy of *secundum quid* described by Aristotle was quite a simple basic idea–it was simply the error of neglect of qualifications. However, as the logic textbook treatments evolved, through the middle ages and into the modern period, descriptions of this fallacy had become so complicated and obscure that the original idea was buried in all sorts of abstruse philosophical theorizing about essences, accidental properties, and the like. Not surprisingly, the whole category of *secundum quid* fell into disuse, for all practical purposes. And today this phrase, or the category of fallacy it represents does not seem to really mean much of anything to anybody, as part of common language.

An important development historically was that Aristotle's rather abstract and perplexing account of the so-called fallacy of accident led to a variety of different interpretations among subsequent generations of commentators on Aristotle's works. This led to considerable controversy in the middle ages on the subject of accident, and also to the construction of complex metaphysical theories concerning accident, with the introduction of abstruse, scholastic terminology.

As noted previously, what Aristotle said about accident as a fallacy in *On Sophistical Refutations* is puzzling, in that its practical import for the study of

---

[17] Hamblin (1970) supports this contention.

fallacies is unclear. According to Bäck (1987), Aristotle held a fundamental logical principle in his *Categories* and *Prior Analytics* called the *dictum de omni*, that says (in modern terms) that the predicates of the predicates of a subject are predicates of that subject. An apparent counter-example, or at least problem for this principle is the case of the man who is coming towards us with his face covered *(On Sophistical Refutations* 179b3-179b8): ". . . if I know Corsicus but I do not know the man who is coming towards me, it does not follow that I know and do not know the same man." The Greek commentators on Aristotle saw the problem as one of adding some "qualifying phrase" to the *dictum de omni* that would rule out the counter-example. According to Bäck (1987), an interpretation common to these commentators was to add the qualification that there must be an essential connection between the terms in the *dictum de omni* principle. Hence in subsequent discussions of accident in the middle ages, the discussion of the fallacy of accident had become strongly tied in with the doctrine of essential and accidental properties.

In Boethius' view (Gelber, 1987), the *dictum de omni* had efficacy only in cases of essential predication. In the *De Fallaciis,* attributed to Aquinas, an even more complex solution was worked out that involved three different kinds of predication. Following these developments, other leading medieval philosophers worked out theories of accident, engaging in running controversies on the subject with their predecessors and contemporaries.

According to Bueno (1988), there was also a Byzantine interpretation of the fallacy of accident associated with two commentaries on Aristotle's *On Sophistical Refutations* written by Michael of Ephesus between the 1120s-1130s. This interpretation forgot or ignored the discussions of accident in late antiquity, and launched into a quite different analysis that made the fallacy seem similar to equivocation (Ebbesen, 1981). According to this analysis, we need to distinguish between the subject considered in itself (as a universal) and the combination made up of the subject and its (nonuniversal) accident.

The three great medieval logicians, William of Sherwood, Peter of Spain, and Jean Buridan all disagreed in their explanations of the fallacy of accident. In the Middle Ages then, the fallacy of accident produced what Bueno (1988) called "a bewildering variety of interpretations," leading the Aristotelian scholar Edward Poste (1866) to conclude that the fallacy of accident "has been generally misunderstood."

This confusion was compounded by the Port Royal logicians, who struck out on their own, paying lip service to, but really departing from the medieval traditions, and who defined the fallacy of accident in a way that makes it indistinguishable from the fallacy of ignoring qualifications, or *secundum quid.* At this point, the initially clear and coherent Aristotelian fallacy of *secundum quid* was thrown into confusion and disarray by being systematically mixed in with the fallacy of accident, in the logic textbooks. The result can be seen in the modern treatments of Whately, DeMorgan, and Mill.

The Port Royal account of the fallacy of accident given in Arnauld (1964) is particularly disorienting, because it gives examples that seem more like mixtures of *secundum quid* with other fallacies.

We commit [this] kind of sophism when we make an unqualified judgment of a thing on the basis of an accidental characteristic. This sophism is called *fallacia accidentis* by the Schoolmen. For example, people commit this fallacy when they deprecate the use of antimony on the ground that when misused antimony produces bad effects. This fallacy is also committed by those who attribute to eloquence all the ill effects it works when abused or to medicine all the faults of ignorant doctors. (p. 259)

What is referred to here seems, at least partly, to be the *argumentum ad consequentiam,* or argument from consequences, a species of subpart of practical reasoning that argues from the goodness (or badness) of its consequences to the goodness (or badness) of a proposed course of action. This type of argument can be correct, though it is defeasible in nature. If a proposed action has bad consequences, for example, then, other things being equal, that is an argument against the action. However, the same type of argument can also be used wrongly, for example, in a case where good consequences that outweigh the bad are ignored or suppressed as relevant considerations.[18] You can see, however, that *secundum quid* is partly involved in such cases, where there has been a neglect of qualifications concerning consequences.

The account gets even more disorienting when it seems to confuse the fallacy of accident with what is usually called the *post hoc* fallacy: "Again we fall into this incorrect reasoning [accident] when we take as a genuine cause what is simply an occasion or circumstance."

It is no doubt true that the *secundum quid* fallacy of ignoring qualifications is connected to argumentation from consequences, and also to causal argumentation, in important ways. Nevertheless it is very confusing to mix examples in together that seem primarily to commit errors that are related to these other two distinct types of argumentation, and call them cases of the "fallacy of accident." Given that the history of the subject had degenerated into this deep muddle, it is small wonder that the modern textbooks, which often do adhere in a doctrinaire way to tradition, often do not make much sense in their treatment of hasty generalization, accident, *secundum quid,* and related fallacies.

One exception to the rule was a widely used textbook (Joseph, 1916) that gave a very clear, basically Aristotelian account of the fallacy of *secundum quid,* clearly distinguishing it from accident, and treated accident as a separate fallacy. Putting the question of accident aside, at least this one text went against the trend and preserved the basic thrust of Aristotle's original account of the fallacy of *secundum quid.* However, it was no use. Subsequent texts kept propounding the old, traditional treatment to new generations of students.

The only effective way to combat these entrenched traditions is to provide a clear analysis that really explains the error of *secundum quid* as a faulty kind of inference drawn from a confusing or transposing of two types of generalizations, universal and defeasible. But this task presupposes the prior task of explaining how presumptive generalizations function dynamically within presumptive reasoning.

---

[18] See Windes and Hastings (1965) and also the general account of practical reasoning in Walton (1990, *Pract. Reas.*).

NONMONOTONIC REASONING AGAIN

Deductive logic is monotonic in the sense defined in chapter two, meaning that if you add a new premise to a deductively valid argument, the argument remains valid. Researchers in artificial intelligence have recently begun to pay a good deal of attention to nonmonotonic reasoning, because of their interest in practical reasoning (e.g., robotics), where a machine has to carry out practical, everyday tasks involving variable circumstances. Typically, practical reasoning is dynamic, as we saw in chapter one, meaning that new circumstances alter a case, and once the agent (knowledge base) is provided with the new information describing these circumstances, it may be "logical" for the agent to infer a new conclusion, instead of the old one, concerning the reasonable course of action in the circumstances.

A problem with many generalizations expressed in everyday conversations is that they are expressed in a *generic* fashion without an explicit quantifier being stated, like "all," "some," "many," and so forth. The standard example is the statement "Birds fly." This statement is clearly meant to be a generalization, but it may depend on the context whether it should be taken to mean "All birds fly," "Some birds fly," or "Typically, birds fly." Normally, it would be understood to be meant in the third way, because we all know, and presume others know, that there are some birds that do not fly.

As Beardsley (1950) pointed out, the use of abstract terms in common speech systematically obscures how limited a generalization is meant to be.

> . . . we sometimes speak of "capitalism," when we are unwilling to make up our minds whether we mean *all* capitalists or *most* capitalists. We write, "Science says . . . ," instead of "*Scientists* say . . . ." (How many? Who? Which scientists?); "Religion," instead of "people who belong to religious organizations"; "The Government," instead of "persons in the government," and so on with many other convenient, but sometimes confusing, terms. (p. 415-416)

Beardsley added that these convenient ways of speaking are "necessary tools of thought" and we should not always mistrust them. But it is easy to be confused by them, or to abuse them, by covertly inflating a generalization without realizing it, or by being the victim of an inadequately supported generalization in argumentation. You should only rely on them tentatively, keeping an open mind to new evidence.

The classical case of nonmonotonic reasoning typically cited as an example (called the "canonical example") is the following inference (Case 2.2).

Case 2.2:   Birds fly.
Tweety is a bird.
Therefore, Tweety flies.

Now suppose that Tweety is a penguin. It seems that both premises are true, but the conclusion is false. But that is impossible if the inference is deductively valid.

To solve this problem, we interpreted the major premise as a *default (defeasible)* proposition, meaning (as defined in chapter 2) a proposition that can still be true (or at least hold plausibly), subject to legitimate exceptions that can exist without (necessarily) refuting it. Thus, according to Reiter, the major premise is best interpreted as a plausible reasoning pattern of a kind that is inherently open to exceptions. It is represented (Reiter, 1987) by patterns like "Normally birds fly," "Typically, birds fly," or "If x is a bird, then assume by default that x flies." Such a proposition is defeasible, meaning that if, in a particular case, Tweety is a penguin, or an ostrich, or a bird with a broken wing, etc., then the defeasible proposition can still hold, in general.

In nonmonotonic reasoning then, a conclusion is subject to default if, in a particular case, new information comes in that makes it clear that the case is exceptional. Thus, suppose the train of reasoning in the inference just above has been carried out, but then a new premise is added.

> Tweety is a penguin.

And suppose that, as additional information, we know that a penguin is a type of bird that definitely does not fly. We have to conclude that the first inference is now subject to cancellation (default), and that the new conclusion to be derived is the opposite of the original one.

> Therefore, Tweety does not fly.

But the whole train of reasoning was not simply contradictory or "illogical" *per se*. It represented an advance of new knowledge about the particular circumstances of a case, that made us modify our findings. Once we learned that Tweety, in this case, was an exceptional type of bird with respect to flying–a kind of bird that did not fit the normal or typical pattern in this respect–we took back or defaulted the original conclusion.

We can understand how nonmonotonic reasoning is properly used in argumentation by seeing that it is a species of presumptive reasoning that can be correctly used to shift a burden of proof in dialogue. In a type of dialogue where the goal is to prove something, there is a requirement or standard of the weight of proof called the *burden of proof*, meaning that a participant in the dialogue has an obligation to prove an argument of a particular strength or weight, in order to fulfill the goal. The burden of proof is defined globally, in any given context of dialogue, as part of what defines the goal for that type of dialogue. But burden of proof is also defined locally, at the level of a given speech act in a dialogue. For example, if a participant in a critical discussion makes an assertion, then he or she is normally obliged to prove that assertion, if challenged by the other party. The speech act of assertion normally incurs a burden of proof to back up or prove that proposition, according to the global standard of proof required for that type of dialogue.

The speech act of presumption reverses the normal burden of proof arrangement for assertion in dialogue, as shown in the analysis in chapter two. A presumption is brought forward by its proponent in a dialogue as a commitment that is supposed to be acceptable, in the absence of evidence to the contrary. Presumptions can be justified on procedural or practical grounds, even though the evidence is insufficient to support a proposition's acceptance. But the kind of acceptance or commitment appropriate for a presumption is tentative and provisional.

For example, by law, it is normally required that death be proved before inheritance can take place. But if a person is missing for a designated period–seven years, in some jurisdictions–then it may be presumed, for purposes of setting claims on the estate–that the person is dead. However, such a presumption is defeasible. If definite knowledge comes in that proves that the person in question is alive, then the presumption of death is rebutted.

Presumptive reasoning, as shown in chapter four, is closely related to a type of argument called the *argumentum ad ignorantiam* (argument from ignorance), traditionally held to be a fallacy. However, arguments from ignorance are not always fallacious. In many cases, absence of knowledge to prove a proposition constitutes good presumptive grounds for tentatively accepting that proposition as a commitment (subject to default should new information into the dialogue that reverses the conclusion drawn earlier). Presumptive reasoning enables practical reasoning to go ahead in variable circumstances where knowledge is incomplete.

Researchers in Artificial Intelligence (AI) have put forward various technical solutions that attempt to formalize nonmonotonic reasoning. However, it would be a mistake to think that there could be some single formula or requirement that would solve the problem. The reason is that although some types of exceptions to default propositions can be defined in some cases, in general the new information in a case could be of a kind that was impossible to anticipate. For example, we might try to classify all the different kinds of nonflying birds, like penguins, ostriches, and so forth. But perhaps, in another case, Tweety might be a nonflier for some reason we couldn't have reasonably anticipated (e.g., he might have a broken wing).

How presumptive reasoning is used, correctly or incorrectly in a given case, depends on the context of dialogue, the speech act in which the inference was put forward in the dialogue, and on the type of argumentation scheme appropriate for that inference.[19] Whether a presumptive inference is correct or fallacious in a particular case therefore depends on the global burden of proof in a context of dialogue, and the proper assignment of roles to the participants with respect to meeting the obligations appropriate for that assignment. In some types of critical discussion, for example, the one party may have the burden of proof while the goal of the other may only be to ask critical questions. Fallacies can occur, in such a context, where there has been an error of reasoning or the use of a deceptive tactic of argumentation that conceals an illicit shift in the burden of proof.

What AI has discovered, then, is something philosophers should have known all along, and would have known, if they had not gotten so confused in passing along the subject-matter of the fallacies or sophistical refutations. Aristotle described the fallacy of *secundum quid* very well, even giving good and clear examples, and proving a useful practical test for applying his analysis to

---

[19] This analysis of presumptive reasoning has been put forward more fully in Walton (1992, *Plaus. Arg.*).

particular cases. Now AI has given us a push to recognize presumptive, defeasible arguments as based on a distinctive kind of reasoning of a nonmonotonic type, we should overcome our past deductivist-inductivist bias and blindness to the importance of presumptive reasoning in logic. Part of this reawakening should involve the recognition of the *secundum quid* as an important type of error or fallacy, worth study in its own right.

A MODEL TREATMENT

If Aristotle had the basic fallacy of *secundum quid* right then, how should the logic textbooks describe it? What they should do is separate it off from any treatment of related would-be fallacies like accident, converse accident, and so forth, and treat it under the heading of the *fallacy of ignoring qualifications (secundum quid)*. Whether accident and converse accident should be treated at all is a separate question, but at any rate, the kinds of metaphysical issues raised by attempting to treat the fallacy of accident should not be allowed to intrude on the treatment of *secundum quid* as a fallacy.

Joseph, in his textbook *An Introduction to Logic* (1916) took a very favorable approach, which began by recognizing the fallacy of accident has commonly been expounded in a confusing way that is ill defined, in a way that fails to distinguish it from the fallacy of *secundum quid* (p. 588). Joseph redefined the fallacy of *secundum quid* in a clear and simple way that is easily recognizable as a common type of error: "It consists in using a principle or proposition without regard to the circumstances which modify its applicability in the case or kind of case before us." The following case is given as an example.

Case 5.9:   Water boils at a temperature of 212° Fahrenheit; therefore boiling water will be hot enough to cook an egg hard in five minutes: but if we argue thus at an altitude of 5,000 feet, we shall be disappointed; for the height, through the difference in the pressure of the air, qualifies the truth of our general principle. (p. 589)

The problem in this case is one of neglect of qualifications in dealing with an exceptional situation, in relation to a general principle that holds in normal situations (standard conditions).

It is interesting to note that Joseph stressed the practical nature of the principle stating that water boils at 212° F, adding that "boiling water will be hot enough to cook an egg in five minutes." This principle is defined for the kind of standard conditions one would normally be expected to encounter in practical activities in daily life. But in an unusual set of circumstances, (e.g., at a higher altitude than one might normally expect), it fails.

The fallacy of *secundum quid,* so conceived, is the failure to recognize the nonabsolute character of the principle in admitting of exceptional cases. This type of failure could be represented by the following kind of inference.

Water, in standard conditions, boils at 212°F.
This water, at 5,000 feet above sea level, is at a temperature of 212° F.
Therefore, this water is boiling.

The fallacy of *secundum quid* is committed by the arguer who looks at or treats the previous inference as though it were on a par with the following type of deductively valid inference.

All persons are mortal.
Socrates is a person.
Therefore, Socrates is mortal.

This inference is deductively valid, meaning that it is logically impossible for the premises to be true and the conclusion false. In sharp contrast, the previous inference (concerning water) fails to have this property. In a particular case, it is logically possible that the premises are true and the conclusion is false. Indeed, the special situation where the water is at 5,000 feet above sea level, is just such a case in point. Here, the premises may be true while the conclusion of the inference is false.

Joseph's (1916) general description of the fallacy of *secundum quid* is also very clear in identifying a readily recognizable type of common error of reasoning, and is worth quoting in full.

> A proposition may be stated *simpliciter,* or without qualification, either because the conditions which restrict its truth are unknown, or because, though known, they are thought seldom to arise, and so are neglected; and we may proceed to apply it where, had it been qualified as the truth required, it would be seen to be inapplicable. Perhaps it holds good normally, or in any circumstances contemplated by the speaker; the unfair confutation lies in taking advance of his statement to bring under it a case which, had he thought of it, would have led him to qualify the statement at the outset. But it is not only in disputation that the fallacy occurs. We are all of us at times guilty of it; we argue from principles that hold good normally, without even settling what conditions constitute the normal, or satisfying ourselves that they are present in the case about which we are arguing. (p. 589)

Again, Joseph's way of describing the fallacy is very nice, because you can see exactly what the error is. It has to do with two ways of stating a proposition, or putting a proposition forward in argumentation. You can state it *simpliciter,* presumably like the proposition "All men are mortal." was meant to be put forward in the previous inference. It was, at least presumably, put forward without qualification, as a universal generalization that admits of no exceptions. One contrary case makes it false. In another type of case, you can state a proposition in a qualified way. It holds in normal circumstances, but not *every* contrary instance refutes or falsifies it. If the counter-example can be shown to be an exceptional case, then the principle can still stand. What is meant by "stand" here, however, is holding in normal or standard conditions, subject to exceptions.

In formal logic, like syllogisms, we are used to dealing with universal gener-alizations that are meant to be *unlimited,* in the sense that they are immediately proved false by a single counter-instance. However, in practical reasoning in everyday conversation, very few generalizations are meant to be taken as unlim-ited. As Beardsley (1950) noted: ". . . outside the exact sciences, there are rela-tively few statements beginning with 'All' or 'No' that are true." Exceptions noted by Beardsley are statements that are true by definition, and very restricted univer-sal statements like, "All the people in this room have dark hair." Generally, ordinary speech is full of sweeping statements that are understood by speaker and hearer not to be unlimited.

The fallacy of *secundum quid,* as Joseph describes it, is clearly recognizable as a common kind of error of reasoning, well worth including in the list of informal fallacies. Also, the account of it he gives appears to be very close, in general outline, to the kind of fallacy Aristotle described as *secundum quid* in *On Sophistical Refutations.* If this is right, then it would seem to be true indeed that the majority of writers of logic textbooks between Aristotle and Joseph (and after Joseph, as well) have well and truly made a mess of things.

In defense of the textbook authors, it should be said that they have been working under the disabling lack of any theory of presumptive reasoning, or even any recognition that this is a distinctive type of reasoning in its own right, differ-ent from deductive and inductive reasoning as a type of argumentation. In fact, presumptive reasoning is vitally important to understanding the logic of most of the major informal fallacies traditionally included in the logic textbooks.

The problem then is not the fault of the individual textbook writers, who have often done surprisingly well, but the lack of an underlying theory to guide their efforts. However, the lack of theory can also, at least partly, be explained by the historical bias against taking any kind of opinion-based reasoning seriously in logic, ever since the condemnation of the sophists as having no regard for the truth precisely because they advocated that opinion-based presumptive reasoning is a legitimate kind of argumentation.

DYNAMIC REASONING

In many cases, the type of reasoning associated with informal fallacies is a pre-sumptive kind of reasoning that is not inherently wrong or fallacious *per se,* but is inherently defeasible, and subject to correction. This type of reasoning is inher-ently open-ended and tentative in nature. One of the main problems with it is that it is often taken in an absolutistic or dogmatic way. And that goes against its basic nature as being inherently nonmonotonic. With this kind of reasoning, an arguer should always keep an open mind, and be ready to concede that his or her argument is subject to correction or qualification, should new evidence or counter-indications enter the dialogue.

Such is also the case generally with practical reasoning, because the circum-stances of a particular case tend to be subject to changes in this kind of reasoning. Practical reasoning moves forward until it confronts a situation where it can go ahead no further. There is lack of knowledge to resolve the problem. So now, the reasoning must proceed *ad ignorantiam*. What does it do? It begins to operate on the basis of presumptive reasoning. Perhaps, for example, it can consult a source of knowledge to get an expert opinion. Here the *ad verecundiam* type of argument comes in. Experts make mistakes. Reasoning from the "say so" of an expert is inherently fallible as a type of argumentation. Still, given the right conditions, acting on the advice of an expert could be quite reasonable and nonfallacious.

You can think of practical reasoning as having a subject, an agent or system that contains a set of commitments. During the sequence of dynamic reasoning, the system brings in new information and goals which add propositions to its commitment set. In other instances, it retracts commitments, for example when it finds evidence that refutes one of its previous commitments.

Or another choice would be for the system to proceed to act, and by trial and error, collect new information that would be useful. Seeing the consequences of the various attempts it has made, the system can perhaps learn some new, useful information by feedback, and thereby correct and improve its attempts to steer a course toward its goal. This way of proceeding may involve circular reasoning. Presumptions are acted upon, and if they work in practice, they are given an additional weight of presumption. This process is, if not circular, a spiral path of increased sophistication of the reasoning of the system.

Often, this process of groping and improvement of reasoning must act on presumptions derived from customary ways of acting, and other presumptions based on propositions that are generally accepted, but cannot be proved. This is the *argumentum ad populum*.

Typically, the reasoning takes the form of *argumentum ad consequentiam*. As the system sees or predicts consequences of its actions that would likely lead toward its goals, it labels these consequences good or favorable, and tries to bring them about if possible. Similarly, if the system recognizes or thinks that certain consequences will abort or prevent its goals, it labels these consequences bad, and tries to avoid them. Using this kind of consequential reasoning, the system argues with itself to the effect, "This is likely to be a good consequence. Carry it out!" Or "This is likely to be a bad consequence. Try to avoid it!" The system here is using the argumentation schemes for argument from consequences (see chapter 6).

Another common type of argumentation is the slippery slope. The system tries to look ahead, and see, if possible, the long term consequences of its projected actions. If it sees that taking one step would lead to another, and so forth, and the whole chain would lead to a disastrous outcome, the system will warn itself against taking such a first step.[20]

The system is typically moving ahead on the basis of heuristic rules of thumb and presumptions that cannot be conclusively verified. They may turn out to be false or inapplicable in the given circumstances confronted by the system, as its knowledge of those circumstances develops. Hence, the system moves ahead on the basis of nonmonotonic reasoning that will encounter defaults and exceptions. This is where the *secundum quid* fallacy comes in, because the system must always be alert and open to the possibility of default, as it reasons along. The system must beware of depending too heavily, or dogmatically on the rules

---

[20] This fallacy is analyzed in Walton (1992, *Slip. Slope*).

of thumb it must operate on. The system must remain flexible, and be ready to retract commitments, where new evidence comes in to justify correction or default.

Reasoning of this kind must generally be open to new evidence that may come in, in the future, and it cannot be anticipated exactly which way this evidence will tend to go. Hence, it is a failure of the system if it becomes closed to the admitting of new evidence, as the sequence of reasoning goes along. If the system becomes too rigid or closed in this fashion, the reasoning becomes dogmatic. That is, it becomes stuck or fixed, and is unable to cope with argumentation properly.

On the other hand, it is an opposite kind of problem if it becomes too flexible, and continually evades commitment by hedging, maintaining that each set of individual circumstances is unique, and so forth. This kind of attitude is reflected in the kind of approach that always avoids reaching any definite conclusion in reasoning on the grounds that such a course would be "authoritarian" or "arbitrary." This is the opposite fault of dogmatism. This point of view holds that every argument is just as good as any other argument. Often espoused on grounds of toleration, freedom, and right to one's own opinion, this attitude maintains that my argument is equally valid, no matter how good your argument against it is. Dynamic reasoning must steer a middle course between these two extremes or failures, if it is to be any good. It must be prepared to recognize that an argument is good in certain respects, while leaving open the possibility that this argument may later turn out to be bad in other respects.

Dogmatism is an attitude, not a kind of tactic of argumentation, but the closing off of argumentation that is characteristic of dogmatism is also associated with how many of the fallacies work as sophistical tactics. The dogmatic arguer tends to treat argumentation as a quarrel, where the goal is to defeat the other party by pushing for the one side with too strong and rigid a commitment.

Just looking at the one-liner examples so often used by the textbooks, it is not apparent how anyone is ever fooled by the fallacy of hasty generalization. If hasty generalizations are so widespread as a species of fallacy in everyday reasoning, how is it that people are persuaded to accept them? Some insight into this question is yielded by a case presented by Beardsley (1950). In this emotionally charged argument, one can perceive a kind of progression or escalation of a dogmatic attitude from "some" to "all" woven into the discourse.

Case 5.10:   I was outraged when I read in your letter column a plea for higher pay, signed by three grade-school teachers. When I think of the devotion to duty which we mothers have a right to expect from those to whom we entrust our children, it seems to me a shocking thing to find that some of them are so mercenary. We housewives do not complain about our lot; but if many of the teachers are apparently interested more in their pay than in their work, then it is time we did something about it. I always believed that most teachers thought of their work as a service, and enjoyed doing it, but now it seems that

> most of them are dissatisfied because they don't have enough
> money to spend–and look at the long vacation they get, too!
> Teachers are certainly ungrateful–next thing we know, the
> teaching profession will be screaming for a union! (p. 415)

As Beardsley noted, the generalization in this passage proceeds from "three" to "some" to "many" to "most" to "teachers" in the sense of "all teachers." This progressive exaggeration towards absolutistic argumentation is disguised, or made easier to overlook, by the *ad hominem* argumentation in the passage, and by the emotional and quarrelsome nature of the dialogue generally. The hasty generalization is made easier to swallow, and harder to detect, by its being woven into the fabric of extended discourse.

The argumentation in Case 5.10 is not only a pyramidal buildup, a gradual-istic argument that goes to stronger and stronger generalizations. It is also an emotional progression that splits a controversy sharply into two sides. House-wives are portrayed as "good guys," and increasingly, teachers are vilified, portrayed as "bad guys." Progressively, an *ad hominem* attack is built up against the teachers. Teachers are "mercenary"–"more interested in their pay than in their work." They are "ungrateful" and soon they will be "screaming" for a union.

The writer of this discourse makes it clear that she has a conflict of opinions with the point of view expressed in a previous column. This leads us to expect a critical discussion, with argumentation given in favor of this writer's (opposed) point of view. However, as the argumentation in Case 5.10 proceeds, we see it shifting toward an outright quarrel, as the teachers are attacked personally through escalating *ad hominem* argumentation.

This shift, and the progressive nature of the emotional buildup of the quarrel in Case 5.10 serve to conceal the hasty generalization, and to make it more acceptable to the reader who is caught up by the emotional appeal. The claims get more and more extreme toward the end. And such claims would perhaps not be very plausible in themselves, if stated by themselves. But, for the emotionally committed reader who is brought to be sympathetic with the point of view of the author, in context, they somehow seem to be more persuasive or acceptable.

Many of the traditional fallacies are tactics that block legitimate goals of dialogue because they involve legitimate kinds of argumentation that are pressed ahead too aggressively in a context of dialogue, allowing a respondent insufficient room to ask legitimate critical questions or pose objections. The *ad verecundiam* is again a good example. The tactic used here is to invalidate the respondent's objections to your argument which has been based on expert opinion, by sug-gesting that whatever the respondent says, it can have no weight at all against the opinion of the experts in the field in question. The suggestion is that the respon-dent really has no right to speak out on such a question. For, as a nonexpert, the respondent has no access to the evidence at all. So if he or she does speak out, it merely shows impudence and bad judgment. The tactic here involves a kind of poisoning the well effect which is also evident in other traditional fallacies like the *ad hominem*. With the *ad hominem*, there is generally a kind of disqualifying suggestion present that the person attacked is not a sincere contributor to the dialogue, and that therefore the arguments can be discounted or even ignored, in advance of whatever they happen to be.

In the past, dynamic reasoning has not been well understood or accepted as a kind of reasoning that can be legitimately or correctly used in good arguments. Any kind of reasoning that was not recognizable as either deductive or inductive was regarded as being generally fallacious. There was a kind of mistrust of any presumption-based reasoning on the grounds that you can never absolutely rely on it to prevent reasoning from true premises to a false conclusion. After all, you might turn out to be wrong, and if your standard of rigor is high, then such "subjective" argumentation would not really be solid proof of your conclusion.

We must come to recognize however that this fallible and tentative aspect of presumptive reasoning is simply part of its nonmonotonic nature. It should be seen as a special kind of reasoning in its own right that can be used rightly to fulfill a burden of proof in the right context of dialogue on a practical basis. It should give way to more conclusive, deductive, or inductive proofs where these are available. But it still should be regarded as a useful kind of argumentation that is, in many cases, correct within its limitations, when harder evidence that would solve or eliminate a practical problem is not available.

Underlying the study of *secundum quid* as a fallacy, there is a general, theoretical issue for logic involving relativism. Once we recognize presumptive reasoning based on generalizations subject to exceptions, based on the way things can normally be expected to go in a typical situation, aren't we really opening the door to subjective reasoning as a legitimate type of argumentation? Isn't this really a kind of relativism which loosens the rigor of logic? Here we come back to the ancient controversy surrounding the condemnation of the sophists.

PROTAGOREAN RELATIVISM

What did Protagoras of Abdera mean by his famous saying, "Man is the measure of all things, of things that are that [or "how"] they are and of things that are not that [or "how"] they are not." Plato, in the *Theaetetus* interpreted this saying by offering the following example: When the same wind appears cold to one person, and warm to another person, then that wind is cold to the person to whom it seems cold, and warm to the person to whom it seems warm. The example gets the idea across of some kind of relativism, but what really follows?

Was Protagoras saying that when when two people have a conflict of opinions, it does not follow that what the one said is true, while what the other said is false? According to Kerferd (1967), that is exactly the inference we can draw from Plato's example of the doctrine of Protagoras: "It follows that all perceptions are true and the ordinary view is mistaken, according to which, in cases of conflict, one person is right and the other person is wrong about the quality of the wind or anything else." Because very little of Protagoras' written work has survived, it is hard to confirm such conjectures fully, but Kerferd thought that this inference can be taken to represent the position held by Protagoras.

Typically, the saying of Protagoras has been taken as expressing a form of relativism that is so radical that it is open to self-refutation by the "turning of the tables" *(peritrope)* argument: If the doctrine of Protagoras were true, then those who hold that it is false are holding the truth. In other words, the doctrine of Protagoras refutes itself because, according to this very doctrine, the proposition "The doctrine of Protagoras is false," cannot be said to be false. The problem seems to be that the Protagorean doctrine cannot successfully defend itself against any attacks that deny it is true.

Plato pointed out in the *Theaetetus* that surely if Protagoras could "pop his head up through the ground," he would have an answer to this problem. Whatever Protagoras might say, there is a way to meet the turning of the tables argument by interpreting his doctrine in a particular way. Perhaps what the saying could mean is that whenever there is a genuine conflict of opinions, it is not appropriate to say that the one opinion is true and the other false, but it could be appropriate to say that the one opinion is better than the other.

But what does it mean to say that one opinion is "better than" another? On this question, Protagoras did have definite views, according to Kerferd (1967):

> In the case of conflict about perceived qualities all perceptions are true. But some perceptions are better than others, for example, the perceptions normally found in a healthy man as distinct from those found in a man who is ill. It is the function of a doctor, Protagoras held, to change a man who is ill so that his perceptions become those of a man who is well. Likewise, in moral, political, and aesthetic conflicts it is the function of the Sophist as a teacher to work a change so that better views about what is "just" and "beautiful" will seem true to the "patient"–better, that is, than those which previously seemed true to him. All the "patient's" views are equally true, but some are better than others. (p. 506)

Kerferd added that better views, according to Protagoras, are not just views that seem better, but views that really are better, because they have better consequences.

Perhaps then, what the doctrine of Protagoras means is that in a genuine conflict of opinions, when there is room for argument on both sides, you may not be able to conclusively show that the conclusion of the one side is true and the conclusion on the other side false, but in many cases you may be able to show that the argument on the one side is "better" or "stronger" than the argument on the other side. If so, this finding may be perfectly good grounds for committing yourself to the conclusion of the argument that is stronger, at least provisionally (subject to correction).

The problem that remains, however, is that commitment of this type is always tentative and provisional, because by its nature, we cannot be sure that, at some point in the future, the argument that was formerly the weaker has now become the stronger. The better view is the one that has better consequences up to this point. But in the future, there could be further consequences of both views that would make the other view "better."

This way of interpreting the Protagorean point of view is not going to satisfy all the would-be table-turners then. They are still going to feel that we cannot really accept the man-measure doctrine as true, because we can't be sure of it–it could still turn out to be false. The Protagorean point of view is only successful to the extent that it can reassure those doubts by saying that generally, with conflicts of opinion, it is a matter of weighing the stronger argument against the weaker, and then committing to the opinion that is the conclusion of the stronger argument. Judged by its own standard, the man-measure doctrine would seem to be a practical, heuristic principle which we cannot be sure is true, but which nevertheless can be justified on grounds of its good consequences.

Because of the lack of definitive guidance from the small corpus of sayings or extant writings attributable to Protagoras, it is possible to interpret Protagorean relativism in a stricter, or stronger way, and also in a looser, or milder way.

Strict Protagorean Relativism: For every conflict of opinions, it is not possible to prove (conclusively) that the one opinion is true and the other false.

Mild Protagorean Relativism: For some conflicts of opinions, it is not possible to prove (conclusively) that the one opinion is true and the other false.

The mild relativism seems much more harmless and less controversial, but it is still a significant kind of relativism. According to mild relativism, there are different contexts of dialogue, or conversational frameworks in which arguments are proved, refuted, supported, and so forth. If a conflict of opinion occurs, say, in a political debate, then it is not possible to prove that the opinion on the one side is true, or that the opinion on the other side is false. In this context of dialogue, the conflict of opinions is about two different points of view. One could be better supported by argumentation in that context. Yet it does not follow that we should say that this opinion is "true" or has been "shown to be true." Like the warm and cold wind conflict of opinion, the difference is one of points of view.

But the mild relativism is compatible with the contention that in other contexts of dialogue, for example, in a scientific inquiry, it is possible to prove that one opinion or conjecture is true whereas its opposite is false. This type of conflict of opinions can be resolved by a conclusive proof or disproof of one of the contentions. For example, such a conflict might concern the pair of propositions "The earth is round" *versus* "The earth is flat" or "Two is a prime number" *versus* "Two is not a prime number." Here it is not a question of which of the pair is better, "healthier," or more plausible as a point of view. One of the pair is demonstrably false, and there is no need to weigh relative strengths of argumentation on both sides in a more relativistic way.

The context of dialogue is crucial in setting a reasonable burden of proof to be fairly used to evaluate arguments using, or concluding in generalizations. For example, in a scientific inquiry, standards may be quite high, and any generalization not proven in a statistically well-researched fashion may be held to be highly suspect. By contrast, in dealing with everyday practical problems on the basis of familiar experience, anecdotal evidence could be good enough to meet a burden of proof, and generalizations that are much more rough-and-ready could be allowed.

As Beardsley (1950) pointed out, however, often science has a way of improving on and even supplementing practical wisdom.

> This is why, as thinking becomes scientific, it tends to demand larger numbers of instances before generalizing; and even so, the generalization is very tentative. And that is why so many common-sense generalizations are continually being overturned by more patient and persistent research. Such generalizations may concern the most familiar objects of everyday experience, yet everyday experience is haphazard and limited. "Everyone knows" how to bring up children and what to do for a cold. But popular convictions about children, medicine, and food are full of "old wives' tales" that are based on a little fragmentary evidence but that won't stand up under a searching examination. Hence the careful inquirer is constantly discovering that "what everyone knows" is in fact not true. (p. 414)

Plausible generalizations are often pre-scientific guides to action based on custom, precedent, or practical wisdom. They may be far from perfect, but still they may have enough practical value as working presumptions to make them a useful, if tentative basis as guides to action. In a critical discussion, presumptive generalizations can have enough of a basis to serve as premises.

According to mild relativism, there are different contexts in which arguments occur. In an inquiry, you may be able to definitively prove that a particular proposition is true, or alternatively show that it cannot be proved. In a critical discussion on a controversial issue, you, quite rightly, do not expect to meet that kind of standard. It is enough, for practical purposes, to show that the one opinion is better supported by argument than the other.

The mild form of relativism is quite compatible with the thesis that the most significant conflicts of opinion that matter in one's life are generally of the second type. So it is a significant type of relativism with some "bite." Moreover, by postulating different contexts for argumentation, it is really quite a deep kind of relativism, and far from being trivial.

It needs to be recognized then that the move toward informal logic, from a formalistic, deductivist conception of logic, does involve a shift toward a relativistic conception of the concept of a reasonable argument. But the question is what form of relativism is involved. And is it a kind of relativism that logic can live with, as an objective, scientific discipline. These questions are brought very much to the forefront by our consideration of the *secundum quid* fallacy as a type of error of dynamic reasoning that can be identified, analyzed, and evaluated objectively in particular cases.

CONCLUSIONS

Analyzing *secundum quid* is a nontrivial problem, because dynamic reasoning, although it is associated with many informal fallacies, can be used correctly in some cases. However, Aristotle's practical test for evaluating specific cases was already the basis of a good solution, because he advocated looking at each individual case on its merits, starting with the conclusion, to see whether the inference that was drawn is of the kind that requires the taking of exceptions and qualifications into account or not.

The analysis of this Aristotelian fallacy presented earlier is pragmatic in nature, because the context of dialogue has to be used in judging whether a strict (universal) or qualified (defeasible) generalization is appropriate in a given case where an argument has been put forward. Drawing a conclusion by inference from either a strict or a qualified generalization can be a reasonable kind of argument. But the fallacious kind of case occurs where the proponent of the argument draws out the conclusion presenting the argument as though it were a strict (deductive) inference based on deductive reasoning, whereas in reality, in the given case a defeasible (qualified) interpretation of the generalization in the major premise is appropriate.

But what about inductive generalizations? They fall in between absolute (universal) generalizations and presumptive (defeasible) generalizations. It could also be the same type of fallacy, or a similar one, to jump from a universal to an inductive generalization, or from an inductive generalization to a presumptive one. Or perhaps these could be two different fallacies.

In this chapter, we have not attempted to give an analysis of inductive generalizations, or to study in detail the associated fallacies and problems of using this type of generalization in argumentation. However, it does seem reasonable that they should be included, as well, under the fallacy classification of hasty generalization.

The fallacy of hasty generalization needs to be understood not simply as a flaw or error in one type of reasoning, but as a kind of scalar fallacy where reasoning is pushed forward from one of five levels to another.

1. **Argument from Example:** "This [one] F is a G." Here, one case is cited as an example or illustration of something that shares both properties F and G.

2. **Particular Claim:** "Some F are G." This type of claim is not really a generalization (or much of one), because one instance is enough to verify it.

3. **Plausible (Defeasible) Generalization:** "Typically, F are G." This type of claim is defeasible. It says that normally you can expect F to be G in a typical case, but an F may fail to be a G in an exceptional case.

4. **Inductive Generalization:** "Most [many] F's are G's." This type of claim is based on data that is collectible and/or countable. "How many?" is a very important consideration. Where a specific number (normally expressed as a fraction between 0 and 1) is given, the claim is called a statistical generalization.

5. **Universal Generalization:** "All F are G." This type of claim is falsified by any (even a single) counter-instance–any case of something that is an F but not a G.

As we go up the scale here from level 1 to level 5, the type of reasoning becomes stronger and stronger–more "absolute" as the generalization becomes more demanding to prove, and less tentative. As we go up the scale, larger numbers of instances are required in order to sustain the claim. And smaller numbers of instances serve to overturn or refute the claim.

The most common types of errors cited by the logic textbooks, however, concern the shifting back and forth among levels 3, 4, and 5. It is primarily at these levels where the cases occur that come under the categories of hasty generalization and *secundum quid*.

There are three kinds of errors or faulty types of inference involved, represented in Fig. 5.1 by the three arrows (arcs).

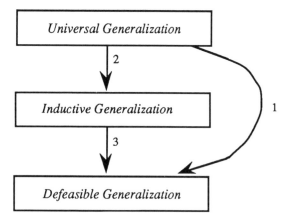

FIG. 5.1. Three types of Hasty Generalization Errors.

Error 1 is the fallacy of ignoring qualifications to a defeasible generalization *(secundum quid)* of the type that has been the primary target of analysis in this chapter. As a general term to cover all three kinds of errors, *hasty generalization* would suit very well. Error 3, of going from an inductive to a defeasible generalization, could perhaps best be treated as a special type of case, or subfallacy of the general fallacy of ignoring qualifications. Perhaps it could be called the *inductive variant* of the *secundum quid* fallacy. Finally, Error 2, which does not relate to defeasible reasoning at all, is best treated as the distinctively inductive subspecies of the fallacy of hasty generalization. Perhaps it could be called *hasty inductive generalization*.

The two most common types of fallacies of hasty inductive generalization cited in the textbooks are called criticisms in Walton (1989, *Inf. Log.*) because, in many cases, and even typically, they are not (in practice) such bad faults that they deserve to be labelled generally as fallacies. The criticism of *insufficient statistics*

(Walton, 1989, *Inf. Log.*) is appropriate when a sample selected is so small that the generalization based on it is worthless as a conclusion. The criticism of *biased statistics* is appropriate in cases where the distribution of the property in the generalization does not properly match the distribution of the property in the sample (Walton, 1989, *Inf. Log.*). In extreme cases, where the failure is systematic or persistent, and not just a slip, these two kinds of errors in arguing to or from an inductive generalization can be classified as fallacies. At any rate, it may be appropriate to classify them as subspecies of the fallacy of hasty inductive generalization, and that is the proposal we will suggest. Then we would have the system of classification in Fig. 5.2.

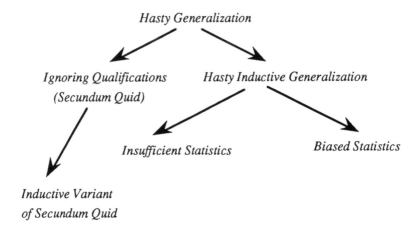

FIG. 5.2. Subspecies of Hasty Generalization.

Should we call the *secundum quid* type of error the fallacy of *neglecting qualifications,* the fallacy of *ignoring qualifications,* or the fallacy of *ignoring exceptions*? In some cases, the fallacy seems more like a sophistical tactic of argumentation than merely an error of reasoning. Perhaps, in such cases, it could even be called the fallacy of *suppressing qualifications.* To choose a middle way between the weaker "neglecting" and the stronger "suppressing," the more neutral term "ignoring" is not bad. Let us therefore use as the standard terminology, the *fallacy of ignoring qualifications* (in Latin, *secundum quid,* in Greek, *para to pe*).

According to this proposed terminology and system of classification, the fallacy of accident is to be treated as a separate kind of fallacy that has no place in this system of analysis of hasty generalization and its subfallacies. While not trying to analyze the so-called fallacy of accident, a job best left for another occasion, we do conclude that it is questionable, and remains to be shown, whether accident is a major informal fallacy that ought to be covered by (at least intro-ductory) texts on informal logic. The kinds of cases presented by Aristotle as examples of the fallacy of accident do appear to be genuinely philosophically and logically interesting. But they look more like logical paradoxes or puzzles,[21] more of theoretical interest than of interest as representing common errors of reasoning or sophistical tactics that are important to detect and be on guard against in argumentation in everyday conversations.

Whether the kinds of inferences that Aristotle studied under the heading of the fallacy of accident are very important or not to include in the textbooks as com-mon and influential errors of reasoning remains to be seen. My initial suspicion is that they are like the case of the fallacy called *amphiboly*. It is included in a lot of the textbooks, but the examples given have never persuaded one that here is an error worth taking care to warn students of informal logic about as a common and tricky pitfall in argumentation. If accident and amphiboly should be taken seri-ously, then the burden of proof should be on those who would make a case for continuing to accord them prominence as fallacies to be featured in elementary logic textbooks.

By contrast, it is immediately apparent, even from the cases studied here, that *secundum quid,* the fallacy of ignoring qualifications, is a very common error in everyday argumentation that often leads to confusion, mischief, and significant instances of misleading and bad reasoning.

The big problem has been that the deductivist-inductivist bias in logic in the past has been associated with a general failure to even recognize dynamic pre-sumptive reasoning as a legitimate kind of argumentation in its own right. Small wonder then that faults and fallacies of ignoring qualifications have never been systematically presented in a useful way in the textbooks. The first step in coming to study how dynamic reasoning fails in some cases is to see how it can be used correctly in argumentation. But this requires looking at argument from a new point of view–a Protagorean relativism that accepts presumptive reasoning as legitimate generally in argumentation, subject, of course, to exceptions.

---

[21] Bueno (1988) supports this interpretation.

CHAPTER SIX

ARGUMENT FROM CONSEQUENCES

The *argumentum ad consequentiam* or argument from consequences may be broadly characterized as the argument for accepting the truth (or falsehood) of a proposition by citing the consequences of accepting (or rejecting) that proposition. However, the *argumentum ad consequentiam* is often more narrowly and negatively conceived as the argument for rejecting a proposition by citing undesirable (bad) consequences that might follow from its acceptance. Here "bad" primarily means undesirable for the proponent of the argument for acceptance of the proposition, although the consequences might be undesirable for others as well.

The *argumentum ad consequentiam* tends to be classified as a fallacy by those informal logic textbooks that include it.[1] However, other writings on argumentation have seen it as a reasonable (nonfallacious) type of argument.[2] Still other sources have treated it as sometimes fallacious and sometimes not.

A typical example of the use of the *argumentum ad consequentiam* is the following case.

Case 6.1:   Two politicians are arguing about the issue of whether a woman should have the right to an abortion. The pro-life politician argues against this proposition on the grounds that the fetus has a right to life. The pro-choice politician replies: "If you take that view, you will not be elected."

This reply can be held to be a fallacious *argumentum ad consequentiam* on the grounds this citing of negative consequences by the second arguer is really irrelevant to the question of whether the first arguer's argument (based on the alleged right to life of the fetus) is any good or not.

If the second politician's reply is interpreted as an argument designed to refute the point of view of the first politician, it does seem to be somehow irrelevant. It also has shades of the *argumentum ad baculum* (appeal to threat) and the

---

[1] *Argumentum ad consequentiam* would seem to be a modern addition to the list of fallacies. I have found no substantial references to this fallacy in historical textbooks or other writings on fallacies before its mention in twentieth-century sources. The most plausible exception is the account of a fallacy in DeMorgan (1847, pp. 276-277)–see later–but the fallacy referred to is a subfallacy as opposed to being the basic fallacy of *argumentum ad consequentiam*.

[2] Perelman and Olbrechts-Tyteca (1971, p. 266).

argumentum ad populum (appeal to popular sentiment) mixed in as part of the suspect or fallacious nature of the move.

But could the reply of the second politician be interpreted merely as a piece of practical advice–a kind of warning, rather than an attempt to refute the first politician's argument? If so, the *argumentum ad misericordiam* in this case might not be so clearly fallacious at all.

Moreover, the idea that considering consequences is always irrelevant to discussing the worth of a proposed policy or proposition of values seems to fly in the face of common sense and common practices. One view, utilitarianism, even has it that consequences are all-important in deciding moral issues.

Is *argumentum ad consequentiam* then really a fallacy or not? If this type of argument is only fallacious in some cases, or under certain conditions, what are those conditions? How can we verify that it is fallacious, if there are no good grounds for saying so? These unanswered questions pose serious and interesting problems.

THE CLAIM THAT IT IS FALLACIOUS

Rescher (1964) explained the fallacy of *argumentum ad consequentiam* by making a division between two factors–the truth of a conclusion, and the consequences that would be likely from accepting it. According to Rescher, "logically speaking," the second factor is irrelevant to the first. Therefore, arguing from the second factor to the first is a logical leap that is fallacious.

> In an *argumentum ad consequentiam* ("appeal to consequences") the premises deal only with the consequences that are likely to ensue from accepting the conclusion, and not with its truth. Logically speaking, it is entirely irrelevant that certain undesirable consequences might derive from the rejection of a thesis, or certain benefits accrue from its acceptance.[3]

This view of the *argumentum ad consequentiam* makes it a fallacy of irrelevance. Consequences are held to be always irrelevant to the logical acceptance of a conclusion as a thesis that is true or false. Here we have a sharp bifurcation between practical concerns with consequences and logical concerns with truth, as a basis for the analysis of the *ad consequentiam* fallacy.

Rescher (p. 82) offered two examples of this fallacy.[4]

Case 6.2:   Vegetarianism is an injurious and unhealthy practice. For if all people were vegetarians, the economy would be seriously affected, and many people would be thrown out of work.

---

[3] Rescher (1964, p. 82).

[4] Rescher may have changed his mind in his later writings (1985; 1988) on the balance between practical and theoretical reasoning in argument.

Case 6.3:   The United States had justice on its side in waging the Mexican war of 1848. To question this is unpatriotic, and would give comfort to our enemies by promoting the cause of defeatism. (p. 82)

These cases show clearly what Rescher is driving at. There could be some grounds for reservations, however, in accepting Rescher's thesis that *argumentum ad consequentiam* is always a fallacy. In Case 6.2, the premise that vegetarianism would affect the economy badly appears to be only weakly relevant to the conclusion that vegetarianism is an injurious and unhealthy practice, for two reasons. One reason is that the main consideration is how vegetarianism as a practice would directly affect the health of people, never mind its indirect effects on health through the economy. The other reason is that it is not a very plausible or strong argument that a shift to vegetarianism would have such a drastic and bad effect on the economy. Perhaps then, such a weak degree of relevance is what is referred to by classifying Case 6.2 as a fallacy of irrelevance.

But classifying Case 6.2 as an *ad consequentiam* fallacy on the grounds that undesirable consequences are "entirely irrelevant" is puzzling. For, given that the discussion is about whether vegetarianism is an "injurious and unhealthy practice," surely some consequences of vegetarianism could be highly relevant. Supposing it were to be argued that vegetarianism is likely to lead to unhealthy consequences because it can be shown that it leads to osteoporosis in many cases. This *argumentum ad consequentiam* does not seem to be fallacious, at least simply on the grounds that such "undesirable consequences" are "entirely irrelevant" to acceptance of the conclusion at issue. It is simply far too strong to say that the *argumentum ad consequentiam* is a fallacy because undesirable consequences or benefits are always irrelevant to the acceptance or rejection of a thesis.

Case 6.3 is more plausibly portrayed as a fallacious argument. It certainly seems like a bad argument, initially. The premise that questioning the American side in the Mexican War of 1848 would presently "give comfort to our enemies" seems highly implausible, and in no way relevant to the historical or moral issue of which country "had justice on its side" in that war.

But if we were to change the case by considering a case of a war we are currently engaged in, it might not be so easy to take it for granted that practical considerations of "giving comfort to the enemy" are altogether irrelevant to the discussion–see Case 6.10 later, for example. With Case 6.3 then, we have a problem if the consequences cited are "irrelevant": What does this mean, and how could we prove it? What it seems to mean is that the point about "giving comfort to our enemies" makes no real contribution to the critical discussion of the issue of who had the more just cause in the War of 1848. But what does "make no real contribution" mean here? The fallacy, so construed, seems to be an error of reasoning, a shift from one type of reasoning to another. The case began with a critical discussion of the issue of justice in the War of 1848 and then shifted, through the introduction of the *argumentum ad consequentiam* to consideration of practical consequences or effects of continuing with one side of the discussion. This shift seemed fallacious because to Rescher because concern with the truth of the conclusion at issue shifted to (an irrelevant) concern with the consequences of holding (or questioning) this conclusion.

Hackett Fischer (1970) described the fallacy of *argumentum ad consequentiam* as the "attempt to prove or disprove a reasoned argument by reference to the consequences which flow from its acceptance or rejection." Fischer's treatment of *argumentum ad consequentiam* presumes that this type of argument is a fallacy.

An example of the fallacy of *argumentum ad consequentiam* cited by Fischer (1970), concerned the argument of a 19th-century German historian Hermann von Holst, in his book, *The Constitutional and Political History of the United States.* In an argument quoted by Fischer, von Holst claimed that the policy of U. S. President James K. Polk was a good one because it led to the "advancement of civilization" in California.

Case 6.4:   In the hands of Mexico [he wrote] California was not only as good as lost to civilization, but it also lay exposed, a tempting prey, to all the naval and colonial powers of the world. . . . In whatever way the ethics of ordinary life must judge such cases, history must try them in the light of their results, and in so doing must allow a certain validity to the tabooed principle that the end sanctifies the means. Its highest law is the general interest of civilization, and in the efforts and struggle of nations for the preservation and advancement of general civilization, force not only in the defensive form, but also in the offensive, is a legitimate factor. (p. 301)

But Fisher saw this argument as a fallacy of *ad consequentiam*. Even granting von Holst's premise that "Mexico's loss was civilization's gain," does not follow "that a line of reasoning is valid or invalid because we happen to approve or disapprove of its consequences." Fischer's objection appears to be that this argument is being used by a "chauvinist" historian to support the American war with Mexico, a one-sided approach.

To support this interpretation, Fischer went on to cite a case where Polk's expansionism was supported by an *ad populum* combined with the *ad consequentiam* argument. In this case, a historian supported Polk's policy by claiming that it would be impossible to find an American citizen who would "desire to undo President Polk's diplomacy. . . ." What Fischer appears to be suggesting is that the *ad consequentiam* argument is unfairly biased and one-sided. It appeals to conservative Americans, but you can bet it would not be found to be such a persuasive argument with Mexican citizens.

What is implicit in this case is that Fischer's treatment of the argument presumes a context of dialogue where there could be a conflict of opinions and interests. What are favorable consequences from the point of view of a supporter of the American side may be viewed as unfavorable consequences from the point of view of someone who supports the Mexican side.

Fischer faults the argument in Case 6.4 on two grounds. First, he contended that the premise "Mexico's loss was civilization's gain" is a dubious assumption, "not likely to survive a cultural comparison of Los Angeles and Mexico City." Second, he contended that the conclusion based on this premise does not follow, because it depends on the fallacious presumption that "a quality which attaches to an effect is transferable to the cause." The fallacy here (quoted earlier) is the erroneous inference that a line of reasoning is valid because we approve of its practical consequences. Just because the incorporation of California into the U. S. had some good effects (arguably), it does not follow that the reasoning behind Polk's expansionist policy was sound, or can be justified on the grounds of its practical consequences.

What are we to say of this evaluation of Case 6.4? Can it be classified as an instance of the *ad consequentiam* fallacy for the reasons given by Fischer?

Fischer is right to note that the premise and also the inference based on it in Case 6.4 should be subject to doubt and further discussion. However, this interpretation presumes that the case is set in the context of a controversial discussion to which there are two sides. The premise is not only dubious, but also chauvinistic in representing the Mexican point of view in a prejudicial and objectionable way. Much depends on what you mean by "civilization" or "civilized," and the question is quite open to discussion and objections. Blocking off such a discussion would be fallacious.

Moreover, the argument in Case 6.4 is highly objectionable on moral grounds. In effect, it is an argument to justify the use of force in the name of the dubious principle that the end justifies the means. It is all right, according to this argument, for a bigger country to use force to preserve its civilization by taking an offensive against a smaller country. This argument cries out for condemnation.

However, it is one thing to say that this argument is morally objectionable, quite another thing to say that it commits a fallacy. The latter claim presumes that there is some inference or chain of reasoning in the argument that is erroneous.

But what about the inference? Is it so faulty that it should rightly be called a fallacy? For sure it is a weak and defeasible inference–subject to rebuttal and counter-argument. Even if we grant that Polk's expansionist policy had this one (supposedly) good effect, it remains quite possible that it had all kinds of bad effects as well, particularly from the Mexican point of view. Did the good effect outweigh the bad effects, or vice versa? The ultimate validation of the argument rests on this question.

Even so, the inference is not totally worthless, provided that, for the sake of argument, we grant the premise that the "civilization" of California resulting from its incorporation into the U. S. was arguably a good thing. The argument alleges that this outcome was one good thing resulting from Polk's policy. Hence, as far as the argument in this particular case went, it was claimed that Polk's policy worked out in a favorable way because of this allegedly good outcome.

Of course, it is quite another question whether Polk's policy was, in general, a good policy in itself, as a principle for international relations or foreign policy–as Fischer put it a "Good Thing." Whether the policy was a Good Thing, generally and in itself, would depend on all its ramifications as applied to all the different kinds of situations to which it would be applicable. It might have good consequences as applied in some cases, bad consequences in others. Even in a single case–like that of the annexation of California–the principle presumably would have all kinds of consequences, some of them arguably good and some of them arguably bad.

In sum, Fischer's inference could be correctly described, in relation to Case 6.4, as a weak argument. A defeasible and weak inference based on a one-sided and dubious premise. But is this enough to call it a fallacy? It should be called a fallacy not on the grounds of its objectionable and one-sided premise, but because it is based on a faulty inference. However, in this case the inference is weak, and subject to reasonable rebuttal in subsequent dialogue, but not so systematically erroneous or subject to strong refutation that we should properly call it a fallacy. As applied in Case 6.4, the argument from consequences is a weak argument which cites only one (arguably) positive consequence of the policy in question. But the fact that it does cite this one arguably positive consequence is, at least in principle, a *prima facie* point in its favor. The use of the *ad consequentiam* argument is not intrinsically wrong in this case. It is not a fallacy, or a fallacious kind of argumentation in itself. It is simply a case of this type of practical argumentation being used in an unconvincing way in the given context of dialogue. The argument is very weak, and subject to doubt and rebuttals as used in this context. But that does not make the argument from consequences fallacious *per se*. Nor does it make its use in this particular case a fallacy.

In Case 6.3, the *argumentum ad consequentiam* was used, in effect, to shut off the legitimate flow of dialogue by blocking it in a dialectically inappropriate way. This made Case 6.3 more plausible as a candidate to be classified as a sophistical tactics type of fallacy. With Case 6.4 however, the use of this blocking technique was not so evident. Hence it seems less plausible to classify it as a sophistical tactics type of fallacy, or even as a fallacy at all.

So the concept of fallacy which appears in Case 6.3 is inherently dialectical, having to do with the right to continue a critical discussion by bringing forward argument and evidence that is appropriate and relevant for that type of discussion. A fallacy, on this view, is associated with a kind of shift from one stage or type of dialogue to another, and not just with a single defective or weak inference, an error of reasoning where the conclusion fails to follow from the premises.

One key difference between Case 6.3 and Case 6.4 is this. In Case 6.3, the bad consequences referred to are those of questioning the thesis put forward by the proponent (that the U. S. had justice on its side in the War of 1848). The proponent is arguing *(ad consequentiam)* that if the respondent accepts the opposite thesis, (or even questions the proponent's thesis) bad consequences will occur. Therefore the respondent had better accept the proponent's argument without any further discussion of it. In Case 6.4, the good consequences referred to are (allegedly) outcomes of an action that actually took place in the past (the annexation of California by the U. S.). The proponent is arguing that this action was good (justified) because of its good outcome. He or she is not arguing that there will be bad consequences of taking the opposite view, or not accepting the view he puts forward.

Here is the key difference then. In Case 6.4, the consequences cited are not alleged to be consequences of the respondent's failure to embrace the proponent's thesis put forward in his argument. In Case 6.4, the consequences are the (alleged) outcome of the event itself, which was argued to be a good thing by the proponent because of these consequences.

In Case 6.3, the consequences are the outcome of one of the participants adopting a particular point of view in the dialogue. There is an inherently dialectical involvement in the production of the consequences of one type of dialogue to another.

VIEWS OF THE AMSTERDAM SCHOOL

The account of the *ad consequentiam* fallacy given by van Eemeren, Grootendorst and Kruiger (1987) is a little puzzling.

> The *argumentum ad consequentiam* . . . is a fallacy in which unfavorable light is cast on a thesis by pointing out its possible consequences, without the rightness of the thesis itself being disputed. For example: You may think it would be nice if the shops were open in the evenings, but abolition of the hours of trading regulations would leave shop staff open to exploitation. (p. 90)

But is the rightness of the thesis itself being disputed in this case or not? If the policy of allowing the shops to be open in the evenings would really leave shop staff open to exploitation (as seems possible as a consequence), then the thesis that this policy should be allowed is "disputed" by this consequence. If so, the given example about the shop hours is not an instance of the *argumentum ad consequentiam* fallacy. But this is puzzling, since van Eemeren, Grootendorst, and Kruiger evidently do intend their example to be an instance of this fallacy.

The other puzzling aspect of this account of the fallacy is the general question—how do we know, in general, when the rightness of a thesis in an argument is disputed, or not, by pointing out its possible consequences? Our uncertainties on ruling on the case given by van Eemeren, Grootendorst, and Kruiger pose a more general problem. How can we judge that the rightness of a thesis is not disputed by pointing out consequences, so we can determine that an *argumentum ad consequentiam* fallacy has been committed?

Van Eemeren and Kruiger (1987) seemed to recognize a type of nonfallacious argumentation from consequences which they call the "argumentation type to convince by the causal." However, they do not specifically label this type of argumentation as *argumentum ad consequentiam,* nor do they discuss its potential for fallacious employment.[5]

---

[5] Van Eemeren and Kruiger (1987) do refer to an argumentation type of "pointing to the consequences of a certain course of action" as one type of argumentation based on the causal relationship.

The argumentation scheme for the argument to convince by the causal has been given by van Eemeren and Kruiger (1987) as follows.

For X, Y is valid because
For X, Z is valid, and
Z leads to Y. (p. 74)

As an instance of this scheme, they offer the following case: "Ella can get any man she wants, because she looks fantastic (and if a woman looks fantastic, all men are attracted)." It is not stated what the variables X, Y, and Z stand for here, but the following interpretation seems reasonable: "For Ella, getting any man she wants is valid because for Ella, looking fantastic is valid, and looking fantastic leads to getting any man she wants [or perhaps, more generally, for any woman, looking fantastic leads to getting any man she wants]. The exact details of how this argumentation scheme is supposed to work pose many puzzles. Is "looking fantastic" an event or state of affairs? If so, how can it be "valid"? And what are the variables, X, Y, and so forth supposed to stand for anyway? It would not seem that they are meant to be propositional variables. Could they be a part of some theory of actions or practical reasoning? If so, we need to know more how they fit into such a theory of reasoning about actions.

Van Eemeren and Kruiger seem to be onto something here, at any rate. They appear to be recognizing a special type of argumentation scheme to be used in arguing about the possible consequences of a proposed or discussed course of action. They postulate a set of critical questions relevant in assessment of argumentation of this type.

Is Z valid for X?
Does Z really lead to Y?
Can Z lead somewhere else?
Can Y not be the result of something else? (p. 74)

The idea seems to be that the scheme for argument from consequences (or "to convince by the causal") can be a legitimate (nonfallacious) use of argumentation in a context of dialogue to the extent that it is used properly against an opponent's side in the dialogue to legitimately raise the critical questions cited earlier.

According to van Eemeren and Grootendorst (1987), the *argumentum ad consequentiam* consists of "testing the truth or acceptability of a standpoint by pointing out desirable, or undesirable consequences," for example, "This can't be true because it would destroy everything this country stands for." Note that this case, in general outline, is very similar to Case 6.3, also cited as a fallacious *argumentum ad consequentiam*. Van Eemeren and Grootendorst add however, that whether an argument of this type is fallacious or not depends on the kind of proposition to be tested. If the proposition to be tested concerns a future course of action being considered, the *argumentum ad consequentiam* might not be fallacious at all. If the proposition is something to be tested in a scientific inquiry, pointing out its desirable or undesirable consequences may not be relevant to establishing it as true or false. In this latter context, arguing that a scientific hypothesis should be rejected because it has bad political or financial consequences, for example, could be a fallacious argument from consequences.

The suggestion made here is that there are two different kinds of propositions which can be put forward to be tested in argumentation. But what is the difference between these two types of propositions? And how can you know which one is being put forward in an argument? The one type of proposition concerns a future course of action to be considered. The other type of proposition is to be established as true or false. The distinction seems to be between a practical proposition that has to do with actions, and a theoretical type of proposition that has to do with truth and falsehood.

This suggestion brought forward by the Amsterdam School appears very reasonable, and holds promise to be a key to resolving the problems posed by the *argumentum ad consequentiam* as a fallacy. The fallacy seems to arise through the illegitimate shift from the one kind of "proposition to be tested" to the other. What is the difference between these two ways of testing a proposition? Once we understand this, we will be a good way toward solving the basic problem of the *ad consequentiam* fallacy.

PRACTICAL AND DISCURSIVE REASONING

In Case 6.1, the suspicion of *ad consequentiam* fallacy arose because there was a theoretical ethical issue to be discussed, and then one participant shifted to a practical issue of the consequences of holding one point of view in the discussion. The same kind of questionable shift was the root of the problem. Citing consequences is not in itself necessarily problematic nor fallacious. It is this shift from one kind of reasoning to another that makes the *argumentum ad consequentiam* fallacious.

Suppose that in Case 6.1 the pro-choice politician had replied using a different *argumentum ad consequentiam* than the one used in Case 6.1: "If we adopt the policy of not allowing women the right to an abortion, there will be "back-alley" abortions which will result in injuries and loss of life." This is an argument from consequences used against the thesis of the pro-life politician. But it is not obvious that it is fallacious. Certainly it is not fallacious in the same way that the *argumentum ad consequentiam* in Case 6.1 is. And it could be maintained that, at least in principle, it is a reasonable kind of argumentation from consequences.

In many instances, argumentation from consequences is a legitimate and also very common kind of reasoning. When two or more individuals are arguing about some proposed or contemplated course of action, it is appropriate for each of them to cite possible consequences of the action that this individual sees as relevant. It can be argued by the one side that positive consequences of the action support the case for going ahead with action, and by the other side that negative consequences undermine or detract from support for the action.

Consider the following critical discussion of whether mandatory retirement at age 65 should be enforced by the courts.

Case 6.5:   **Roy:**   Well, you know what's going to happen if we don't
                           have mandatory retirement. Huge numbers of people
                           are not going to retire at age 65, and the unemploy-
                           ment situation for young people will be made much
                           worse. New jobs for younger people will not open up.

              Nancy: That's not true. The effects will be negligible, because
                           you are only talking about a very small number of
                           people who will want to stay in their jobs at age 65.
                           The impact will be minimal, and anyway, forcing
                           someone to retire for no reason other than their age is
                           a violation of equality.

In Case 6.5, Roy and Nancy have a difference of opinion which turns on an
argument from consequences. They are arguing for or against a policy on the
grounds of whether its consequences will be good or bad.

Another very common context of dialogue for reasonable argumentation from
consequences is advice-giving dialogue.[6] For example, an expert who has been
consulted may advise a layperson, "Don't go ahead with that course of action,
because if you do it will have highly negative consequences from your point of
view." A financial expert might counsel you, for example, that a particular action
you are thinking of–like investing in a particular stock–would not be a prudent
thing for you to do at this time, on the grounds of the possible or likely negative
consequences for you, should you take this action.

Argumentation from consequences can occur in different types of dialogue,
and whether or not the argument is reasonable depends on the type of dialogue the
arguer is supposed to be engaged in. The *argumentum ad consequentiam* often
occurs in a critical discussion. But a critical discussion can be about a conflict of
opinions concerning whether a particular proposition is true or false. Or in other
cases, a critical discussion could be about actions–the conflict of opinions could
concern the issue of whether a particular action is prudentially reasonable or not.
The one participant *(pro* side) advocates carrying out this action as prudentially
reasonable. The other side *(contra)* doubts this proposal, and has the burden of
raising critical questions against it (or in the stronger type of conflict, the burden
of refuting it).

In the action-oriented type of critical discussion, the dispute can also be recast
as a clash of points of view *vis á vis* a proposition at issue–so described is the
proposition that the action in question is one that ought (practically) to be
brought about. Even so, the two types of critical discussions can be differentiated.
In the nonaction type, the proposition does not reduce to an action. It is a proposition that is simply true or false *per se.* In the action type of critical discussion,
the proposition is a practical ought-proposition that contains an imperative. The

---

[6] See Walton (1990, *Pract. Reas.*) on advice-giving dialogue as a context of practical reasoning.

proposition in this type of case is one that asserts that a particular course of action is prudentially reasonable in the circumstances.

But what is the difference between these two types of critical discussion? It is not an essential difference between the two types of dialogue in themselves, as basic types of dialogue. Both are critical discussions. It is a difference between what the two types of dialogue are about. One concerns reasoning or evidence needed to prove that a proposition is true or false. This type of reasoning brings forward factual or other kinds of evidence which bears on the truth or falsehood of the proposition to be proved, questioned, or refuted. The other concerns reasoning that shows that a particular course of action is prudentially reasonable for an agent to carry out in a given set of circumstances. One concerns practical reasoning to a conclusion about actions. The other concerns reasoning to a conclusion that needs to be shown to be true (or false)–never mind whether this conclusion is practically reasonable or not.

The key difference between these two types of argumentation in a critical discussion concerns two different types of reasoning contained within the argumentation. One is a kind of theoretical or truth-theoretic reasoning which we called discursive reasoning. The other is a kind of action-directed prudential reasoning which we called practical reasoning. The key differences between them have already been summarized in chapter one.

So, is the fallacy of *argumentum ad consequentiam* an error of reasoning or a dialectical fallacy that is a sophistical tactic of some sort? Rescher's treatment seemed more inclined to put it in the category of an error of reasoning type of fallacy–a shift from one type of reasoning to another. However, another textbook has portrayed it as a sophistical tactic.

Thouless (1930) identified the *argumentum ad consequentiam* as a device of "crooked thinking," but, at the same time, recognized that it is also often used in a nonfallacious way. Thouless did not use the expression *argumentum ad consequentiam*, but described the argument as the device of *commending or condemning a proposition because of its practical consequences to the hearer*. This description is a very nice way of summing up the gist of the *argumentum ad consequentiam*, showing that Thouless recognized and emphasized two of its key features. The dialectical aspect is nicely brought out by putting the argument as one addressed to a hearer, and centering on the consequences for the hearer. And Thouless also recognized that the argument from consequences can be positive (commending a proposition) or negative (condemning a proposition) in nature.

Thouless insightfully saw the argument from consequences as a device for making the acceptance of a doubtful proposition "easier" by "wording it in such a way as to make it appeal to the prejudices" or to the previously indicated "thought habits" of an audience. As such, it need not always be fallacious as an argument, but clearly it is a device or strategy that is commonly used as a deceptive trick. Thouless, in fact, thought the argument from consequences to be a powerful kind of appeal which is used very commonly, and also very effectively in political argumentation. The kind of case he had in mind was the argument that appeals to personal interests and consequences of the individual voter in a political speech.

Case 6.6:   A very considerable part of political propaganda is made up of
                this kind of appeal. Whether he is attacking national expenditure
                on armaments or on social services, a speaker can get a ready
                response by pointing to its effects in increased taxation. Our
                objection to increased taxation is primarily a very individual and
                personal one, that as we pay more in taxes we have less to spend
                on ourselves and our families. Even when the speaker makes a
                relatively impersonal basis to his appeal by emphasizing the
                effect of high taxation as a burden on industry, we can safely
                guess that it is the effect on themselves that his audience are
                thinking about. That is the true reason for the success of the
                speaker in carrying conviction. (p. 230)

According to Thouless, the effectiveness of this kind of appeal is strongly
enhanced by the difficulty, for each member of the audience personally affected in
such a case, to be "sufficiently detached emotionally from his own affairs" to
reflect on an issue on national policy in a nonbiased way.

What is revealed here is a curious link with the bias type of *ad hominem*
argument. The argument from consequences, in a case like the one sketched out
by Thouless, contains a personal appeal to the interests of the respondent which
has an emotional response that may be difficult for the respondent to resist–all the
more so because the *ad hominem* nature of the argument is nonexplicit, and may
not even be recognized as such by the respondent. The antidote, according to
Thouless, is to cultivate an "attitude of detachment of mind" when trying to arrive
at a conclusion on an argument that contains "matters which touch us personally."

Thouless' account of the *argumentum ad consequentiam* is revealing and
informative precisely because he has exposed a subtlety underlying how it is used
as an argumentation tactic. Thouless has shown us that the argument from consequences is so highly effective in persuading an audience because it appeals
directly–yet in a way that may be nonobvious and somewhat underhanded–to the
personal interests of that audience. In the case he cites, it is in fact the financial
interests of the audience that are appealed to.

But there is still room to examine the question of why the argument from
consequences is fallacious (when it is so), according to the account given by
Thouless. For the fact is that, as he himself conceded, there is nothing inherently
wrong with a proponent commending or condemning a proposition because of its
practical consequences on the respondent in a dialogue. Whether such an argument
should be judged fallacious or nonfallacious in a given case depends on the
context of dialogue.

If the dialogue is a negotiation between two parties, then for one of them to
commend or condemn a proposition, because of its practical consequences for the
other party, could be quite a normal and reasonable move in the argument that is
part of the negotiation. Appealing to personal financial interests of the hearer is
what negotiation is all about. Hence an argument from consequences that is not,
at least for that reason alone, fallacious.

On the other hand, if the dialogue the participants are supposed to be engaged in is a critical discussion, the dialectical shift to a negotiation type of dialogue, where the argument from consequences was used to appeal to the financial interests of the hearer, could be a fallacy. It could be a fallacy precisely because the shift to negotiation is an irrelevant move from the point of view of the original critical discussion–a kind of move that does nothing to forward the goal of the critical discussion, or even obstructs this goal by shifting to another type of dialogue. Here we have a fallacy precisely because of the shift. The appeal to personal interests may appear appropriate, and indeed be appropriate in the context of a negotiation. But the problem is that the participants are supposed to be engaged in a critical discussion of an issue (generally apart from the question of how it would affect each of them personally or financially).

The problem then for evaluating Case 6.6 is one of what type of dialogue the participants are supposed to be engaged in. Does the political discussion on national expenditures on armaments or social services legitimately include financial appeals to the personal interests of the audience or not? In other words, does the political debate include negotiation–like appeals to special interest groups, and so forth–or not? This is the key question for evaluating the *argumentum ad consequentiam* as a fallacy, and generally it is reasonable to presume that political debate–in election campaigning, and other kinds of political dialogue–does legitimately include this aspect of negotiation and appeal to personal interests.

So we can see here that we need to go deeper beneath the surface of Thouless' account to come to grips with the question of whether and why the *argumentum ad consequentiam* is a fallacy in some cases. According to Thouless, this tactic of argumentation is "propaganda" because it appeals to personal interests of a respondent or audience. But is appealing to personal interests of a respondent or audience in an argument necessarily fallacious? No, it is not. In negotiation dialogue, it is perfectly acceptable and appropriate. Even in a critical discussion, arguing from premises your opponent is personally committed to is quite normal, reasonable, and appropriate. It is only where this tactic is abused, or carried to extremes in various ways, that it is correct to condemn it as fallacious.

It would appear then that an adequate understanding of the *argumentum ad consequentiam* as a fallacy requires that we look at it not only as an error of reasoning, but also as a sophistical tactics type of fallacy that involves a dialectical shift. It does involve practical reasoning, but the key question of evaluating a particular case is to see whether or not the use of practical reasoning is appropriate in the given context of dialect. In some cases, practical considerations of consequences are appropriate, but in other cases, there could be an illicit shift from discussing a general issue to an irrelevant consideration of consequences.

PRAGMA-DIALECTICAL NATURE OF ARGUMENT
FROM CONSEQUENCES

One can easily see how argumentation from consequences fits into and arises out of the framework of practical reasoning by considering the role of critical question, Q4, (see chapter 1) in the shifting of burden of proof in a dialogue. The respondent cites negative consequences against the proponent's proposal for action based on practical reasoning. The proponent can counter by carrying on the dialogue in various ways. The proponent can deny that there are the cited negative consequences. But alternatively, he or she could also reply quite properly by arguing that there are positive consequences that outweigh the negative consequences, even without challenging the existence of the cited negative consequences. In such a case, it would be a classic example of *pro* and *contra* argumentation from consequences. So construed however, the *ad consequentiam* type of argument is not a fallacy *per se,* but rather a dialectical type of argumentation that can be stronger or weaker on either side, depending on the particulars of a given case. So conceived, the argument from consequences is both practical (pragmatic) and dialectical as a type of argumentation.

The practical and dialectical nature of argumentation from consequences as a species of nonfallacious argument was, early on, recognized and identified by Perelman and Olbrechts-Tyteca (1969) and by Windes and Hastings (1965). Both accounts recognized it as a species of action-directed reasoning used in a context of dialogue when there is a conflict of opinions on how to proceed prudentially in a situation of reasoned deliberation.

Perelman and Olbrechts-Tyteca (1971) called the *pragmatic argument* a type of argument where an act is evaluated in terms of its favorable or unfavorable consequences. They see this type of argument not as fallacious *per se,* but as being valid in some cases and invalid in other cases. They also see it as a dialectical type of argument used by a proponent and challenged or opposed by a respondent. Perelman and Olbrechts-Tyteca noted the following two properties of this type of argument: (a) it can be developed only by presuming agreement between the proponent and respondent on the value of the consequences, and (b) the respondent (opponent) claims the right to choose from among the consequences deemed "worthy of consideration in view of the object of the debate." In general, the proponent cites the positive consequences in favor of his pragmatic argument and the opponent cites the negative consequences, taken to go against the pragmatic argument.

What Perelman and Olbrechts-Tyteca called the pragmatic argument may be taken to be broadly equivalent to what is generally called the argument from consequences (or *ad consequentiam)* argument. However, their account of this type of argument makes it clear that they see it in a pragma-dialectical way, as a species of practical reasoning used in a context of dialogue. They see it as a two-sided type of argumentation, or dialectical exchange, where the proponent's side is opposed to the respondent's side.

Windes and Hastings (1965) also treat the argument from consequences as a dialectical exchange, pointing out that many political debates on issues of social policy take the form of opposed positive versus negative argumentation from consequences. In their account too, argumentation from consequences can be reasonable or unreasonable, and is not necessarily fallacious. The proponent of a course of action cites the favorable or good consequences of the action to support the conclusion that the action should be carried out. The opponent cites the unfavorable or bad consequences of the action to support the conclusion that it should not be carried out.

Windes and Hastings (1965) also pointed out, however, that the opponent has three additional techniques of argumentation available. The opponent can: (1) attack the proponent's argument for his or her contention, (2) propose an alternative to the proposed course of action, or (3) argue that, on balance, the alternative has a better ratio of favorable versus unfavorable consequences as compared to the proponent's proposed course of action. Hence, argumentation from consequences can be a correct (reasonable) use of practical reasoning in dialogue. But whether it is used reasonably or not depends on the given context of dialogue.

Consider the following example of the argument from consequences, where the context is one of advice-giving in an election campaign.

Case 6.7:   **Candidate:** I plan to tell the people in my next speech that I'm not going to raise taxes.

Adviser: If you are going to say that, you had better be committed to it, because one of the consequences of your saying it is that people are going to hold you to it. If, later, you raise taxes, people are going to criticize and even ridicule you for it. My advice would be not to say it in the first place.

In this case, the adviser's argument is an *argumentum ad consequentiam,* but it seems to be a reasonable, that is, nonfallacious argument. Certainly the advice given to the candidate could be reasonable, and as a piece of advice, it is relevant to the subject of discussion between the two participants in the dialogue. For as our analysis of Case 6.6 made clear, the candidate's raising the issue of taxes in the political speech definitely does involve an argument from consequences. So consequences, in such a speech, are a legitimate issue.

Possibly, one could object to the adviser's line of argument as "fallacious" on the following grounds, however. In the campaign speech, the candidate should say what he or she honestly believes, and express the real position on the issue of taxes. But the adviser is counselling the candidate not to say this, on grounds of political expediency. According to the adviser, such a course of action will lead to bad consequences that will be difficult to deal with, possibly leading to political ruin. This does not really bear on the question of whether it is right to raise taxes or not. It is not relevant to what the real issue should be in the dialogue.

Put this way, the problem seems to be one of practical expedience versus the question of whether an utterance is truly right or wrong, in itself, as an expression of belief or opinion. It may be right for the candidate to make this declaration if it is his or her real opinion, but is it politically expedient for the candidate to say it at this time? The adviser says "No."

But to judge whether the adviser's argument from consequences is relevant, you have to take a careful look at the context of dialogue. The adviser's job is to give practical advice on how to win the election and on practical matters of how to achieve political goals. This task clearly involves questions of expediency and practical matters of means and ends. Therefore the advice–in the form of an argument from consequences–seems quite relevant and proper as a part of the dialogue.

Moreover, the adviser's argument legitimately points out the implications of the commitment made by the candidate if he or she was to make a public declaration that taxes will not be raised. Such a commitment would be difficult to retract, once made, and the adviser is making a legitimate kind of commentary by pointing out the dialectical implications of such a speech act to the candidate. The adviser is pointing out to the candidate that later, the candidate may find himself or herself facing a conflict of commitments when practical circumstances may force the candidate to raise taxes. As long-term political advice, this could be very good counsel. Hence it would be a mistake to dismiss it as fallacious argumentation. It fits in with the context of dialogue very well. It does not go against the goals of the type of dialogue the participants are supposed to be engaged in, which would be the mark of a fallacy. Is the dialogue supposed to be about truth or expediency (ends and means, or practical reasoning)? This is the question of what normative models of dialogue are contained in political discourse. The answer, here in this case, is that it is partly about both. If so, questions of expediency (consequences) are not irrelevant.

The question of whether the use of an *argumentum ad consequentiam* in a given case is fallacious or not depends on whether practical reasoning is an appropriate type of reasoning to introduce into the discussion. This, in turn, depends on what the discussion was supposed to be about in the first place. The question, in short, is one of the context of dialogue in which the *argumentum ad consequentiam* was used.

In Case 6.7, the context of dialogue indicates that questions of practical expedience are relevant. The adviser could have chosen to reply that the policy of not raising taxes is unjustifiable or bad *per se*. The adviser chose not to take up this discursive line of reply, however, but to take the practical line of evaluating the consequences of such a pronouncement. But this reply was not a fallacious shift. The context of dialogue of advice-giving includes consideration of the practical consequences of what the candidate proposes to say in his or her speeches.

APPROPRIATE DIALECTICAL SITUATIONS

It has seemed, so far, that the *argumentum ad consequentiam* is a fallacy is not best conceived of exclusively or generally as a species of failed inference from premises to a conclusion, but also as a dialectical fault. A fallacy is a violation of a rule of reasonable dialogue, according to the Amsterdam School. But beyond this, in some cases a fallacy can be a speech act that would be appropriate as a contribution to one type of dialogue, but is inappropriate or out of place in another (given) dialogue. An example of a dialectical shift of this sort is the following case. It is not a fallacy, but is a general example of a dialectical shift or inappropriate move in a dialogue. In this case, a teacher reported he saw one of his students, with a man, looking under the hood of her car.

Case 6.8:   Thinking I might be of assistance, I walked over and cheerfully
               said: "Well, I see the old clunker has conked out again! Don't
               worry, we'll get it started!" I was surprised to see the look of
               shock on her face as she turned to me. Puzzled, I asked the man
               if he had already found out what was wrong. Slowly, he straigh-
               tened up. "Well," he drawled, "I *was* thinking of buying it!"[7]

In this case, the speaker advanced a speech act that he took to be appropriate to
the situation, and helpful to the student. Given the actual context of the dialogue
which was underway between the student and the man she was engaged in discussion with, the speaker's move was inappropriate and out of place. It turned out to
have bad consequences for the student's aims in that discussion.

    It will be our contention that when the *argumentum ad consequentiam* is a
fallacy, it is at least partly because of an underlying inappropriateness of its use
in a context of dialogue–a dialectical shift like that exemplified in Case 6.9 is
involved.

    George, a British chaplain is engaged in preparing a sermon on the causes of
war. It is August, 1940, during the summer of the Battle of Britain. George is
discussing the arguments in his proposed sermon with his fellow minister,
Arthur.

Case 6.9:   **George:** Well, you have to look at this thing in a
                            reasonable perspective. I have come to the con-
                            clusion that the Treaty of Versailles really was
                            unfair to the Germans, and that this was an
                            important cause of the war, all things con-
                            sidered.

               Arthur: Holy smoke, George! What a bad argument. If
                            you say that, Goebbels will leap on it as a
                            propaganda triumph. Not only will it support
                            the enemy side, it will dispirit and even enrage
                            our own troops and population. You may even
                            get shot as a traitor. Your argument about the
                            cause of the war is refuted, and wholly without
                            justification.

Here it seems that Arthur is making an unwarranted logical leap from citing the
bad consequences of George's putting forward an argument in his speech, to the
conclusion that the argument is unjustified or based on false premises.

    Suppose, however, that Arthur had put his objection in a different way,
responding to George's same argument with the following reply.

---

[7] Pettis (1989).

Case 6.10:   **Arthur:**   Holy smoke, George! Don't even think of saying something like that in your sermon. It may be true– I mean you may have a valid point there about the causes of the war and perhaps you could give some reasonable arguments for it. But this is not the right occasion to put forward that particular argument. Goebbels will exploit it, our troops and population will be dispirited, and they will (understandably) be enraged about it.

In Case 6.10, Arthur can be interpreted as giving George practical advice about the appropriateness of advancing this kind of argument in the context of the sort of speech that George is going to be giving. There will be bad consequences, according to Arthur. By pointing out these likely consequences, Arthur is asking George whether it is worth bringing about these very bad consequences, given the aims of his speech. George can then decide, as a question of conscience, whether the negative value of these consequences is worth whatever good aims he may have had in mind in attempting to bring up this particular argument in his speech.

In Case 6.10 then, Arthur is not rejecting George's argument about the causes of World War II. What he is doing in his reply is something quite different. He is questioning whether the dialectical context is right or appropriate for George to present his argument. This is a matter of the appropriateness of the dialogue situation for the presentation of George's argument, not a matter of the rightness or wrongness of George's argument. Arthur is giving George practical advice about the presentation of his argument, not criticizing the correctness or incorrectness of the argument *per se*. Indeed, Arthur makes his stance quite explicit by declaring that he is willing to concede that George "may have a valid point" about the causes of the war. He is not disputing this historical or moral argument, and his reply addresses quite a different point of criticism.

Arthur's reply is addressed not to claiming that there is a weak link or lack of evidence in George's premises to support his conclusion. Arthur's reply is broader than that in its aim. Arthur is making a point about the context of dialogue of George's argument. He is pointing out that, given current popular sentiments, George's audience and the British public will not only not accept it. They won't even really listen to it, and they will likely punish George for daring to make such a suggestion. Thus Arthur is warning George by giving him a piece of practical advice about the likely consequences of presenting this argument at a particular time and place.

The important point made by this case is that argumentation in the form of a critical discussion is not always appropriate. Some may think that critical discussion of an issue is good in itself and an absolute dialectical right. But this is a kind of fallacy, which could be called *the philosopher's fallacy*,[8] for in some

---

[8] To the best of my recollection, this fallacy was invented by Erik Krabbe. At any rate, it came up in a discussion between the author and Erik Krabbe in Wassenaar in early 1990, where it was

situations critical discussion is not appropriate or useful, for practical reasons. An example would be the ethical theorist who finds his neighbor in a dangerous situation. Instead of helping the neighbor out of it (which he could have done), the ethical theorist engages his neighbor in a philosophical discussion of the problem. As a result, the neighbor is hurt. The fault here was a failure to recognize that this was not the right occasion for engaging in critical discussion.

In Case 6.10, Arthur is conceding that George has a right to his point of view. But he is pointing out to George that, practically speaking, not every situation provides a proper forum for George to express those views and get a fair hearing and good discussion of them.

However, the problem posed by this case is an interesting and fundamental one that does not appear to have been much discussed in the literature on argumentation. It concerns the right of freedom of speech and the practical question of dialectical limitations on the prudential exercise of that right. Another case may illustrate the nature of the problem.

Case 6.11:   Marcia is an expert in medical ethics who is employed as an ethics adviser and counsellor in a clinical setting. She personally has a strong opinion that suicide is morally acceptable and that the popular stigma against it is not based on good arguments. She is introduced to a new patient, Bernie, who has just been told he has cancer. Marcia knows that Bernie's wife and children are terrified that Bernie might commit suicide. He has threatened to do it, and has the means to do it. Bernie asks Marcia, "So what do you think on the moral issue of whether it is all right to commit suicide or not?"

Marcia knows, or should know, that if she expresses her point of view in a critical discussion on the morality of suicide, it might possibly have the consequence that Bernie commits suicide. It is also likely that Bernie's wife and children would probably blame Marcia for causing the suicide. Moreover, freely expressing her positive views on the topic of suicide, even in a critical and balanced discussion, could very well be a violation of Marcia's professional obligations not to knowingly cause harm to a patient. Marcia has a right to her views, but nevertheless there is a practical question about how and when she should express them, it seems.

In some cases, argument from consequences is legitimate as a kind of reasoning. To think of it as always being a fallacy could be a bad policy which would make it impossible to reply to false charges of having committed this fallacy.

---

characterized as the fallacy of engaging in a protracted critical discussion in a situation where this type of dialogue is inappropriate, or represents a shift from the type of dialogue the participants should really be engaged in. Typically, this original type of situation would be of a practical nature, so that a critical discussion would not be a relevant or appropriate type of dialogue for the situation.

Case 6.12:   Biologist Mary was bitten by an abnormally aggressive beaver during the course of her research on beaver dams. Brought to Doctor Dave for treatment, she was given anti-rabies injections. Missing two days of work as a result of the injections–which made her temporarily sick–she accused Doctor Dave of committing the fallacy of *argumentum ad consequentiam,* saying: "Instead of being a scientific physician and finding out the facts, (i.e., whether this beaver was rabid or not), you just went ahead and acted on possible consequences to guard yourself against a potential of malpractice suits."

How could Doctor Dave defend himself against this charge of having committed the *ad consequentiam* fallacy? One way would be for him to argue that he had to act on the presumption that Mary had, or may have had rabies, on grounds of her safety. As caregiver to his patient, as well as being a "scientific physician" he had to take practical considerations into account–by the time it had been certainly determined whether the beaver had rabies or not, Mary would have been infected by the virus, if she had it, and would have probably died, despite any treatments that could be given to her. Thus, Dave would be conceding that he acted on argumentation from possible consequences on practical grounds of safety, but that such an argument was not fallacious. Dave could argue that he acted on presumption in the absence of hard evidence, but that this was the proper approach for him, as a physician, to take in this case.

In this case, there was a very real conflict between discursive and practical considerations. Doctor Dave was faced with a practical problem of caring for this particular patient. But his reasoning in dealing with the problem involved a factual premise–the question of whether Biologist Mary had been infected with the rabies virus or not. Doctor Dave would eventually find the answer to this factual question by means of discursive reasoning based on empirical findings.

But a conflict arose because Doctor Dave would not get this knowledge in time for it to be practically useful to help in making his present decision. Here, practical considerations of the patient's safety loomed large, so Doctor Dave concluded that he had better act–in the absence of certain knowledge–on the basis of presumption. In this case, practical presumption took priority over the purely discursive resolution of the question by the relevant scientific and empirical evidence.

Doctor Dave defended his reasoning against Biologist Mary's charge of fallacy by appealing to the priority of the practical in the context of the situation.

Case 6.12 raises philosophical questions on which kind of reasoning should have primacy–discursive or practical. Rescher (1985) has argued that generally discursive reasoning should have primacy, but that practical reasoning has a place where information is not sufficient, or where, for other reasons, discursive reasoning is not sufficient to resolve a problem or issue. Rescher (1988) has also shown, however, that practical reasoning requires cognitive input from discursive reasoning. The precise relationship and balance of practical versus discursive reasoning in a general theory of reasoning remains controversial, however. It is enough for our purpose to say that practical reasoning should *in some cases* be given priority over discursive reasoning in argumentation. It follows from this thesis that *argumentum ad consequentiam* is not always fallacious.

The general issue of the primacy of practical versus theoretical reasoning is hard to resolve. But it is not really necessary to come to a resolution of this issue, given that the practical problem is to have criteria for evaluating particular cases. It is enough for a critic to be able to say: "In this case, practical reasoning is relevant, hence *argumentum ad consequentiam* is, in principle, a reasonable line of argument to take up." This will not enable us to determine, in every case, whether an *argumentum ad consequentiam* is fallacious or not. But it enables us to make such a determination in enough cases to be useful.

CONSEQUENCES OF PUTTING FORWARD
A POINT OF VIEW

One case of the *fallacy of argument ad consequentiam* cited by David Hackett Fischer concerned a book that was a psychoanalytic interpretation of Martin Luther by a psychiatrist, Erik Erikson. The use of argument from consequences to reject Erikson's interpretation was attributed to G. R. Elton, a historian, author of *The Practice of History*. The following case, citing the use of fallacious *argumentum ad consequentiam* on the part of Elton, is directly quoted from Hackett Fischer (1970).

Case 6.13:   One example is the verdict which an English historian, G. R. Elton, passed upon Erik Erikson's psychoanalytic interpretation of Martin Luther. "I cannot feel that the much-praised Freudian effort of E. H. Erikson, *Young Man Luther: A Study in Psychoanalysis in History,* contributes anything of value to an understanding of Luther or his age," Elton wrote, "In so far as it has been responsible for John Osborne's play, it may even need condemnation." (p. 301)

Hackett Fischer commented that Elton is entitled to his opinion, but that his second sentence is "illegitimate." Hackett Fischer suggested that you can grant Elton's premises, but you should not grant the incorrect conclusion drawn from these premises. You can grant that Erikson's essay was responsible, "in some degree," for Osborne's play. And you can grant that Osborne's play "calls for condemnation as a historical work." But Fischer denied that you can correctly reason from these premises to the conclusion "that Erikson's monograph should be condemned for the deficiencies which may have been based upon it."

But what exactly is the fallacy here? If the suggestion is that we cannot blame Erikson because a bad play was subsequently based on his work, then it may be an eminently reasonable one. Osborne's play is (presumably) an independent work, and should be judged on its own merits, unless there is evidence to the contrary.

But the question of the fallacy of *ad consequentiam* is not a question of individual praise or blame for actions. The fallacy alleged in Case 6.13 turns on the claim that Erikson's argument in his monograph was condemned wrongly because it had Osborne's play as a consequence. This question surely cannot be decided fairly without looking at Erikson's work more closely.

Was Erikson's argument a scientific work by a psychoanalyst that should be judged as a contribution to science? If so, judging it by reference to literary works that it influenced or prompted would be inappropriate, and perhaps even fallacious. Here, there has been a dialectical shift from an argument that was supposed to be a scientific inquiry, to another kind of argument that was put forward in a literary work.

On the other hand, if Erikson's monograph is supposed to be a philosophical work with moral implications concerning how people should act, then it needs to be evaluated differently. Suppose the arguments in it led people to the conclusion that people should not be held morally responsible for their actions, because all actions are based on psychiatric motives. This could lead to all kinds of bad consequences. But whether the arguments in the work could be criticized for these bad consequences depends on how the work is correctly or incorrectly interpreted. If the moral arguments in the works are justifiably interpreted as sanctioning or approving of these bad actions, then it could be right to condemn the work exactly for this reason. There would be no *ad consequentiam* fallacy in such a case.

A parallel case is that of the philosophical works of Nietzsche, used by the Nazis to support the ideas of the "master race" and "supermen." We can rightly condemn these Nazi ideas, but can we blame the writings of Nietzsche for promoting them by helping to give them the appearance of a respectable philosophical basis? This depends on how we interpret Nietzsche's writings, and whether in fact these bad ideas can be found in there.

Thus the question of whether an *ad consequentiam* fallacy exists in a case of this sort is not a simple one, and depends on a careful interpretation of the text of discourse of the original argument. Not only that, it depends on the purpose of the argument in the context of dialogue. Whether the original argument was supposed to be part of a scientific inquiry, or a moral argument judging the rightness or wrongness of actions, is relevant.

The problem in this type of case is that you cannot blame an author for all the unfortunate consequences of his or her literary work, but you certainly can condemn an author's work for some of them, in some cases. The problem is to sort out the one option from the other in a given case. Blaming the author or not is a moral problem, and is not exactly the same problem as the one posed by the alleged fallacy in an argument from consequences. This latter problem is one of judging the worth of the arguments in the literary work by means of citing assumptions concerning the positive or negative consequences that have arisen from the work. This problem is a logical problem of argumentation evaluation. But there is a parallel with the moral problem. Sometimes the bad consequences do rightly count against the original argument and sometimes they should not.

The problem is to sort out the one type of case from the other, on the available relevant evidence.

The moral problem is to judge blame or praise of the author. The logical problem is to judge the worth of an argument, especially an argument that is properly meant to have practical implications, and can be judged (to some extent) by its consequences. These are different problems, but they are related, and often arise in the same kinds of cases. Both kinds of cases can arise in legal argumentation.

In one case of this type, a seventeen-year-old man, Michale Anderson of Pittsburgh claimed that repeated viewings of the violent movie *A Clockwork Orange* had led him to fatally stab and strangle his seventeen-year-old friend, Karen Hurwitz.

Case 6.14:   In a confession to police, Anderson said he "always did bad things" when he wore his black *A Clockwork Orange* T-shirt. He was wearing the shirt when he stabbed Hurwitz, a high school senior.

Anderson's attorney, Jon Botula, said during the two-day trial that his client was incited to kill by repeated viewings of the 1971 film, which starred Malcolm McDowell as the leader of a group of hooligans.[9]

During the trial, Botula showed part of the film to the jury. The film chronicled the brutal "ultraviolence" of marauding gangs of youths that could not be controlled in a futuristic society.

In response to this argument, a specialist in media psychology testifying for the prosecution countered that Botula was using the movie as a "scapegoat."

The question of criminal responsibility posed by this case is whether the film caused this man's violent act in a way that negated his personal responsibility for the act. If so, it is the creators of the film, and not Michale Anderson, who are ultimately responsible for the death of Karen Hurwitz. This court case aside, however, there could also be a practical question of whether such a film contributes to violent behavior in a way that could lead a critic to conclude that the film is a harmful influence. Issues of pornography and censorship often turn on just this sort of argumentation. If such a film is very likely to be a harmful influence, it can be argued on grounds of public safety that it should not be shown. The arguments in the film, in principle, have a right to be expressed under the guarantee of free speech in a democracy. But if showing the film is likely to lead to bad consequences, possibly even including loss of life of innocent persons, then questions of the appropriateness of showing the film to the public can be raised, according to the advocates of censorship.

---

[9] Associated Press (1990).

In this particular case however, there is not enough data given to fairly determine whether there exists an *ad consequentiam* argument, and whether this argument, if it is being used here, is fallacious or not. Does the film contain an argument which could be fairly interpreted as sanctioning violent behavior? This claim could be judged by viewing the film, studying the verbal messages and arguments found in it, and interpreting and analyzing those arguments. But simply from the information given in Case 6.14, the reader is not in a position to carry out such a critical task of evaluation fairly or effectively. It could even turn out that it is highly questionable whether there ever was a reasoned argument concerning violence in the film at all. In such a case, even if it was clear that the film did have negative consequences in leading to violent behavior, there would not be grounds for the claim that the argument in the film is an instance of the *ad consequentiam* fallacy.

The conflict between freedom of speech and censorship is based on the conflict between discursive and practical considerations. Ideas expressed in a work of art that condone or recommend certain kinds of behavior as acceptable should be judged freely by everyone who cares to view the work on how they perceive its merits. But if showing the work could have bad consequences, then the issue of the appropriateness of making it available for public viewing could be a legitimate context of discussion for practical reasoning. Practical questions of the appropriateness of this type of dialogue could be relevant. If so, the *argumentum ad consequentiam* might not be fallacious, even if something as drastic as censorship is recommended, using this type of argument. This is not to justify censorship, but it does provide a logical basis that could be used for this purpose.

The problem in Case 6.14 stems from the same general kind of infelicity diagnosed in Case 6.11. The situation of the dialogue was not right or appropriate for a particular type of argumentation or move in the conversation. If or when such a move were to be made, it would have bad consequences. Therefore, it could be condemned as a dialectical infelicity, and if the *argumentum ad consequentiam* were put forward by a third party as a metadialogue move to warn against making the move in question, in a dialectical forum in which it would be inappropriate, it could be a reasonable and constructive use of the *argumentum ad consequentiam.*

Now we are getting some clues to the nature of the *argumentum ad consequentiam.* Sometimes it is a reasonable argument, sometimes fallacious. When it is fallacious, it is not simply because it is a faulty or invalid inference from a set of propositions (premises) to another proposition (a conclusion) in any context. Its fallaciousness resides in the appropriateness of its use as a move in a given context of dialogue. Used correctly, it can contribute constructively to a dialogue. Used fallaciously or inappropriately, it can block or frustrate the goals of the given dialogue by shifting to an inappropriate kind of reasoning.

DIALECTICAL STRUCTURE OF
ARGUMENT FROM CONSEQUENCES

Correct or incorrect use of the *argumentum ad consequentiam* always presupposes a given context of dialogue which sets the normative requirements for correct use of this argumentation scheme in a particular case. Most often, and characteristically, the context of dialogue is a critical discussion turning on a conflict of opinions on how to proceed with respect to an action or policy being considered. The question is: What is it (prudentially reasonable) to do? There are two sides—the question is whether it is best to carry out action A or not.

When the two parties discuss this question critically, the framework for its resolution should be practical reasoning. It depends on the goals of the party who is contemplating the action, and on the available means for carrying out these goals in a given situation. Here, the necessary condition scheme and the sufficient condition scheme for practical reasoning come into play.

But the structure for resolution of the conflict is dialectical. Once the proponent of the particular course of action, A, has advanced practical reasoning in favor of it, the respondent has the right to reply. In using the *argumentum ad consequentiam* the respondent opts for reply Q4 in the set of critical questions appropriate for responding to practical reasoning: What about the possible or probable consequences of A? When Q4 comes into play, it is questioned whether there might be bad (negative) consequences of bringing about A that should be considered. These bad consequences count as reasons against the prudential reasonableness of bringing about A.

The burden of proof is on the respondent to reply to this questioning. If he or she cannot respond successfully, the argument for going ahead with A fails. Moreover, as Perelman and Olbrechts-Tyteca rightly pointed out, the respondent can take his or her choice of *any* bad consequences. The choice of which consequences are important to consider can be structured in any way he pleases.

The respondent also has an additional option at this point in the sequence of argumentation. He or she can propose an alternative action, A' which does not have such bad consequences at A. The proponent can ignore this proposal, and continue to respond to the prior objection that A has bad consequences. But if the proponent does respond to the proposal critically, it results in a curious reversal of roles—see the right rectangle in level four of Fig. 6.1. The proponent of action A becomes the opponent of action A', and attacks it by arguing that it has bad consequences. The original opponent, in turn, becomes the proponent of A' and is obliged to defend the proposal against a negative *argumentum ad consequentiam*. In such a case, one *ad consequentiam* argument is posed against another.

At level three, however, this alternative is only an optional tactic. The main option for the respondent is to fasten on the argument that A has bad consequences, and must therefore be rejected, for this reason, as a prudential course of action.

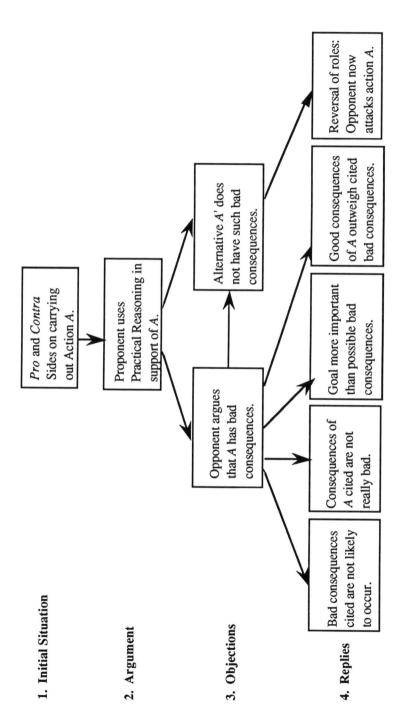

1. **Initial Situation**

2. **Argument**

3. **Objections**

4. **Replies**

FIG. 6.1. Four-stage Structure of the *Argumentum Ad Consequentiam*.

At the fourth level, the proponent has four types of replies available. He or she can directly attack the opponent's use of Q4 by arguing that the negative consequences are not likely to occur. Or the proponent can argue that these consequences are not as bad as the opponent would have us believe. In a third type of move, he or she can concede these consequences may occur, and may be bad, but that they are necessary to achieve the goal, which is a very good goal. The argument here is that the value of achieving the goal is more important than the bad side-effects. This is a comparative argument of values. This type of argument uses the argumentation scheme for practical reasoning by appealing to the goal premise. The fourth option at the fourth level is also a comparative values type of argument. This argument claims that A has good consequences, and that the positive value of these good consequences outweighs the negative value of the bad consequences alleged by the opponent.

In fact, the proponent may be committed to this technique of argumentation early on in stage two when practical reasoning is presented. For example, if part of the sequence of practical reasoning has taken the form of using a sufficient condition scheme, the proponent is arguing that carrying out action A is sufficient for fulfilling or contributing a good goal. In other words, he or she is arguing that carrying out A will have good consequences. In such a case, the proponent is, in effect, engaged in positive argumentation from consequences from the very beginning stages of the dialectical structure of the sequence of argumentation.

The dialectical structure of *argumentum ad consequentiam* has four distinctive stages which form a normative structure. The second stage is the presentation of an argument in the form of practical reasoning by the *pro* side. The *contra* side then has the right to rebuttal by citing bad consequences, using critical questioning move Q4. In the fourth stage, the *pro* side can make a rejoinder to the *contra* rebuttal, using any one of four rejoinders.

At the third stage, the *contra* side, represented by the respondent, can mount a stronger or a weaker form of attack. He or she can merely doubt the proponent's reasoning by bringing forward questions of the form Q4. Or the proponent can try for strong rebuttal by making a more positive attack that is aimed at refutation of the proponent's argument. Windes and Hastings (1965) made this clear when they showed how the opponent (respondent) has different techniques available. The weaker technique is to attack the proponent's argument for contention by citing negative consequences. The stronger technique is to go ahead and propose an alternative course of action. This technique can be carried even further by arguing explicitly that this alternative has a better ratio of good to bad consequences over the proponent's proposed course of action.

The explicit scheme of what is traditionally called the *argumentum ad consequentiam* can take the form of an early move in a dialectical sequence initiated by the *pro* side's practical reasoning.

Pro Side Argument: *Action A has good consequences, (i.e., A leads to a goal G_0 which is good from a point of view of my side).*

But then at the third stage, *argumentum ad consequentiam* is also used by the opponent, but in a negative form.

Contra Side Argument: *Action A has bad consequences, and these bad consequences are a sufficient reason for not carrying out A.*

In citations of the fallacy of *argumentum ad consequentiam* in textbooks, it is most often this negative version that is featured. But in the context of dialogue for this type of argumentation, both positive and negative types of it can occur, at different stages. Whether a given instance of the *argumentum ad consequentiam* is correct or not depends on which stage it has been used in a dialogue.

Figure 6.1 displays all four stages in the dialectical structure of use of argumentation from consequences. This four-part sequence summarizes the whole dialectical context of any use of the *argumentum ad consequentiam* in a given case. To evaluate the *argumentum ad consequentiam* as used correctly or incorrectly, reasonably or fallaciously in that case, a critic must evaluate the given text of discourse for that case in relation to the requirements appropriate for this dialectical structure. Both the *pro* and *contra* sides are obliged to bring forward their practical reasoning moves and responses in the right order as outlined in Fig. 6.1, and in accord with the proper argumentation schemes and techniques of critical questioning as indicated. They must take turns correctly, and make the right sorts of moves, if their arguments are to be judged reasonable and correct for the needs and requirements of good dialogue.

The normative analysis of the dialectical structure of the proper use of the *argumentum ad consequentiam* is still somewhat simplified. A few further details need to be added.

The general form of the argumentation scheme for *argumentum ad consequentiam* (of which a special case is the **Pro Side Argument** mentioned earlier) can be explicated more fully as follows. Let us suppose that the proponent has one particular goal G_0 which is the initial focus of the discussion, but that he also has other goals $G_1, \ldots, G_n$ that are part of the position. All these goals have some value in the proponent's opinion, but it could be a positive or negative value.

Argumentum ad Consequentiam: *Action A leads to G_0, supports G_0, or is consistent with G_0, and leads to, supports, or is consistent with $G_1, \ldots, G_n$, and $G_0, G_1, \ldots, G_n$ have some value.*

These complications reveal a number of subtleties that can play an important part in the proper sequence of dialectical exchanges between the proponent and respondent. In some cases, it is not just one goal that is at issue. Considerations of side-effects can bring other goals, like health or safety for example, into a discussion. These goals may not have been explicitly stated in the original discussion, but they could be relevant. Thus one goal may be pitted against another by the participants in the argument.

Another basic complication concerns the positive or negative character of the argument from consequences. Used in questioning of the Q4 type, the argument from consequences is negative, whereas the **Pro Side Argument** type of use is a positive argument from consequences. As the general form of the *argumentum ad consequentiam* shows, this type of argument can be used in either a positive or a negative format.

Whether or not an instance of use of the *argumentum ad consequentiam* is positive or negative depends on how this type of argumentation is being used by a participant at a given stage of the dialectical structure. Often, for example, the proponent could be using a positive argument from consequences against the respondent's negative argument from consequences. Or it could be the other way around, in another case.

Whether an *argumentum ad consequentiam* is positive or negative depends on the initial description of the conflict of opinions in stage 1 of the structure of the dialogue. This may depend on whether action A is described in positive or negative terms. For example "sitting there" could be described as a positive action (doing something) or as a negative action or omission (not doing anything). Thus the nature of the conflict or difference of opinions between the proponent and respondent have to be clarified carefully at the outset of the discussion. This will determine, subsequently, whether an *argumentum ad consequentiam* is positive or negative in a given case.

SUBFALLACIES OF *ARGUMENTUM AD CONSEQUENTIAM*

The previous section sets out a dialectical structure which can be used as a model of correct use of the *argumentum ad consequentiam*. The right kinds of moves and question-reply sequences for advancing and responding to this type of argumentation are set out in the model. Now comes the question–how is the *argumentum ad consequentiam* misused for sophistical argumentation in relation to this model? That is, how and why is argument from consequences a fallacy?

The simplest type of case of the *argumentum ad consequentiam fallacy* occurs where the context of dialogue is clearly inappropriate (at stage 1 in Fig. 6.1) for using the argument from consequences.

Case 6.15:   Scientists Helen and Ralph are discussing the merits of a new scientific hypothesis proposed by Helen. Ralph argues: "It is a bad hypothesis, because you will not get tenure if you persist in advancing it." Helen replies "It is a good hypothesis, because I will get tenure for advancing it."

In this case, whether the hypothesis in question is good or not as a scientific hypothesis should depend on the scientific evidence for or against it. This is a matter for discursive reasoning within the science in which the hypothesis lies. By ignoring such discursive matters, and instead concentrating on the practical consequences of Helen's having advanced the hypothesis, the participants in the argument have inappropriately used practical reasoning in a given dialectical situation that calls for discursive reasoning. The move from stage 1 to stage 2, and any subsequent moves in the discussion, are illicit. Any such move constitutes a fallacious use of the *argumentum ad consequentiam.*

The cases previously studied, however, are more subtle than this very simple case. For example, in Case 6.1, the discussion about policies on abortion is an appropriate context of dialogue for *pro* and *contra* uses of argument from consequences. The pro-life politician, as already noted, could cite the bad consequences of banning abortion, like "back-alley" abortions with resulting injuries, and so forth. The pro-choice could, in reply, cite consequences that she sees as good, (e.g., the saving of fetuses). Such arguments from consequences could, in principle, be appropriate and nonfallacious, because the original dialogue can be legitimately construed as being about policies concerning the acceptability of certain courses of action. The given context of dialogue is right for practical reasoning.

Why then is the reply, "If you take that view, you will not be elected" judged to be a fallacious *argumentum ad consequentiam?* The key factor here is that, at stage 3, the respondent has shifted to a metadialogue level which does not address the issue of abortion which the dialogue is supposed to be about. The pro-choice politician has shifted the line of dialogue to a higher level, claiming that bad consequences will ensue from the pro-life politician's having advanced a particular argument in the dialogue, in support of that point of view. This higher-level move, in effect, blocks off the dialogue at the lower level. For if the pro-life arguer tries to continue the line of argument in a way that is appropriate for the real dialogue the participants are supposed to be engaged in, it will not do any good against that blocking move. And if he or she tries to ascend to the higher level of disputing the point of whether he or she will be elected or not because of expressing pro-choice views, he or she has consented to abandoning the original line of the initial dialogue and going on to discuss a quite different practical question.

So the fallacy in Case 6.1 is more subtle than the one in Case 6.15. In Case 6.1, practical reasoning was generally appropriate for the dialogue, but by switching the practical reasoning to a different level, the respondent cut off the original, legitimate line of dialectical reasoning that was supposed to take place.

But both Cases 6.1 and 6.15 can be classified as instances of the basic *ad consequentiam fallacy* where *argumentum ad consequentiam* is used inappropriately in a dialogue either (a) because practical reasoning is not appropriate for the context of dialogue, or (b) because there has been a metadialogue shift to a different line of practical reasoning which blocks off the original dialogue.

Two subfallacies of argument from consequences, both different from the basic *argumentum ad consequentiam* fallacy, have previously been recognized by Michalos (1970) and DeMorgan (1847) respectively.

According to Michalos (1970), the *fallacy of uncertain consequences* "is committed when it is erroneously supposed that there are so many *uncertain consequences* attached to the adoption of some new policy, program, or law that it must not be adopted." Michalos offered the following example to illustrate this fallacy.

Case 6.16:   . . . suppose a certain kind of sewage disposal system is proposed for a town. Stanley Stopaction objects to it on the ground that it is bound to produce an unpleasant odor. After hearing a detailed explanation of the system's odor-preventing apparatus, Stanley still objects to it. Now, however, his view is simply that it is *too risky*. He is unable to specify *any* feature that might make it so, but he still insists that the system *could* produce unpredictable consequences which no one would want. Stanley has committed the fallacy of *uncertain consequences*.[10] (pp. 99-100)

In this case, Stanley has committed a fallacy because he has failed to respond properly, according to his obligations required by the dialectical procedures for engaging in this kind of argumentation. Moreover, he has persisted, dogmatically and truculently, in this failure. A (presumably) good reply was made to Stanley, countering his allegation of bad consequences of the proposed new sewer system. Instead of responding to this reply properly, or accepting it and going on to raise other objections, he persists in this Q4-type objection, yet cannot back it up with good evidence.

Stanley made a Q4-type objection at level three in Fig. 6.1. The proponent of going ahead with the new sewer system made the first type of reply at level four, arguing that the bad consequences were not likely to occur. He cited the system's odor-preventing apparatus. Presumably, this was a good and sufficient reply to Stanley's objection. But Stanley refused to concede it, still insisting that the new system was "too risky." But why was it "too risky," unless some defect in the odor-preventing apparatus can be cited? Stanley doesn't attempt to cite any specific defect, however or base his refusal to concede the point on any adequate reason. In persisting with this tactic, he violates the proper procedures required by the normative structure of the dialogue. For he must either (a) concede the reply, or (b) give some reason or some appropriate argument which would rebut the reply, shifting the burden of proof back in favor of his negative *argumentum ad consequentiam*. He has, in effect, failed to acknowledge the proponent's properly given and adequate reply, instead retreating in a dogmatic and truculent tactic of pushing his *argumentum ad consequentiam* ahead too aggressively.

Stanley's attitude is similar to the attitude of the proponent of an unfalsifiable hypothesis who will allow no evidence to count against it–any attempt at reasonable rebuttal is brushed aside as "not counting" against the hypothesis. Stanley keeps insisting the new sewer system is "too risky" even though he has been presented with evidence that the system will not likely have the bad consequences he has cited. He claims the new system *could* produce "unpredictable consequences which no one would want" but he does not cite anything specific to move the argument along any further.

DeMorgan (1847) described a fallacy of arguing from consequences, but it seems to be a special type of *ad consequentiam* fallacy. DeMorgan did not claim

---

[10] Michalos (1970, p. 100).

or imply, however, that argument from consequences is generally fallacious. And indeed, his discussion of this particular type of fallacious reasoning presumes that arguing from consequences is generally a reasonable form of argument. The fallacy DeMorgan described is one of drawing a hasty conclusion from a single consequence, or too few consequences of an action.

> The disposition to judge the prudence of an action by its result, contains a fallacy when it is applied to single instances only, or to few in number. That which, under the circumstances, is the prudent rule of conduct, may, nevertheless end in something as bad as could have resulted from want of circumspection. But upon dozens of instances, such a balance would appear in favour of prudence as would leave no doubt in favour of the rule of conduct, even in the instances in which it failed. The fallacy consists in judging from the result about the conduct of one who had only the previous circumstances to guide him. 'You acted unwisely, as is proved by the result,' is a paralogism, except when it implies 'You did, as it happens in this instance, take a course which did not lead to the desired result.' Take a strong case, and the absurdity will be seen. A chemist makes up a prescription wrongly, and his customer leaves him for another: this other, so it may happen, makes it up still more wrongly, and poisons the patient. Who would venture to say that he acted unwisely, as is proved by the result, in leaving the tradesman whom he knew to be careless, for another of whom he knew no harm.[11]

As DeMorgan described this fallacy, it is a kind of inductive error of failing to find out "that the result which has happened is the one which was likely to happen." (p. 277). One result, by itself "proves very little as to the superior wisdom of the course that produced it." (p. 277). Hence the fallacy is one of basing a generalization or presumption on too few instances to support the weight accorded to it. This fallacy could be called the *fallacy of too few consequences*.

Note, however, that DeMorgan was clearly not saying or implying that argument from consequences is fallacious or incorrect *per se*. In fact, his discussion strongly appears to be based on the presumption that judging "the prudence of an action by its result" is, or can be, a reasonable form of argument when it meets the right requirements. The fallacy is committed where an arguer makes a leap from one (or too few) consequences to an inadequately supported conclusion about "the wisdom of the course which produced it" (or them). This fallacy is a kind of combination of argument from consequences with the fallacy of inadequate statistics or hasty generalization (arguing inductively from too small a sample).

The fallacy of uncertain consequences occurs at the leftmost reply of level 4 in Fig. 6.1. The opponent fails to respond properly to the proponent's legitimate proof that the cited bad consequences are not likely to occur. Instead, he dogmatically digs in his heels and persists in cleaving to the prejudicial view that *some* bad consequences *must* be likely to occur, though he cannot say what they are. This is opting out of the proper sequence of dialogue by failing to concede the proponent's legitimate and well-supported reply. It is a fallacy because it is a

---

[11] DeMorgan (1847, pp. 276-277).

dogmatic refusal to concede a point which makes further legitimate dialogue impossible. No response to it is possible in the sequence of dialogue, other than pointing out its fallaciousness.

The fallacy of too few consequences concerns the judgment of how bad the consequences really are. Are they bad enough to justify the prudential reasonableness of opting for an alternative line of action? At level 3, the opponent suggests going to an alternative that does not have such bad consequences (the arrow to the right at level 3 in Fig. 6.1). But here it is up to the proponent, at level 4 (second box from the left) to argue that the consequences of the proposed action are not really all that bad. The error here is to overlook or misjudge this consideration, leaping ahead too hastily to an alternative that, really, is no better a bet. This fault is not so much a fallacy as an error of reasoning. But it can be a fallacy where the appropriate moves are blocked out by a proponent who is too dogmatic or intransigent to even allow this line of reasoning a place in the sequence of dialogue.

Now we have identified the basic *ad consequentiam* fallacy and some subfallacies. Our list of subfallacies of the *ad consequentiam* is not complete, however. If you look at Fig. 6.1 again, you can see that there could be all kinds of tricky or erroneous ways of violating the proper order and structure of question-reply moves in the sequence of this type of dialogue. Future case studies can now go ahead with the work of identifying and analyzing other *ad consequentiam* subfallacies.

We now turn to the relationship of the *argumentum ad consequentiam* to some major fallacies that are familiar from the standard list of fallacies in the textbooks.

RELATED FALLACIES

The *argumentum ad baculum* is very closely related to the argument from consequences. This connection is especially close in the case of the indirect type of *ad baculum* argument, where an argument from consequences is used as a speech act to indirectly make a threat against a respondent in dialogue. The classic case from Copi (1986) shows this connection very clearly.

Case 6.17:   According to R. Grunberger, author of *A Social History of the Third Reich,* published in Britain, the Nazis used to send the following notice to German readers who let their subscriptions lapse: "Our paper certainly deserves the support of every German. We shall continue to forward copies of it to you, and hope that you will not want to expose yourself to unfortunate consequences in the case of cancellation." (p. 106)

The *argumentum ad baculum* works in this type of case by piggybacking on the argument from consequences. The argument from consequences is used, in the context of dialogue, to convey an indirect speech act that is a threat. On the surface, it is an argument from consequences, but the part of Case 6.17 in quotation marks is an indirect speech act that, at a secondary level of interpretation, expresses a threat. At one level it is a warning, but at a deeper level, it is a threat. The use of this technique is a way for the speaker to "distance" from the making of a threat, an act that may be illegal, impolite, or otherwise unacceptable.

According to Searle (1969), the speech act of *warning* has four essential conditions: (a) the hearer has reasons to believe that the event in question will occur [an event that is not in the hearer's interests], (b) it is not obvious to either the speaker or the hearer that the event will occur, (c) the speaker believes that the event is not in the hearer's best interests, and (d) the act by the speaker counts as an "undertaking" that the event is not in the hearer's best interests. According to Searle, however, warning is a speech act that–unlike the act of requesting–is not an attempt to get the hearer to do an action. Thus "undertaking" does not mean, as used by Searle, that the speaker is expressing that he or she will bring about the event that is not in the hearer's interests, unless the hearer complies with some demand.

By contrast, the speech act of making a threat does essentially require that the speaker is conveying the message that he or she will take steps to bring about this bad event (bad for the hearer) unless the hearer takes steps to avoid this outcome. Making a threat is an attempt by the speaker to get the hearer to carry out an action (or to refrain from some action).

Thus the speech act requirements for a warning and a threat are essentially different. As used in argumentation, the two types of speech acts are distinct. The indirect *argumentum ad baculum* is a device used to put pressure on a respondent in argumentation by covertly making a threat, using an indirect speech act. What appears on the surface to be a warning, is, at a deeper level of the dialogue, really a threat. There is a shift from a prudential argument (an argument from consequences) to the making of a threat.

But there are two points here to be very clear about. One is that the *argumentum ad baculum* is not simply fallacious because it is conveyed through the use of a covert threat. Such a move can be deceptive, but that is not, in itself, a fallacious argument. A threat can be immoral, illegal, impolite, brutal, and so forth, without necessarily being fallacious. The other point is that the *ad baculum,* in such a case, is not a species of the argument from consequences.

On the first point, it should be said that the *argumentum ad baculum* is fallacious where the threat has been used as a sophistical tactic which goes against the goals of dialogue that the participants are supposed to be engaged in. The threat, for example, may be used as an irrelevant distraction in place of giving proper evidence according to the rules for the type of dialogue the speaker and hearer are supposedly engaged in.

On the second point, it should be said that two stages are involved in the fallacious use of the indirect *argumentum ad baculum.* The first stage is the indirect speech act of using the argument from consequences to convey a threat to the respondent. But the second stage is the using of this conveyed threat in the sequence of argumentation to mask or substitute illicitly for a lack of evidence or good reasons to support the conclusion that is supposed to be proved. As Woods (1987) convincingly showed, a bad prudential argument based on a threat can be a failure for various reasons without necessarily being an instance of the *ad baculum* fallacy.

Initially, it is correct to classify the *argumentum ad baculum*[12] as a species of argument from consequences. This classification is not, however, the whole story when it comes to providing a good way of analyzing the fallacy of *ad baculum*. The indirect type of *ad baculum* does incorporate the argument from consequences, but it is simplistic and incorrect to say that the *ad baculum* is fallacious because it is a particular instance of argument from consequences. The *ad baculum* is a fallacy because it violates rules of reasonable dialogue, most often because it has been used as a distraction from the task of fulfilling the proper burden of proof in an argument. It does incorporate the argument from consequences in an indirect speech act.[13] But this is a function of the way it is used as a sophistical tactic of argumentation. It is misleading to claim that the *ad baculum* is fallacious simply because it is a particular instance of the more general fallacy of argument from consequences.

Cederblom and Paulsen (1982) claimed that the *argumentum ad baculum* is a fallacy because it is a "particular instance of the more general fallacy" of "appeal to consequences." According to their account, "If you accept an appeal to force or an appeal to pity, you adopt a certain belief not because of evidence but in order to bring about certain consequences–avoiding harm to yourself or others." The example they represent is the following:

Case 6.18:   If you opposed gun control you'd have a lot better chance of being elected. Why don't you reconsider your position on that issue?[14]

The problem with this case, to begin with, is that it is by no means clear that it is a fallacy. Nor is it clear that it is an *ad baculum* argument that makes a threat or appeals to force. The context of dialogue could be that of the candidate's own adviser giving advice on which positions in the riding might give him or her the best chances of being elected. In the context of this type of discussion, there would be no fallacy in Case 6.18, and no appeal to force.

Of course, in other contexts of dialogue, the argument in Case 6.18 could amount to a threat which should count as a fallacy. But in order to fit this bill, several requirements would have to be met. There is no evidence at all from the information given on the text of discourse in Case 6.18 that any of these requirements has been met. Case 6.18 could be interpreted many ways. But because the burden of proof required to substantiate the charge of fallacy has not been met, it is unfair to classify it as either an *ad baculum* argument or as a fallacy.

Note, however, the similarity with Case 6.1, which was classified as an *ad consequentiam* fallacy. Case 6.18 could be a fallacious argument too if the context were a critical discussion of the issue of gun control between a proponent

---

[12] It may be plausible to so classify other fallacies as well.

[13] At least, this is true of the indirect *ad baculum*.

[14] Cederblom and Paulsen (1982, p. 102).

and a respondent who have taken opposed sides on the issue. It could, so interpreted, be a case of the fallacy of *ad consequentiam*, or even possibly a case of the fallacy of the indirect use of the *ad baculum*. The problem is that we are not given enough information about the context of dialogue to determine, one way or the other, whether such charges are well-founded.

Note also another key difference between Case 6.1 and Case 6.18. In Case 6.18, the speech act requesting reconsideration of the arguer's position is put in the form of a question. This makes it less open to the charge of being a fallacious move in the dialogue, other things being equal. The basic problem with Case 6.18 then, a problem which it shares with Cases 6.13 and 6.14 (and to some extent, with Case 6.1) is the lack of enough information given about the context of dialogue, to firmly pin down the charge of fallacy.

Another of the major recognized fallacies that appears to be a species of *argumentum ad consequentiam* is the slippery slope fallacy.

According to the analysis of the slippery slope argument given in Walton (1992, *Slip. Slope*), this argument turns out to be an extension of argumentation from consequences. In a slippery slope argument, a chain of consequences is driven onward from a given "first step" of action toward some dangerous or "horrible" ultimate outcome. Because the outcome is bad for the proponent advocating or considering this first step, by a *modus tollens* sequence of "backward" inferences, the conclusion is inferred that the proponent should not take this first step.

"Consequences" are not always (narrowly) causal consequences in a slippery slope argument. There are four basic kinds of slippery slope arguments: (1) *sorites* or linguistic, (2) causal, (3) precedent, and (4) all-in slippery slope arguments (Govier, 1982). Even so, many or all slippery slope arguments can be seen as based on the *argumentum ad consequentiam*, depending on how the term 'consequence' is defined.

The following example is an all-in type of slippery slope argument that combines elements from all of (1), (2) and (3). But causal considerations are very important in it, and it can be seen as based, to a significant degree, on argumentation from consequences. The dialogue was a parliamentary debate on whether the use of marijuana should be legalized.

Case 6.19:   Tolerance to cannabis leads the chronic smoker to increased usage and on to more potent drugs. Decriminalization of marijuana would unleash a drug problem more severe than we have ever known.

But is the slippery slope argument a fallacy? Walton (1992, *Slip. Slope*) argued that it can be a reasonable kind of practical argumentation in some cases, or a weak, faulty, or even fallacious argument as used in other cases. In Case 6.19, the argument leaves out many intervening steps and scientific evidence that would be needed to make it strong enough to meet persuasive requirements of burden of proof. It does not follow, however, that because a slippery slope argument is weak, it must be fallacious. Case 6.19 is open to legitimate critical questions.

But, in principle, these questions could be met with appropriate replies that would support the reasonableness of the slippery slope argument as used in Case 6.19.

Little, Groarke, and Tindale (1989) agreed that there can be good as well as bad instances of the slippery slope argument. They judge slippery slope arguments as stronger or weaker in a given case, depending on "whether the causal connections posited really hold and whether the final consequence has been properly judged to be desirable or undesirable" (p. 241). The way that Little, Groarke, and Tindale defined the slippery slope argument, as an argument "used to show that certain actions should be performed or avoided because of their long-range consequences" (p. 240), shows how it can be classified as a species of argument from consequences.

At any rate, we have further confirmed the contention of chapter three that the slippery slope argument is quite often a species of *argumentum ad consequentiam.* It is an extension of the *argumentum ad consequentiam* that adds on the idea of a "slippery" sequence of linked consequences leading to one ultimate negative disastrous outcome. Hence the study of the slippery slope fallacy can greatly profit from the insights derived from our analysis of the dialectical structure of the *argumentum ad consequentiam.*

The slippery slope and the indirect *ad baculum* argument are also, in many cases, very closely related. The slippery slope argument is often used as a threatening scare tactic by a proponent who paints an ominous picture of what *might* happen in the dim and uncertain future if things go badly–a kind of pessimistic argument which exploits fear of the unknown future. Both the slippery slope and the *ad baculum* fallacies are quite often species of argument from consequences that have been used fallaciously for all kinds of reasons that merit study as special fallacies in their own right. But the underlying structure of the *argumentum ad consequentiam* provides their basis.

A case described by Beardsley (1950) combines these elements under a kind of argumentation tactic Beardsley calls *alarm,* described as a kind of fallacious appeal to emotion instead of violence.

Case 6.20:   *Alarm.* "Crime waves sweeping across the nation in the wake of progressive education . . . the man next to you on the bus may be a secret agent of the Kremlin . . . the clergy, the teaching profession, the army, Hollywood–infiltrated with subversive elements." By calling up such specters as these, the speaker aims to put us in a state of unreasonable fearfulness. What he *suggests* is that the policy he opposes will inevitably lead to these fearful consequences, but he does not stop to *prove* that the consequences will follow. Instead, he makes us so frightened at the very thought of them that we will be scared to try any policy even remotely suggestive of the possibility of such consequences.[15]

---

[15] Beardsley (1950, p. 285).

Of course, raising an alarm need not necessarily in itself be a fallacious kind of argument. But used as a species of argumentation from consequences, one can easily see how it could be abused, or used as a sophistical tactic. The similarity with Case 6.16, the case of Stanley Stopaction, should come to mind. Stanley could not cite any specific negative consequences that made the proposed new sewer system too risky, but still insisted that it had to be too risky–a kind of appeal to fear which was not backed up by evidence. In Case 6.16, a fallacy could be involved for similar reasons. The person who raises the alarm calls up "specters," or fearful possible consequences by suggestion, rather than by presenting any real evidence that such fearful consequences are realistically likely. The by now familiar failure occurs at the leftmost reply in level 4 of Fig. 6.1– a failure to show that the projected bad consequences are likely to occur.

THE PROJECT OF EVALUATION

The normative model of the *argumentum ad consequentiam* presented earlier is a useful tool in aiding a rational critic to approach a particular case and judge, in relation to the given text of discourse and context of dialogue, whether the use of this argument can fairly be evaluated as fallacious or not.

Case 6.9 was a fallacious use of the *argumentum ad consequentiam*, whereas Case 6.10 was not, because Arthur's reply in Case 6.9 shifted to the metadialogue level and (inappropriately) shifted to a consideration of negative consequences at that level. Arthur could have cited the consequences of the Treaty of Versailles– that it made the Germans feel resentful, and so forth. But instead, he shifted to the consideration of the practical consequences of George's stating that point of view in his future sermons or other public speeches.

Case 6.9, therefore, is a classic case of the basic *ad consequentiam* fallacy. Arthur's reply makes an illegitimate shift to the wrong kind of consequential argumentation, using it inappropriately (in the context of dialogue) to try to rebut George's argument about the fairness of the Treaty of Versailles. What clinches the fallacy is Arthur's reply to George, "what a bad argument." It is clear that Arthur is trying to attack George's argument by this *ad consequentiam* reply, and not just to question the prudence of George's putting forth his argument in a public forum.

In Cases 6.13 and 6.14, we were not given enough information on the text of discourse or context of dialogue to arrive at a fair and complete resolution of the question of whether the use of the *argumentum ad consequentiam* was fallacious or not. There was a strong suspicion of fallaciousness in these cases, but it would be prejudicial to claim "fallacy" without sufficient evidence to back up such a serious charge.

Case 6.7 was not judged to be a fallacy even though the *argumentum ad consequentiam* was routed through the metadialogue level–the adviser cited the consequences of the candidate's saying something in the proposed election speeches. The reason why this case is not a fallacy is that the given context of dialogue is one of advice-giving by a campaign adviser. Hence the practical question of the possible consequences of taking a public position on an issue are a legitimate and appropriate shift from discursive to practical reasoning in the sequence of argumentation.

Case 6.11 showed, however, that even when raised to the metadialogue level, the *argumentum ad consequentiam* need not necessarily be fallacious. Challenging the dialectical appropriateness of a proposed speech or move in an argument on grounds of the practical consequences of making this kind of move can be quite legitimate as a kind of argumentation.

As Case 6.12 showed, thinking of argumentation from consequences as always or inherently fallacious would be a bad theory which would make it impossible to reply to false or unjustified charges of fallacy. Case 6.12 also showed that the appropriateness of practical reasoning in a situation where it has been pitted against discursive reasoning depends on the given situation and context of dialogue. When a discursive inquiry into the facts is insufficient to resolve an urgent practical problem, it can be reasonable and justifiable to act on the basis of practical presumptions. Here the argument from consequences is a presumptive kind of reasoning. But as such, it can be reasonable and nonfallacious.

The problem in Case 6.2 was that it seemed that the argument addressed consequences that were only indirect or tangential, rather than discussing the more direct consequences that are more to the point. It may be that vegetarianism on a wide scale, especially if brought about quickly, would throw large numbers of people out of work. But surely that could be dealt with, and more importantly, it is tangential to the main issue of whether vegetarianism is "injurious and unhealthy" because of its direct effects as a diet. Would it lead to protein deficiency or other nutritional and health problems because of its direct effects on those who choose it? This question seems like the major issue to be addressed first, and these other considerations of employment, because they are secondary, seem to get in the way when given priority, as Case 6.2 suggests. But is the imbalance of priorities blocking the legitimate flow of dialogue in the argument in Case 6.2? Unless there is evidence that this is so, Case 6.2 should not be classified as an instance of the fallacious use of the *argumentum ad consequentiam*.

If there is a subfallacy or error to be suggested by this case, it is the fault of hitting on the wrong kinds of consequences, relatively indirect or less relevant consequences, at the expense of considering more direct and significant consequences that should be of primary concern. However, it is not clear that this is a distinct type of subfallacy in its own right as a question of judging the significance of consequences for resolving a practical issue.

This work is part of a broader program including the development of the theory of practical reasoning, the theory of errors of reasoning, and the theory of fallacies as sophistical tactics used in dialogue argumentation (see Walton (*Inf. Log.*, 1989; *Pract. Reas.*, 1990; *What Reas.*, 1990; *Begg. Quest.*, 1991; and *Prag. Theory*, 1995). This research has studied one particular fallacy, the *argumentum ad consequentiam*, and argued for seven main theses with respect to it.

1. The *argumentum ad consequentiam* is not fallacious *per se*. It can be used correctly in some cases, incorrectly or inadequately in other cases.

2. When it is a fallacy, it is a pragma-dialectical fallacy that relates to the context of dialogue in which the argument has been used, and it should be judged in relation to normative models of reasonable dialogue. The fullest understanding of the fallacy requires seeing it as a kind of sophistical tactic involving a dialectical shift.

3. The basic fallacy is partially explained as an error of reasoning on the basis of a distinction between practical reasoning and discursive reasoning, and how these types of reasoning are used in argumentation. There are also a number of other errors of reasoning associated with faults of practical reasoning.

4. The fallacious instances of *argumentum ad consequentiam* are the severe cases of misuse where there is a serious, underlying, systematic error or sophistical tactic.

5. A distinction needs to be kept in mind between fallacies and flaws or faults that result in weak, unjustified arguments, or errors that are not fallacious.

6. Particular cases should be judged on their merits, in relation to the application of a normative model of dialogue to a text of discourse in the given case.

7. Some other important traditional fallacies, especially *ad baculum* and slippery slope arguments of some kinds, are based on *argumentum ad consequentiam*.

Not all questions about the *argumentum ad consequentiam* have been answered. But enough insight into its structure has been gained to serve as a practical aid to help in evaluating particular cases, and to serve as a solid and fertile basis for future research.

REFERENCES

Aristotle. (1928). *The Works of Aristotle Translated into English,* W. D. Ross (Ed.). Oxford: Oxford University Press.

Aristotle. (1939). *Topics.* (Trans. E. S. Forster). Cambridge, MA: Harvard University Press.

Aristotle. (1955). *On Sophistical Refutations (De Sophisticis Elenchis).* (Trans. E. S. Forster). Cambridge, MA: Harvard University Press.

Arnauld, A. (1964). *The art of thinking* (Trans. James Dickoff and Patricia James). Indianapolis: Bobbs-Merrill. [First published in 1662]

Associated Press. (1990, August 25). Life Sentence for Murder. *The Globe and Mail,* C4.

Audi, R. (1989). *Practical reasoning.* New York: Routledge.

Bäck, A. (1987). Philoponus on the Fallacy of Accident. *Ancient Philosophy, 7,* 131-146.

Barth, E. M., & Krabbe, E. C. W. (1982). *From Axiom to Dialogue.* New York: De Gruyter.

Barth, E. M., & Martens, J. L. (1977). *Argumentum Ad Hominem:* From Chaos to Formal Dialectic. *Logique et Analyse, 77-78,* 76-96.

Beardsley, M. C. (1950). *Thinking straight.* Englewood Cliffs, NJ: Prentice-Hall.

Begley, K. and Fitzgerald, K. (1986, September 1). Freud Should Have Tried Barking. *Newsweek,* 65-66.

Black, M. (1970). *Margins of Precision.* Ithaca, NY, and London: Cornell University Press.

Blair, J. A. (1988). What is Bias? In T. Govier (Ed.), *Selected Issues in Logic and Communication* (pp. 93-103). Belmont: Wadsworth.

Blair, J. A. (1991). What is the right amount of support for a conclusion? In F. H. van Eemeren, R. Grootendorst, J. A. Blair, & C. A. Willard (Eds.), *Proceedings of the Second International Conference on Argumentation,* Vol. 1A (pp. 330-337). Amste,dam: SICSAT.

Brinton, A. (1985). A Rhetorical View of the *Ad Hominem. Australasian Journal of Philosophy, 63,* 50-63.

Brinton, A. (1986). Ethotic Argument. *History of Philosophy Quarterly, 3,* 245-257.

Brinton, A. (1987). Ethotic argument: some uses. In F. H. van Eemeren, R. Grootendorst, J. A. Blair, & C. A. Willard (Eds.), *Argumentation: Perspectives and Approaches* (pp. 246-254). Dordrecht and Providence: Foris Publications.

Bueno, A. A. (1988). Aristotle, the Fallacy of Accident, and the Nature of Predication: A Historical Inquiry. *Journal of the History of Philosophy, 26,* 5-24.

Byerly, H. C. (1973). *A primer of logic.* New York: Harper & Row.

Campbell, S. K. (1974). *Flaws and fallacies in statistical thinking.* Englewood Cliffs: Prentice-Hall.

Cederblom, J., & Paulsen, D. W. (1982). *Critical reasoning: understanding and criticizing arguments and theories.* Belmont, CA: Wadsworth.

Chazin, S. (1989, June 25). Learning to Appreciate the Dandelions in Life. *The New York Times,* 32.

Clarke, D. S., Jr. (1985). *Practical inferences.* London: Routledge.

Clarke, D. S., Jr. (1989). *Rational acceptance and purpose.* Totowa, NJ: Rowman and Littlefield.

Cohen, M. R., & Nagel, E. (1934). *An introduction to logic and scientific method.* New York: Harcourt Brace & World.

Collins, A., Warnock, E. H., Aiello, N., & Miller, M. L. (1975). Reasoning from incomplete knowledge, In D. G. Bobrow & A. Collins (Eds.), *Representation and Understanding: Studies in Cognitive Science* (pp. 383-415). New York: Academic Press.

Copi, I. M. (1982). *Introduction to Logic* (6th ed.). New York: Macmillan.

Copi, I. M. (1986). *Introduction to Logic* (7th ed.). New York: Macmillan.

Copi, I. M., & Cohen, C. (1990). *Introduction to Logic* (8th ed.). New York: Macmillan.

Cuomo, M. L. (1984, October 25). Religious Belief and Public Morality. *The New York Review of Books,* Vol. 31, 32-37.

de Cornulier, B. (1988). Knowing Whether, Knowing Who, and Epistemic Closure. In M. Meyer (Ed.), *Questions and Questioning* (pp. 182-192). Berlin: Walter de Gruyter.

Degnan, R. E. (1963). Evidence. *Encyclopaedia Britannica,* 15th Ed., Vol. 8, 905-916.

DeMorgan, A. (1847). *Formal Logic.* London: Taylor and Walton.

De Pater, W. A. (1968). La Fonction du Lieu et de l'Instrument dans les Topiques. In G. E. L. Owen (Ed.), *Aristotle on Dialectic: The Topics* (pp. 164-188). Oxford: Oxford University Press.

Doyle, A. C. (1932). *The Complete Sherlock Holmes,* Vol. 1. New York: Doubleday, Doran & Co.

Ebbesen, S. (1981). *Commentaries and Commentators on Aristotle's Sophistici Elenchi,* 3 Vols., Leiden: E. J. Brill.

Editorial (1992, March 28). Aquarium Stops Catching Killer Whales. *Winnipeg Free Press,* A3.

Engel, S. M. (1982). *With Good Reason: An Introduction to Informal Fallacies* (2nd Ed.). New York: St. Martin's Press. [1st Ed., 1976].
Evans, J. D. G. (1977). *Aristotle's Concept of Dialectic.* Cambridge: Cambridge University Press.
Fearnside, W. W., & Holther, W. B. (1959). *Fallacy: The Counterfeit of Argument.* Englewood Cliffs: Prentice-Hall.
Fischer, D. H. (1970). *Historians' Fallacies.* New York: Harper & Row.
Fogelin, R. (1987). *Understanding Arguments.* New York: Harcourt Brace Jovanovich.
Gelber, H. G. (1987). The Fallacy of Accident and the *Dictum de Omni:* Late Medieval Controversy over a Reciprocal Pair. *Vivarium, 25,* 110-145.
Golding, M. (1984). *Legal Reasoning.* New York: Knopf.
Govier, T. (1982). What's Wrong with Slippery Slope Arguments? *Canadian Journal of Philosophy, 12,* 303-316.
Grice, H. P. (1975). Logic and Conversation. In D. Davidson & G. Harman (Eds.), *The Logic of Grammar* (pp. 64-75). Encino, CA: Dickenson.
Hamblin, C. L. (1970). *Fallacies.* London: Methuen.
Harding, H. F. (Ed.) (1952). *The Age of Danger: Major Speeches on American Problems.* New York: Random House.
Hastings, A. (1963). *A Reformulation of the Modes of Reasoning in Argumentation.* Doctoral dissertation, Northwestern University, Evanston, Illinois.
Hinman, L. M. (1982). The Case for *Ad Hominem* Arguments. *Australasian Journal of Philosophy, 60,* 338-345.
Hintikka, J. (1981). The Logic of Information-Seeking Dialogues: A Model. In W. Becker and W. K. Essler (Eds.), *Konzepte der Dialektik* (pp. 212-231). Frankfurt am Main: Vittorio Klostermann.
Hintikka, J., & Saarinen, E. (1979). Information-Seeking Dialogues: Some of Their Logical Properties. *Studia Logica, 38,* 355-363.
Imwinkelried, E. J. (1981). *Scientific and Expert Evidence.* New York: Practising Law Institute.
Imwinkelried, E. J. (1986). Science Takes the Stand: The Growing Misuse of Expert Testimony. *The Sciences, 26,* 20-25.
Johnson, R. H., & Blair, J. A. (1983). *Logical Self-Defense* (2nd Ed.). Toronto: McGraw-Hill Ryerson Limited.
Johnstone, H. W., Jr. (1978). *Validity and Rhetoric in Philosophical Argument.* University Park, PA: Dialogue Press of Man and World.
Joseph, H. W. B. (1916). *An Introduction to Logic* (2nd Ed.). Oxford: The Clarendon Press.
Kerferd, G. B. (1967). Protagoras of Abdera. In P. Edwards (Ed.), *The Encyclopedia of Philosophy* (Vol. 5, pp. 505-507). New York: Macmillan.
Kienpointner, M. (1987). Towards a Typology of Argumentation Schemes. In F. H. van Eemeren, R. Grootendorst, J. A. Blair, & C. A. Willard (Eds.), *Argumentation: Across the Lines of Discipline* (pp. 275-287). Dordrecht: Foris.
Kienpointner, M. (1992). *Alltagslogik: Struktur und Funktion von Argumentationsmustern [Everyday Logic: The Structure and Function of Argumentation Schemes].* Stuttgart: Fromman-Holzboog.
Kneale, W., & Kneale, M. (1962). *The Development of Logic.* Oxford: Oxford University Press.
Krabbe, E. C. W. (1990). Inconsistent Commitment and Commitment to Inconsistencies. *Informal Logic, 12,* 33-42.
Kubie, L. S. (1954). Some Unsolved Problems of the Scientific Career. Part II, *American Scientist, 42,* 104-112.
Levinson, C. C. (1983). *Pragmatics.* Cambridge: Cambridge University Press.
Lewis, C. T., & Short, C. (1969). *A Latin Dictionary.* Oxford: Clarendon Press.
Lipton, P. (1991). *Inference to the Best Explanation.* London: Routledge.
Little, J. F., Groarke, L. A., & Tindale, C. W. (1989). *Good Reasoning Matters.* Toronto: McClelland and Stewart.
Marks, J. (1988). When is a Fallacy not a Fallacy? *Metaphilosophy, 19,* 307-312.
Michalos, A. C. (1970). *Improving Your Reasoning.* Englewood Cliffs, NJ: Prentice-Hall.
Moore, W. E. (1967). *Creative and Critical Thinking.* New York: Houghton Mifflin.
Motherwell, C., & Fraser, G. (1990, December 19). Supreme Court Backs Mandatory Retirement. *The Globe and Mail,* A1.
Perelman, C., & Olbrechts-Tyteca, L. (1969). *The New Rhetoric: A Treatise on Argumentation* (2nd Ed.). (Trans. J. Wilkinson & P. Weaver). Notre Dame: University of Notre Dame Press. [First published in 1958 as *La Nouvelle Rhétorique: Traité de l'Argumentation*]
Pettis, David M. (1989, December). Honest Engine? *Reader's Digest,* 59.
Pollock, J. L. (1991). A Theory of Defeasible Reasoning. *International Journal of Intelligent Systems, 6,* 33-54.
Popper, K. R. (1963). *Conjectures and Refutations.* London: Routledge & Kegan Paul.
Poste, E. (1866). *Aristotle on Fallacies or the Sophistici Elenchi.* London: Macmillan and Co.
Rachels, J. (1986). *The End of Life.* Oxford: Oxford University Press.

Reinard, J. C. (1991). *Foundations of Argument.* Dubuque, Iowa: William C. Brown.
Reiter, R. (1987). Nonmonotonic Reasoning. *Annual Review of Computer Science, 2,* 147-186.
Rescher, N. (1964). *Introduction to Logic.* New York: St. Martin's Press.
Rescher, N. (1976). *Plausible Reasoning.* Assen-Amsterdam: Van Gorcum.
Rescher, N. (1977). *Dialectics.* Albany: State University of New York Press.
Rescher, N. (1985). *Pascal's Wager: A Study of Practical Reasoning in Philosophical Theology.* Notre Dame, Indiana: University of Notre Dame Press.
Rescher, N. (1988). *Rationality: A Philosophical Inquiry into the Nature and Rationale of Reason.* Oxford: Oxford University Press.
Robinson, R. (1971). Arguing from Ignorance. *Philosophical Quarterly, 21,* 97-108.
Runes, D. D. (1964). *Dictionary of Philosophy* (15th ed.). Paterson, NJ: Littlefield, Adams & Co.
Sainsbury, R. M. (1988). *Paradoxes.* Cambridge: Cambridge University Press.
Salmon, W. (1964). *Logic.* Englewood Cliffs, NJ: Prentice-Hall.
Salmon, M. H. (1984). *Introduction to Logic and Critical Thinking.* San Diego: Harcourt Brace Jovanovich.
Schank, R., & Abelson, R. (1977). *Scripts, Plans, Goals and Understanding.* Hillsdale, NJ: Lawrence Erlbaum Associates.
Schellens, P. J. (1987). Types of Argument and the Critical Reader. In F. H. van Eemeren, R. Grootendorst, J. A. Blair, & C. A. Willard (Eds.), *Argumentation: Analysis and Practices* (pp. 34-41). Dordrecht: Foris.
Schwartz, J., Rogers, M., & Sandza, R. (1988). Steve Jobs Comes Back. *Newsweek,* October 24, 46-51.
Searle, J. (1969). *Speech Acts.* Cambridge: Cambridge University Press.
Searle, J. (1975). Indirect Speech Acts. In P. Cole & J. L. Morgan (Eds.), *Syntax and Semantics* (Vol. 3, pp. 59-82). New York: Academic Press.
Simpson, R. L. (1985). *A Computer Model of Case Based Reasoning in Problem Solving.* Doctoral Thesis, Report # GIT-ICS-85/18. Atlanta: Georgia Institute of Technology.
Thouless, R. H. (1930). *Straight and Crooked Thinking.* London: English Universities Press.
Ullman-Margalit, E. (1983). On Presumption. *The Journal of Philosophy, 80,* 143-163.
Vanderveken, D. (1990). *Meaning and Speech Acts.* Cambridge: Cambridge University Press.
van Eemeren, F. H., & Grootendorst, R. (1987). Fallacies in Pragma-Dialectical Perspective. *Argumentation, 1,* 283-301.
van Eemeren, F. H., & Grootendorst, R. (1989). A Transition Stage in the Theory of Fallacies. *Journal of Pragmatics, 13,* 99-109.
van Eemeren, F. H., & Grootendorst, R. (1992). *Argumentation, Communication and Fallacies.* Hillsdale, NJ: Lawrence Erlbaum Associates.
van Eemeren, F. H., & Kruiger, T. (1987). Identifying Argumentation Schemes. In F. H. van Eemeren, R. Grootendorst, J. A. Blair, & C. A. Willard (Eds.), *Argumentation: Perspectives and Approaches.* Dordrecht: Foris Publications.
van Eemeren, F. H., Grootendorst, R., & Kruiger, T. (1987). *Handbook of Argumentation Theory.* Dordrecht: Foris.
Walton, D. N. (1985). *Arguer's Position.* Westport, CT: Greenwood Press.
Walton, D. N. (1987). *Informal Fallacies.* Amsterdam: John Benjamins Publishing Co.
Walton, D. N. (1988). Burden of Proof. *Argumentation, 2,* 233-254.
Walton, D. N. (1989). *Informal Logic.* Cambridge: Cambridge University Press.
Walton, D. N. (1989). *Question-Reply Argumentation.* New York: Greenwood Press.
Walton, D. N. (1990). Ignoring Qualifications (*Secundum Quid*) as a Subfallacy of Hasty Generalization (*Sec. Quid*). *Logique et Analyse, 129-130.* 113-154.
Walton, D. N. (1990). *Practical Reasoning.* Savage, Maryland: Rowman and Littlefield.
Walton, D. N. (1990). What is Reasoning? What is an Argument? *The Journal of Philosophy, 87,* 399-419.
Walton, D. N. (1991). *Begging the Question: Circular Reasoning as a Tactic of Argumentation.* New York: Greenwood Press.
Walton, D. N. (1991). Bias, Critical Doubt and Fallacies, *Argumentation and Advocacy, 28,* 1-22.
Walton, D. N. (1992). *Plausible Argument in Everyday Conversation.* Albany: State University of New York Press.
Walton, D. N. (1992). *Slippery Slope Arguments.* Oxford: Oxford University Press.
Walton, D. N. (1995). *Arguments from Ignorance.* University Park, PA: The Pennsylvania State University Press.
Walton, D. N. (1995). *A Pragmatic Theory of Fallacy.* Tuscaloosa: University of Alabama Press.
Walton, D. N., & Krabbe, E. C. W. (1995). *Commitment in Dialogue.* Albany: State University of New York Press.
Whately, R. (1836). *Elements of Logic.* New York: William Jackson.

Whately, R. (1963). *Elements of Rhetoric.* Ed. Douglas Ehninger, Carbondale and Edwardsville, Southern Illinois University Press. [Reprint of the 7th British edition published by J. W. Parker in London, 1846]

Windes, R. R., & Hastings, A. (1965). *Argumentation & Advocacy.* New York: Random House.

Windes, R. R., and Kruger, A. N. (1961). *Championship Debating.* Portland, ME: J. Weston Walch.

Woods, J. (1987). *Ad Baculum,* Self-Interest and Pascal's Wager. In F. H. van Eemeren, R. Grootendorst, J. A. Blair, & C. A. Willard (Eds.), *Argumentation: Across the Line of Discipline* (pp. 343-349). Dordrecht: Foris Publications.

Woods, J., & Walton, D. (1978). The Fallacy of *Ad Ignorantiam. Dialectica, 32,* 87-99. [Reprinted in Woods and Walton (1989, pp. 161-173)]

Woods, J., and Walton, D. (1989). *Fallacies: Selected Papers, 1972-1982.* Dordrecht: Foris.

Zadeh, L. (1987). *Fuzzy Sets and Applications.* New York: Wiley.

AUTHOR INDEX

212

Subject Index

T

Tactics, 44, 87, 95, 120, 128, 131, 159, 192
    of argumentation, 57, 85, 130, 158, 180,
        204
            weakness of, 131
    of attack, 57
    defensive, 129
    offensive, 129
    scare, 98, 204
    shift of, 129
    sophistical, 16, 129, 201
Terminology
    negative or vituperative, 54
Theaetetus, 160-161
Threat, 9, 96, 200-202
Topos, 5
Tutiorism, 38
Tweety case, 21, 41, 151-153

V

Vagueness, 45, 53-55, 66, 102, 104-108
Validity, 5-6, 9-13, 146, 151, 171

W

Warning, 73, 75, 77, 98, 100, 110, 169, 185,
    201
Warrant, 53-54
    Toulmin, 5
Wittgenstein, 4, 9